BAD JUDGMENT

PATRONS OF THE OSGOODE SOCIETY

The Society also thanks the Law Foundation of Ontario
and the Law Society of Upper Canada for their continuing support.

Bad Judgment

The Case of
Mr Justice Leo A. Landreville

WILLIAM KAPLAN

University of Toronto Press
Toronto Buffalo London

© University of Toronto Press Incorporated 1996
Toronto Buffalo London

An Osgoode Society edition of
Bad Judgment
has been published simultaneously.

Printed in Canada

ISBN 0-8020-0836-4

Printed on acid-free paper

Canadian Cataloguing in Publication Data

Kaplan, William, 1957–
Bad judgment : the case of Mr Justice Leo A. Landreville

Co-published by the Osgoode Society for Canadian Legal History.
Includes index.
ISBN 0-8020-0836-4

1. Landreville, Leo Albert, 1910–   . 2. Judges –
Ontario – Discipline – Case studies.   3. Misconduct
in office – Ontario – Sudbury – Case studies.
4. Northern Ontario Natural Gas (Firm) – Corrupt
practices.   I. Osgoode Society for Canadian Legal
History.   II. Title.

KE416.L35K3 1996   343.713'03534   C95-932693-6
KF345.Z9L35K3 1996

University of Toronto Press acknowledges the financial assistance to its
publishing program of the Canada Council and the Ontario Arts Council.

To the memory of my grandfather,
Bernard Kaplan,
14 March 1897–2 March 1975,
and in honour of my grandmother,
Nadia Kaplan

Contents

Foreword

THE OSGOODE SOCIETY
FOR CANADIAN LEGAL HISTORY

The purpose of The Osgoode Society for Canadian Legal History is to encourage research and writing in the history of Canadian law. The Society, which was incorporated in 1979 and is registered as a charity, was founded at the initiative of the Honourable R. Roy McMurtry, former attorney-general for Ontario, and officials of the Law Society of Upper Canada. Its efforts to stimulate the study of legal history in Canada include a research support program, a graduate student research assistance program, and work in the fields of oral history and legal archives. The Society publishes (at the rate of about one a year) volumes of interest to the Society's members that contribute to legal-historical scholarship in Canada, including studies of the courts, the judiciary, and the legal profession, biographies, collections of documents, studies in criminology and penology, accounts of significant trials, and work in the social and economic history of the law.

Current directors of The Osgoode Society for Canadian Legal History are Jane Banfield, Tom Bastedo, John Brown, Brian Bucknall, Archie Campbell, Susan Elliott, J. Douglas Ewart, Martin Friedland, Charles Harnick, John Honsberger, Kenneth Jarvis, Allen Linden, Virginia MacLean, Wendy Matheson, Colin McKinnon, Roy McMurtry, Brendan O'Brien, Peter Oliver, Paul Reinhardt, James Spence, and Richard Tinsley.

The annual report and information about membership may be obtained by writing to The Osgoode Society for Canadian Legal History, Osgoode

Hall, 130 Queen Street West, Toronto, Ontario, Canada M5H 2N6. Members receive the annual volume published by the Society.

William Kaplan has written the history of an event of considerable importance in the history of the Canadian judiciary. For many years Canadian lawyers and many non-lawyers have known something of the story of the near-impeachment and forced resignation of Mr Justice Leo Landreville of the Supreme Court of Ontario. Over the years the truth has mingled with myth, and a full and accurate account was greatly needed. Kaplan not only has provided an authoritative account but has done so in a fascinating style that captures and intrigues the reader from first sentence to conclusion. *Bad Judgment* is a model study of an episode of far-reaching and continuing significance, one that will be of interest to all Canadian judges and lawyers.

R. Roy McMurtry
President

Peter N. Oliver
Editor-in-Chief

Acknowledgments

This book is part of a larger project, the biography of Ivan Rand. In writing that biography it became clear to me that Leo Landreville and his stock option was a story of its own, and one that should be told.

As in every undertaking of this kind, a great many people made many contributions along the way. Leo Landreville gave me unrestricted access to his voluminous personal papers. He made no editorial demands of any kind, other than asking to see a final copy of the manuscript. A number of friends and colleagues read the manuscript and made many useful comments and helpful suggestions. J.L. Granatstein read an early draft, and encouraged me in the endeavour. Blaine Baker, Robert Bothwell, Earl Cherniak, QC, Mr Justice Dan Chilcott, Barry Wright, and my closest and best counsel, Michael N. Kaplan, commented on the penultimate draft. Christopher Moore, who is writing the official history of the Law Society of Upper Canada, reviewed the final draft. He made a number of useful suggestions, even though we differ in our interpretation of events. Martin Friedland also reviewed the manuscript, and generously shared with me a copy of his unpublished study of judicial independence and accountability in Canada. G. Norman Hillmer reviewed the final draft of the manuscript line by line, and improved it in a great many ways. Rosemary Shipton made a tremendous editorial contribution, while Maraya Raduha assisted with the final preparation of the manuscript. To all of them go my thanks.

I am also grateful to the Hon. John Arnup, the Hon. Frank U. Collier,

Yves Fortier, QC, Gordon Fairweather, the late Gordon Henderson, Donald C. MacDonald, the Hon. John Matheson, Barry Pepper, QC, and J.J. Robinette, QC, each of whom gave me one or more lengthy interviews about their roles in this matter.

Research assistance was provided by Debra Armstrong, Graham Rawlinson, Torsten Strom, and Rebecca Thomson. Rawlinson, a doctoral candidate in history at York University, deserves particular mention and recognition for his substantial contribution to this book.

At the Faculty of Law of the University of Ottawa, Dean Donald McRae and his successor, Sanda Rodgers, gave this project their full support. I had the privilege of working as a professor at the Faculty of Law between 1986 and 1995, and benefited greatly during that time from my association with a number of fine scholars and convivial colleagues, one of whom, Jamie Benidickson, made helpful comments on the first draft of this book.

Dr Charles Rand gave me unrestricted access to his father's personal papers, including Ivan Rand's 'Landreville file.' I would also like to thank the staff at the National Archives of Canada, in particular Peter Delottinville and Paul Marsden. Professor Chris Armstrong, who is engaged in his own larger study of securities regulation in Canada, shared with me some of his Landreville research and pointed me in the right direction at the Ontario Archives, where Stormie Stewart removed barriers initially precluding access to the records of the Ontario Securities Commission and the attorney general. Leon Warmski was, as usual, helpful during my many visits. The staff at Trent University Archives assisted with the Leslie Frost Papers, while Susan Binnie at the Archives of the Law Society of Upper Canada facilitated my research in law society files. Research materials and interview notes will be deposited in due course at the University of Toronto Archives.

The research for this book was financially assisted with grants from the Social Sciences and Humanities Research Council of Canada, the Osgoode Society, and the Law Foundation of Ontario. Madeline Glazer administered the various grants in aid that I received, and did so with her customary grace and efficiency. Barbara Main and Francine Daoust provided excellent secretarial assistance.

At the University of Toronto Press it was a pleasure, once again, to work with Bill Harnum and Virgil Duff. A special edition of this book has been published by the Osgoode Society, and it is appropriate for me to express my thanks to Peter Oliver and Marilyn MacFarlane. A number of anonymous reviewers read the book for both UTP and the Osgoode Society, and I am grateful to them for their comments and suggestions. I would also like to thank my agent, Linda McKnight.

WK, November 1995

BAD JUDGMENT

Prelude

Room 182 at Osgoode Hall was no ordinary judge's chambers, and its occupant, Leo A. Landreville, was no ordinary judge. Landreville, Franco-Ontario's representative on the Superior Court bench, was a small, well-dressed man who had made it big in northern Ontario. His Sudbury law office had been the busiest in town, the income from it being handsomely supplemented by his many successful investments. A life-long Liberal and successful local politician, the culmination of his political career had been his election, in December 1954, as mayor. His two-year term had been interrupted, however, by a telephone call from Ottawa. Would Landreville accept a judicial appointment? Yes, he decided, after much soul-searching and considerable thought, he would. On 13 September 1956 Leo A. Landreville, at forty-six, became the youngest judge at Osgoode Hall.

Landreville had a second home in Cuernavaca, 'Landra Villa,' he called it, and he decorated his Osgoode Hall office in a Mexican motif. He worked at a large semicircular walnut desk with leather inlay. The carpet was vivid red, and the walls were covered with straw. A ceramic-inlaid coffee table, sofa, bar, hi-fi, and several occasional chairs completed the furnishings. Outside, Landreville parked his Cadillac Brougham. He and his wife lived at the newly built and very fashionable Benvenuto Place and joined the Granite Club. Life could not have been better. Landreville had no worries in the world – except for one little secret.

This story begins in northern Ontario.

1

Northern Ontario Natural Gas

His busy, bustling office could have been in any Canadian city or town, but Leo Landreville's law chambers were in Sudbury, Ontario, and this story is, in many ways, a northern one set in a place called northern Ontario. By the 1950s northern Ontario had a definite identity within Canada's most populous province, an identity that stemmed above all from the land. The Canadian Shield's 'rugged, hilly, lake-pocked plateau,'[1] with its endless stands of deciduous and coniferous trees, countless lakes, and rocky outcrops, created a natural border with the south, while the Hudson Bay lowlands to the north boasted one of the most forbidding climates in the world.[2]

Native Canadians came first. For perhaps 10,000 years, they have fished, hunted, traded, and made war on the shores of the big lakes of northern Ontario. Europeans chased fur-bearing animals into the area in the seventeenth and eighteenth centuries: the British from the north, via Hudson Bay, and the French from the south and the St Lawrence River. The newcomers initially found little reason to stay in the region – other than missionary work. Natural resources, however, changed that. By the 1840s, demand for timber in the British Isles spurred development and settlement in the North. Settlers trickled in and, after Confederation in 1867, Ontario's government began a long but eventually successful battle to have its provincial boundaries encompass this vast area. The Canadian Pacific Railway pushed through the region in the 1880s, bringing farmers and lumberers to many newly established communities. Development led to the discovery of a new resource: minerals.

Copper and nickel were discovered near Sudbury in the 1880s, silver at Cobalt in 1903, and gold near Timmins in 1909. Northern Ontario, or 'New Ontario' as it was briefly known at the turn of the century, became firmly fixed in the public mind as a provincial treasure chest. Its rapidly developing mines, its apparently endless forests, and its rivers, which held the promise of unlimited and inexpensive electricity, all made northern Ontario a land of opportunity.

Despite this economic potential, however, most of the hundreds of thousands of immigrants who flowed into Canada in the nineteenth and twentieth centuries made their way south and settled in the rich agricultural lands. Taming the north was a job for a hardy few. Still, increasing numbers of newcomers, finding opportunities in mines and forests, headed north and joined a society that was markedly different from that of the south. Finns, Ukrainians, Italians, Germans, Poles, and a few other 'foreign' groups made up about a quarter of northern Ontario's population by the 1920s. French Canadians, migrating most often from overcrowded farms in Quebec, formed another quarter of the population. Aboriginal peoples and Canadians from British stock completed the picture. This mix made northern Ontario, which had a population of just over half a million in 1951, a very different place from the rest of the province, which remained, until the 1950s and 1960s, overwhelmingly British in outlook and stock. In sharp contrast, northern Ontario was bilingual and multicultural before politicians in the rest of the country had even heard of the concepts, or discovered ways to use them to garner votes.

To be sure, the social mix made for some problems, resulting in cultural conflict in northern Ontario's unions, churches, and politics. Overall, there was a sense of otherness in Ontario's north – a sense that decisions and disbursements were made in the south for the south. Franco-Ontarians in the north like Leo Landreville knew this feeling well. Along with French speakers in Ontario's eastern counties, they were the victims of successive anti-French policies of the provincial government. Regulation 17, passed by the legislature at Queen's Park in 1912, severely restricted French-language education rights. The intent of the provision was obvious, and fortunately it was most often honoured in the breach. Though eliminated in 1927, it symbolized a widespread sense that French Canadians were not truly welcome in Ontario. A legacy of bitterness about the infamous law remains to this day.[3]

Still, northern Ontario was, for all its problems, a land of opportunity, a frontier that was exciting, risk-laden, and filled with potential. John Diefenbaker's 'Northern Vision' campaign during the 1958 general election struck a popular and timely chord with Canadians. Diefenbaker called for a 'Canada of the North,' and promised massive investment in transportation and communication to create a 'new soul for Canada' that would 'safeguard our independence' and 'restore our unity.'[4] Diefenbaker, who always had a keen eye for a bandwagon, typically promised much more than he could or would deliver, but it was an impressive vision, and it deliberately echoed John A. Macdonald's National Policy of the previous century.

The attempt to reorient Canada northward was less successful. Yet investment did increase, and roads made many northern communities less remote. In the 1950s and 1960s scientific exploration was funded as never before, and the budget of the Department of Northern Affairs increased annually. Northern resource industries boomed and, fuelled by postwar military and consumer goods markets, Ontario's mineral, timber, and power production exploded. New discoveries were matched by new investment in resource towns. Places like Kenora grew rapidly, and other communities appeared out of nowhere. Overall, the population of northern Ontario expanded at a record rate during the 1950s.[5] But the new northerners were serving the same function as those of the previous generation: getting resources out of the north for delivery and consumption in the south and elsewhere. Still, the north was a place where business could be done and fortunes made by men with savvy, guts, and an eye for opportunity. The building of a trans-Canada natural gas pipeline provided one such opportunity.

In the early 1950s the market for natural gas was minuscule, outside a few small centres in Alberta. More Canadians burned wood than natural gas for fuel, while oil and coal were the fuels of choice in most Canadian cities and towns. All that changed by the middle of the decade. Natural gas was an inexpensive and efficient fuel, and, because of advances in technology, it could now be transported long distances by pipe. Gas pipelines were being planned and built all over the world: a giant pipeline, 15 metres in diameter, was on the drawing board to take gas from the Caspian Sea to Moscow, while another network of pipelines was beginning to tap both North Sea and Sahara Desert reserves.[6] Western Canada had huge proven reserves. Ontario, which had suffered a critical coal shortage during and after the Second World War, was an obvious market for the natural gas, but the real market was the energy-starved United States. All that was needed was a pipeline to transport the gas to eastern markets.

Accordingly, by 1950, several groups of businessmen were seeking permission to build natural gas pipelines out of Alberta. It was widely assumed that the millions needed for financing would largely come from the United States and would be contingent on the pipeline bringing gas south. Alberta gas producers, indifferent to Ontario's needs, were fully in favour of a north-south route. They wanted to get the gas to America's industrial heartland as quickly and as inexpensively as possible. That meant exporting the gas to the United States via Emerson in Manitoba down to Minneapolis and Milwaukee, and then over to Chicago and Detroit. This route also left open the possibility of reimporting any left-over gas across the Niagara River, about 5 kilometres north of the Lewiston Bridge. Southern Ontario and Quebec would have service, but not northern and northwestern Ontario.

Conventional wisdom held that there were no markets for natural gas in Ontario's north. The population and the industrial base were insufficient to justify the large capital cost of building a pipeline across the Canadian Shield. But building the natural gas pipeline involved more than dollars and cents. It was to become another chapter in the continuing Canadian dream: resistance to continental pressure from the United States through strong east-west links.

Clarence Decatur Howe, minister of trade and commerce, but known as C.D. Howe, Canada's 'Minister of Everything,' was dedicated to the idea that there should always be 'at least one great national enterprise underway and something stirring to get it done.'[7] A trans-Canada pipeline was such a project. It was, Howe and other like-minded Liberals in Ottawa believed, a national undertaking rivalling the building of the Canadian Pacific Railway. Once completed, it would be the longest pipeline in the world, and its construction would create thousands of jobs and bring western energy to the industrial east. On 13 March 1953 Howe announced in the House of Commons that the building of an all-Canadian natural gas pipeline was government policy. There would, he said, be one pipeline, and it would be built entirely on Canadian soil.[8] A new company, Trans-Canada Pipe Lines Limited, was established to build, own, and operate the business. But by the fall of 1954 the company was in trouble.[9]

Trans-Canada Pipe Lines, which planned to bring gas to Winnipeg by 1955 and to begin building a pipeline across Ontario the following year, had invested heavily in personnel and engineering plans. It now needed more money to finance its expansion plans, but the American-owned Alberta energy companies would not cooperate. They refused to sign supply contracts. Eastern utilities, such as Consumers Gas of Toronto, declined to sign purchase contracts, preferring instead to maintain established, and American, sources of supply. Without these agreements in hand, the prospect for Trans-Canada Pipe Lines of raising capital on Wall Street was remote. American money was required, since Canadian capital markets were not capable of finding the required funds. To make matters worse, the intransigence of both producers and purchasers was matched by the interference of some provincial premiers, notably Ernest Manning in Alberta and Maurice Duplessis in Quebec, who went out of their way to discourage the endeavour. It was obvious that many in the gas business were waiting for Trans-Canada Pipe Line's plan to collapse and be replaced with a more logical, less expensive, and more profitable north–south route. Keeping the pipeline out of Ontario's north appeared to be the main item on the agenda for most interested groups.

An all-Canadian route was a 'pipedream,' not a 'pipeline,' the critics claimed. But to the nation-building federal Liberals, the pipeline was another important national link akin not just to the railway but to Trans-Canada Airlines and the Canadian Broadcasting Corporation. Canada, one of its prime ministers once observed, was a country with too much geography and not enough history. Successful prime ministers from John A. Macdonald forward have understood that national unity depended, in part, on national projects that spanned the huge distances separating Canadians. The trans-Canada pipeline was one such project, and in an era of rising concern about the American domination of the Canadian economy it possessed considerable symbolic appeal.

Even though an all-Canadian route was government policy and Trans-Canada Pipe Lines was committed to that route, it was hardly a done deal in the years 1953–6, given the continuing difficulties in raising the required funds. Nevertheless, on 24 July 1954 the Board of Transport Commissioners, the regulatory agency responsible for the railways, airlines, and interprovincial pipelines, released a decision granting Trans-Canada Pipe Lines preliminary approval to build a 3500-kilometre-long pipeline. It was to start about 2 kilometres west of the Alberta-Saskatchewan border and generally follow the main line of the Canadian Pacific Railway from Alberta to Port Arthur and Fort William, past Nipigon, and across to Marathon, Sudbury, and North Bay, then south to Toronto, where one branch would head west to Oakville and another east, this time tracing the route of the Canadian National Railway along the St Lawrence River to Montreal. Before reaching Montreal, however, a branch line would head north to service Ottawa-Hull. A lateral branch would be built from Winnipeg to Emerson, in order to serve Minneapolis, St Paul, and other localities in the United States.

In granting preliminary approval to this 'southern route,' the Board of Transport Commissioners did so over objections from representatives of Ontario's north. They had proposed that the main line should follow a northern route and go north from Nipigon to Geraldton and Hearst, following Highway 11 through Kapuskasing, Smooth Rock Falls, Cochrane, Iroquois Falls (with a lateral to Timmins), Kirkland Lake, Englehart, and Cobalt, then south to North Bay, with a lateral travelling west from North Bay to Sudbury. Trans-Canada Pipe Lines opposed this plan, arguing that it did not make economic sense, and the Board of Transport Commissioners agreed. However, the board left open the possibility that the route could be changed by indicating that it would reconsider its decision if evidence was put before it that the 'northern route' was financially feasible.[10] This was an invitation that the northern municipalities and mayors could ignore only at their peril. If they wanted natural gas, and the jobs and industries that this low-cost versatile fuel was sure to provide, they would have to prove to Trans-Canada Pipe Lines, the Board of Transport Commissioners, and federal and provincial politicians that there was a market for natural gas in the north. To create and service that market, a new company was born: Northern Ontario Natural Gas Limited, or NONG for short.

Ralph Keirstead Farris, a Vancouver businessman, sportsman, oil man, and stock promoter, was the main force behind NONG. A striking looking man, wiry and athletic, with a patrician nose and a full head of hair, Farris was a child of the establishment. He was born on 24 February 1910, one of three sons of a prominent British Columbia politician and past president of the Canadian Bar Association, John Wallace deBeque Farris. The senior Farris, a New Brunswick native, had served as attorney general and labour minister in Liberal provincial governments between 1917 and 1922, and he subsequently became the party's key organizational man in British Columbia. In 1937 he was summoned to the Senate by Mackenzie King, his reward for services rendered. Farris's mother, Evelyn, was the founder of the University Women's Club in Vancouver, the first woman to serve on the Senate of the University of British Columbia, and the first woman to sit on the governing board of a Canadian university, a post she held at UBC for thirty years. His uncle was the chief justice of British Columbia. Ralph Farris's brother, John, would also go on to become the province's chief justice. The family was about as 'establishment' as one could find in British Columbia.

Ralph Farris was educated at the University of British Columbia and at the Harvard Business School. After Harvard, he worked for two years in New York, married a Northwestern University co-ed, and, in 1934, returned to Vancouver and began work as a stockbroker. Five years later, he had his own seat on the Vancouver Stock Exchange.[11]

When the postwar oil boom erupted in Alberta, Farris began to commute to Calgary, learned the oil business, and established the Charter Oil Company, an Alberta gas producer. He invested widely and knew everyone in the industry. In 1953 a middle-aged file clerk, Gordon Kelly McLean, who had never run anything bigger than a crossroads general store, suggested to Farris that they create a company to distribute gas in northern Ontario. As McLean explained it, Trans-Canada Pipe Lines had decided to follow the southern route, basically hugging the shore of Lake Superior, and would bypass the major communities of northern Ontario. The southern route was shorter, but to lay the pipe Trans-Canada Pipe Lines would have to blast a trench through the world's oldest and hardest rock, the Precambrian Shield.[12] In contrast, a pipeline following the northern route could service a large number of northern communities and might even be easier and less expensive to build, since it would require digging through soft clay most of the way. Moreover, the advantage of the northern route from a gas distributor's point of view was that it could service all the northern communities through short laterals attached to the Trans-Canada line. Trans-Canada Pipe Lines Ltd was a primary carrier that would make its money by transporting and then selling gas to local and secondary distributors. From NONG's perspective, this arrangement was perfect. Someone else, in effect, would pay the huge cost of building the pipeline.[13] All NONG would have to do was arrange to sell and then deliver the gas.

Farris was immediately attracted to the idea,[14] although he did not know very much about the geography of northern Ontario. 'I had to send my girl out for a road map,' he later observed, 'to find out what he was talking about.'[15] McLean was not a close Farris associate, nor was he a reputable businessman, having served time in jail for fraud.[16] But he did have one indisputable advantage: his uncle, Philip Kelly, was Ontario's minister of mines. 'Phil' Kelly, an accountant who represented Smooth Rock Falls and adjacent areas in the Ontario legislature, was completely knowledgeable about the north: he knew the industries, he knew the cost of West Virginia coal and fuel oil, and he knew there was an insatiable demand in the north for natural gas. Kelly was the mastermind of the deal. He saw the opportunity, developed the idea, and made an agreement with his nephew to split any profit that resulted.[17] Obviously, given his public portfolio, Kelly's involvement had to be kept quiet. McLean could be more prominently involved, but what the project really needed was an established oil man with a proven track record. Farris was that man, and NONG was formed the following year as a limited company with a handful of investors to bring gas to the north and profits to its promoters, though not necessarily in that order.

Lower construction costs aside, the northern route had a number of other advantages. Northern Ontario was the centre of Ontario's pulp and paper industry and the heart of mining in Canada; it supplied '85 percent of the free world's supply of nickel,'[18] as well as copper, gold, iron ore, and uranium. If companies like Ontario-Minnesota Pulp and Paper Company in Kenora, Spruce Falls Power and Paper Company in Kapuskasing, International Nickel Company of Canada in Sudbury, Du Pont of Canada in North Bay, and Abitibi Power & Paper in Iroquois Falls, Smooth Rock Falls, and Sturgeon Falls could be convinced to switch to gas, there was vast potential for growth and profit. The north was a high-cost fuel area. Natural gas, less expensive and more efficient, could easily compete.

But first, Trans-Canada Pipe Lines would have to choose the northern route. If it did not, NONG would have to build a lateral of its own, travelling north from North Bay, and it would be responsible for all the construction costs, estimated at between $40 and $50 million. This would make the venture financially questionable, to say the least. However, even assuming that Trans-Canada Pipe Lines was willing to follow the northern route, and the Board of Transport Commissioners agreed, financial success was not ensured unless the northern municipalities granted NONG franchise agreements. Only through obtaining agreements with most, if not all, of the northern communities could the necessary economies of scale be achieved. Without them, the scheme could not work.

Farris obviously needed help. McLean, having delivered the idea, was assigned the title of assistant to the president and given office chores at the Toronto headquarters. He was a nuisance more than anything else, although he remained on the payroll for several years. What Farris required was a blue-chip team – to establish the engineering and economic feasibility of the northern route, and to convince the northern municipalities, mayors, and industries to lobby on behalf of the northern route and to sign franchise agreements with NONG.

C. Spencer Clark from Seattle was recruited as NONG's executive vice-president. A Harvard MBA, he was an experienced oil man with a 'slide-rule mind.' He was also chairman of the board of the Cascade Natural Gas Company, a successful gas utility in the Pacific Northwest. Leslie T.

Fournier of New York City was another founding director of NONG. He was vice-president and treasurer of Panhandle Eastern Pipelines Company, one of the largest gas transmission lines in the United States. Blancke Noyes and Leonard Dickson, both of New York, were partners in major American investment banking firms. Fournier, Noyes, and Dickson gave the new company, whose only asset at incorporation was its idea, immediate credibility with Wall Street. J. Chester Grey of Toronto, appointed vice-president and general manager, rounded out the executive ranks. Grey brought years of experience with prominent gas utilities in the United States. Other early investors included Gordon Kelly McLean, his uncle, Phil Kelly, and Matt M. Newall, a Calgary oil man and Farris associate.

NONG was a highly speculative endeavour, but the idea underlying it was ingenious.[19] One company serving the entire north might not offer better service and more competitive rates than a number of small utilities, but, if Farris's plan went according to schedule, he would have a monopoly. From a stock promoter's perspective, a natural gas monopoly would make money – for the early promoters and for successive generations of owners. That is what the NONG play was all about.

It was essential that NONG obtain the franchises for the distribution of natural gas throughout the north. The residential market for natural gas in the north was not only small but seasonal as well. Demand would rise sharply in the winter, and decline just as quickly with the warmer weather. In gas terminology, this created a 'summer valley.' And a 'summer valley' created both problems and possibilities. The demand might be uneven, but a gas utility serving the whole northern Ontario area could dispose of 'valley' gas generated in one city to industries at the other end of the system. The combination of high residential demand during the winter months and regular year-round industrial purchases permitted the near-capacity operation of a northern natural gas distribution system. This high-load factor, combined with the inevitable economies of scale and the realistic expectation that natural gas would quickly become the preferred fuel for large industrial users in the north, seemed to provide the ingredients of success.[20]

NONG had to begin by convincing Trans-Canada Pipe Lines that there was a northern market to be served. It also had to secure Trans-Canada's agreement to sell NONG gas at one billing rate throughout the entire system – a departure in conventional pipeline billing practices – leaving NONG free to distribute that gas among its trading areas as it saw fit. This second objective was readily achieved. Changing the pipeline route was much more problematic. Trans-Canada Pipe Lines had initially ruled out the northern route because its studies did not promise significant demand. NONG saw it differently: 'The organizers of the Company felt that the Northern Ontario market had been largely overlooked in the economic studies that had been made.'[21] NONG set about correcting this impression, and in the spring of 1954 Grey went north. He travelled widely from one community to another, gathering data, and concluded that if NONG could obtain substantially all the municipal franchises and industrial load from North Bay north and west to the Manitoba border, it would be feasible, and probably profitable, to service the area. Grey's report was promising, but more information was required. NONG next retained a Texas consulting company, and it approved the project in terms of construction, future economic growth, and profits:

We have carefully reviewed this project and in consideration of the conservative market estimates and the various efforts to be served, the general business condition of each community, we believe the project to be economically feasible and a sound operational undertaking. The realistic and practical forecasts indicate a fair rate of return on the investments and the ability to give useful and adequate utility service.[22]

The evidence seemed to be on NONG's side, but Trans-Canada Pipe Lines still had to change its planned route. For the better part of 1955, NONG concerned itself with developing markets and mobilizing the people and politicians of the north. 'The organizers of the Company,' the directors reported in their first annual report, 'adopted the conception that a concerted effort on the part of the Northern communities which could be assisted by the Company in accumulating the market information might induce Trans-Canada Pipe Lines to consider changing the route.'[23] It did not take too much persuasion to get the northern municipalities and mayors on side: the implications of allowing the pipeline to bypass the north were unthinkable. It was widely believed that a gas pipeline would initiate a new era of economic growth, in the same way that the railways had brought development and prosperity in the nineteenth century. If the pipeline followed the southern route, northern Ontario would be the last place to get natural gas, if it got it at all. The strategy was for northern Ontario to support the all-Canadian route and the northern route by entering into franchise agreements with NONG.

An important move in that direction was taken in November 1954, when a number of meetings were held in Toronto to which representatives of all northern municipalities were invited to discuss issues of concern relating to the proposed distribution of natural gas. The sessions were convened by Dana Porter, attorney general of Ontario. Ontario was governed by the Progressive Conservatives, which held many northern seats. Porter knew that an election was planned for the following year, and the government, needless to say, wished to maintain its northern support. Arthur Crozier, chair of the Ontario Fuel Board and the former wartime fuel controller, was also there. The OFB, just created in 1954, was under Porter's supervision, and he had instructed Crozier to assist the municipalities and mayors in coming to a decision about the company that should receive the natural gas franchise.

After looking into the matter, Crozier had quickly determined that the capital costs involved in the installation of a municipally owned natural gas distribution system would be prohibitive for every northern municipality and most southern ones. Porter then responded that public ownership was almost certainly out of the question, and he suggested that a regional conference be held without delay to select a single company to distribute gas in the North.[24]

It was clear to Crozier and Porter that if one company was chosen to distribute gas in the north, it could purchase gas from Trans-Canada Pipe Lines at the lowest possible wholesale rate. This arrangement would result in considerable consumer savings. Crozier was also aware that Trans-Canada Pipe Lines needed to know, as soon as possible, how much gas it could expect to sell in the north, if it was to change its plans and obtain approval to follow the northern route. These franchise arrangements were also important for another reason. Trans-Canada Pipe Lines was experiencing considerable difficulty in raising capital. Confirmed franchise agreements with most, if not all, of the northern municipalities would assist the company in obtaining money in New York.

Initially, a number of companies expressed interest in obtaining franchises in the north. Crozier sent a questionnaire to each of them, and the results were shared with all the northern municipalities. NONG was, however, the only company that prepared and circulated a detailed feasibility study. When representatives of seventeen northern Ontario municipalities, including Cochrane, Kapuskasing, North Bay, Sudbury, and Timmins, met in Kirkland Lake in February 1955, they had that study in hand.[25]

The meeting was designed to show Trans-Canada Pipe Lines, the Board of Transport Commissioners, and federal and provincial politicians that northern Ontario wanted natural gas and would take whatever steps were necessary to get it. Porter's earlier instructions were followed without reservation or deviation. After Crozier explained the legal process in granting a franchise, Ralph Farris answered questions about NONG. Three important resolutions were passed: the first declared that public ownership of a natural gas distribution system was not feasible; the second affirmed that natural gas distribution should be left in private hands; and the third committed the northern municipalities to negotiate franchise agreements with one company in order to achieve the necessary economies of scale.[26] Participants agreed to meet again the following month. Farris immediately began a lobbying campaign to ensure that NONG would be their unanimous choice when the mayors next came together.

The second meeting was held in early March 1955. Trans-Canada Pipe Lines, if it was to obtain approval and financing for the northern route, needed government funds, but it also needed firm commitments in hand. Since the first meeting in February, it had urged all its potential distributors to conclude their local contracts so the company could give assurances to its bankers and prospective financiers that it could sell enough gas to make the project feasible. Now the delegates unanimously agreed, with Sudbury abstaining,[27] to enter into franchise agreements with NONG. Farris's lobbying activities had paid off.

In the aftermath of the March meeting, virtually every northern community of any significance or size reached an agreement with NONG. By and large, the terms of these agreements were the same. NONG promised to deliver Alberta natural gas under high pressure through an 85-centimetre line to every northern municipality. At no cost to the taxpayer, pipelines would be installed under city streets, providing there was a customer at least every 30 metres. In most cases, the franchise was granted for twenty years and was subject to renewal. Most northern communities were also given the option, at the expiry of the agreement, to buy NONG out. The deal was too good to be missed.

Still, individual franchise agreements had to be reached, and Grey was put in charge of negotiating the individual arrangements. He set up headquarters at the Royal York Hotel in Toronto and began writing and visiting all the municipalities along the proposed pipeline route. His efforts met with immediate success. By the end of April 1955 NONG had signed distribution deals with sixteen northern Ontario municipalities from North Bay to Hearst. The excitement was palpable. 'The impact and influence of natural gas in Northern Ontario,' Farris later told the North Bay and District Chamber of Commerce, 'will trigger a great development.'[28]

There were, however, two holdouts: Sudbury and the Lakehead. In the Lakehead another company, Twin City Gas, obtained franchises for both Port Arthur and Fort William. Twin City also secured the franchise rights for a number of other northwestern municipalities, including Dryden and Kenora. NONG later overcame this problem by buying an interest in Twin City, and soon thereafter acquired control.[29] That left the Sudbury franchise.

Sudbury had little to recommend it physically, strategically, or aesthetically. Yet this site, 500 kilometres from Toronto, just north of Ramsey Lake on the Canadian Shield, amid a mixture of woods, craggy outcrops, and myriad tiny hills and valleys, was chosen by the CPR in the 1880s as a small depot in its push to finish Canada's first national rail line.[30] That gave the town its start. What made it endure was the Sudbury basin, a rounded, rectangular depression a few kilometres northeast of the train station. The basin lay in a northeast-southwest line, 60 kilometres in length and up to 27 kilometres in width, and it was along the circumference of this depression that the copper and nickel ore that would secure Sudbury's future was found.[31] By the 1950s the mines and mills of Sudbury were operating at near capacity, and their smokestacks symbolized the region and gave it an identity.

The region, like the country, was experiencing a boom.[32] Growth and expansion were everywhere. The new Sudbury shopping centre, the area's first, and the city's fourth funeral home, always a sign of population growth, were under construction. Three banks were opening or building new branches downtown. These new services catered to a burgeoning population: 107,889 called metropolitan Sudbury home in 1956, a whopping 34 per cent increase over 1951.[33] Nickel was the main product, although copper, cobalt, iron ore, platinum, and other precious metals were also mined. The Korean War, and the subsequent nickel stockpiling program of the United States government, had fuelled much of Sudbury's expansion. As long as business was good – and INCO's first-quarter profits and Falconbridge's continued growth proved it was – Sudbury's future was bright.[34]

At City Hall, business activity was reflected in the City Council agenda. Economic development demanded the most time of municipal politicians like Leo Landreville, followed by new problems such as municipal plans, parking shortages, and traffic congestion.[35] Recreation and entertainment in Sudbury in the mid-1950s centred on the new Sudbury arena. Curling and hockey had joined hunting and fishing as the city's leisure activities.

Amid this expansion, a few cautionary notes were sounded that the mines might not always be able to support the city: 'Sudburians have no present cause for worry, nor will their children,' suggested one contemporary commentator, 'but the thoughtful among them will at least take some thought for the coming of that distant day.'[36] As events transpired, that distant day was around the corner, but as the city grew, and the new rapidly replaced the old, few saw any cause for pessimism. The outlook was bright and, with the arrival of natural gas, it would become brighter still – once the franchise had been awarded.

NONG's projections indicated that Sudbury was the largest potential market for its product. The company expected to attract almost 5300 residential customers in its first year of operation in Sudbury. Timmins, the next largest market, had an anticipated customer base of only 3300. Kirkland Lake and North Bay followed with predicted customer bases of approximately 2200 each. There were parallel projections for industrial use. Sudbury was expected to have 144 commercial consumers in the first year, followed by 105 for Timmins, 67 for North Bay, and 61 for Kirkland Lake. In terms of actual volume, the NONG study stated that Sudbury would be the largest overall consumer by far. INCO, a large nickel-producing facility located in the adjoining community of Copper Cliff, accounted for most of the anticipated volume.[37] By the end of 1955, however, Sudbury was the only community, and INCO the only industry of any significant size, that had not yet signed up with NONG.

Sudbury and INCO aside, NONG had been largely successful in proving that there were markets in the north. Nevertheless, Trans-Canada Pipe Lines continued to face difficulties in obtaining financing. New York bankers were not convinced that the company would achieve sufficient gas sales; nor would they accept the proposition that either of the two all-Canadian routes, given the additional expenditures involved, was feasible. Without their support, the money needed to finance the project could not be found. Making the situation even worse, Alberta's opposition to the all-Canadian route had only increased. It was merely a matter of time, the Alberta oil and gas companies believed, before common sense would prevail and western producers would be given the green light to build a pipeline due south to the United States, bypassing Ontario's north. The Canadian market could then be served by exchange imports across the Niagara River. Undoubtedly, building a pipeline south would make the most money. In Canada, however, nationalism has a way of redistributing dollars and cents.

2

The Honourable Leo Landreville

Leo Landreville was born in an Ottawa walkup apartment on 23 February 1910. The youngest of six children, Landreville was the only son, born when his merchant father was sixty years old. Because he was illiterate, Landreville's father stressed the value of formal education for his son, and, after proceeding through Garneau Separate School in Ottawa, Bourget College in Rigaud, and an acting school in Montreal, Landreville enrolled at the University of Ottawa. As hard as Landreville worked on his courses, however, he found academic success elusive. He was the only student in a class of thirty-five to fail in his graduating year. He tried his examinations again the following September, and this time he passed.

Although Landreville did not excel in formal education, he did find his vocation in university. He loved public performance – speaking, debates, acting, and music. His family thought it was only natural that he should become a lawyer, so he enrolled at Osgoode Hall Law School. When he failed first year, one professor advised him that he was not cut out for the law; moreover, his English-language skills were not up to standard. But he did not give up, despite his very indifferent academic results. Most of his grades were in the 30 per cent range, and his highest mark was 56 per cent.[1] Obtaining admission to law school was not as competitive as it later became, however, and Dalhousie Law School agreed to give Landreville a second chance. He enrolled in 1934, again finding academic life difficult and again being distracted by drama and debates. Nearly all his marks were between 50 and 60 per cent, and his only grades above 65 in all three years were 66 per cent in Procedure I and II. He scraped through, never-theless, and in 1937 received his law degree.[2]

Admitted to the Ontario bar the following year, Landreville moved to Sudbury. He had spent his summers there, working in the law chambers of J.A.S. Plouffe, a prominent criminal and civil litigation lawyer. He eventually decided to make Sudbury his home. His widowed mother wanted him to stay in Ottawa, but Landreville would have none of it. 'I visited the city during the holidays,' he told his mother. 'There are young miners in that one-industry town. And what does a strong, active ven-turesome fellow do with his first pay cheque? He makes a down payment on a new car, he buys a bottle of liquor, then finds a girlfriend. That's where I come in to defend him. He has an accident, he gets arrested for impaired driving or worse, his girlfriend becomes pregnant.' Sudbury, on the cusp of an economic boom, was, Landreville concluded, the place for him, 'not Ottawa with his feet on his desk like all the other young lawyers in the midst of the depression.'[3]

The original plan was for Landreville to join Plouffe. In 1936 Plouffe was appointed a district court judge, but he was able to introduce Lan-dreville to a law firm in need of a new man, Cooper and Brodie. When William Marr Brodie, a former Sudbury mayor, suddenly died in May 1937, Landreville filled the breach, and, eventually, the firm became Coo-per and Landreville. In 1950 J.M. Cooper was appointed a district court judge, and the firm became known as Landreville, Hawkins and Gratton.

Landreville was one of five French-speaking lawyers in town, and he soon established a reputation as one of the best. He ensured that his office was staffed with multilingual clerks – Finnish, Polish, Italian, and Ukrai-nian – and he attempted to provide service to all Sudbury's varied clien-tele. Appointed a provincial QC in 1956, Landreville specialized in civil and criminal litigation. 'Leo the Lip' was the way some people referred to him. He defended clients in twenty-nine manslaughter cases, and not one was convicted. His record in murder trials was equally impressive: twelve clients were defended, five were convicted of lesser crimes, six were acquitted, and one was sent to the gallows. He was a courtroom nat-ural, with his smooth manner and well-modulated voice. Landreville also founded and operated a business school and was an able investor, mak-ing considerable money in real estate.[4]

A short, slim, dapper man with a sprightly step, prominent nose, and high forehead, Landreville had a full head of straight black hair and sported a pencil-thin moustache. He always had a smile and was impec-cably groomed. His wife, Gracia Toby, had a reputation as a beauty, and they had two sons and a daughter. Their home at 250 Elm Street West in Sudbury was described by the society columnist in the *Sudbury Star* as 'elegant.' An indefatigable Sudbury booster, Landreville became the city's goodwill ambassador to the world. He clearly enjoyed meeting people, travelling, and the good life, even learning to fly a seaplane and using it for hunting and fishing trips to his fully equipped hunting camp in the far north.[5] He was an expert waterskier and a marksman of note.

Landreville also had a taste for politics, like his colleague Cooper, who sat as an MPP for Sudbury between 1937 and 1943. Landreville ran first as a school trustee, then served as an alderman on Sudbury's City Council. He became a member and finally chair of the Sudbury Hydro Commission. Landreville was a Liberal, through and through, like many Franco-Ontarians. He was leader of the party in the Sudbury area, and stood as a Liberal candidate in the 1951 provincial election. Though he was not successful in obtaining provincial office, he continued to work hard on behalf of the cause. He made many friends, including Lester B. Pearson, the member of parliament for Algoma East, the next riding over. Landreville's work on behalf of the party had not gone unnoticed, and Landreville earned Pearson's thanks. After the 1953 election, Pearson thanked Landreville for his 'help and friendship' during the campaign. 'In return,' Pearson wrote, 'one day I will stand beside you and in front of a sign which will read, not "We Like Mike," but "We Love Leo!"'[6] The two men periodically exchanged warm correspondence, and Landreville treasured the relationship.

On 1 January 1955 Leo Landreville became mayor of Sudbury. During his campaign he had promised to work diligently if elected: 'I believe,' he told City Council, 'that a mayor is not only a chairman at meetings. His prime duty is to know, inform, and give guidance to the members of his council – he must disclose fairly and entirely all aspects of a problem for his members to discuss, to weigh the merits and demerits and decide by majority rule. He must lead fearlessly and not follow sheepishly the proceedings.'[7]

The first meeting of the new City Council was held on 12 January 1955, with Landreville presiding. Landreville's political preoccupation was municipal amalgamation; he wanted to annex several surrounding municipalities and add them to Sudbury's tax base. However, among the issues first discussed was the pipeline franchise and which company should get it. Previously Landreville had, in his capacity as chair of the Sudbury Hydro Commission, favoured the creation of a new public utility to distribute natural gas, but he had been disabused of that notion at the November 1954 meeting in Toronto, when Dana Porter had advised northern politicians that, given the costs, public ownership was not a feasible option. At that time, every bylaw, big and small, had to be sent to Toronto for review before being proclaimed. So, when the attorney general indicated that public ownership was not an option, the matter ended there.

On 13 January 1955 the city solicitor, J.J. Kelly, distributed a memorandum on the natural gas issue for the mayor and members of the Sudbury City Council. Kelly, a young lawyer in his first years of practice, began his report with the observation that a number of companies had filed applications for the distribution of natural gas in the city of Sudbury.

The first consideration to be studied by the Council is whether or not any franchise granted with respect to natural gas should be privately or publicly controlled. If public ownership is considered, it could possibly conflict with another public utility, namely, the Hydro Electric system. In addition thereto, public ownership in the light of the information that I have been able to gather with respect to laying down the gas mains and distribution system, would mean an investment of somewhere in the region of 4 to 4.5 million dollars for the City of Sudbury. For a public utility to be set up to handle this project, it would require the approval of various departments and boards of the Provincial Government to incur such an indebtedness. Private ownership on the other hand, would be responsible for the complete financial adjustments, and would have to submit detailed statements of any financing plan before being permitted to commence gas installation and distribution within the City of Sudbury.[8]

Critical to the consideration of this matter, Kelly pointed out, was the extent of INCO's use of natural gas. The only basis on which a gas line to Sudbury made economic sense was with INCO as a customer, particularly if the northern route was chosen. The pipeline would eventually head south to North Bay, and Sudbury, if it was to be served, would get its gas from a lateral from North Bay of approximately 130 kilometres in length, at an estimated cost to NONG of $6 million. Building a lateral of this length could be justified only if INCO agreed to buy gas. If INCO decided to bring in its own trunk line, or tried to cut a special deal, Sudbury might be left out. However, the city and its largest industry could work together for mutual advantage. Kelly recommended that 'top level conferences' be held with INCO officials to 'ascertain exactly in what way that company proposes to handle the natural gas situation.'[9]

Indeed, INCO was considering building its own trunk line from the main pipeline to its facility at Copper Cliff. Managers believed they could save money by dealing with the wholesaler rather than a retailer. It took time, but Ralph Farris was able to persuade the senior officers of the company, who were based in New York, that this was not so. If INCO bought directly from Trans-Canada Pipe Lines, it would have to pay a uniform rate year round. If it dealt with NONG, it would enjoy access to the cheaper valley gas. Eventually, INCO saw the wisdom of this approach, and the company threw its support behind a deal with NONG – provided that the price was right. Still, the negotiations took several years.[10]

In the meantime, Sudbury had to decide what it was going to do, and Kelly gave City Council some practical advice. Assuming that appropriate arrangements were reached with INCO, he recommended that a licence be granted – not a monopoly. After all, he pointed out, 'Council might find, over a period of years, that another company might be interested in Sudbury, which would render more efficient service.'[11] Kelly's suggestion was undoubtedly well meaning, but it was unrealistic. No company would invest in building the infrastructure necessary for the residential delivery of natural gas in return for a licence that could be readily revoked.

Once the type of distribution arrangement had been decided, a distributor would have to be selected. Three companies had expressed interest: the Merchant Gas Company, NONG, and Intercounty Natural Gas Company Limited. All three had the necessary experience and capital to install and run a gas distribution system. Procedurally, Kelly reported, a number of steps had to be followed: first, City Council had to pass a bylaw; second, the bylaw had to be approved by the Ontario Fuel Board; third, the bylaw had to be submitted to the Sudbury electorate; and fourth, the terms of the franchise, once sanctioned by the electorate, had to be affirmed by the OFB. Only then would City Council be entitled to ratify the agreement.

Sudbury obviously occupied a unique position among the northern municipalities. Together with INCO, it was the largest potential customer for natural gas. City councillors knew that Trans-Canada Pipe Lines desperately needed to make a deal with NONG, so it could prove to potential lenders that there were gas customers in northern Ontario. It was also clear that NONG was the only contender for the northern franchises with the financial clout and engineering expertise to distribute natural gas across and throughout the north. Yet Sudbury was not bargaining entirely from a position of strength. If Trans-Canada Pipe Lines failed to obtain financing, and if the all-Canadian route was lost as a result, Sudbury would not obtain natural gas, at least not in the foreseeable future. It was therefore in Sudbury's interest to ensure that Trans-Canada Pipe Lines succeeded in demonstrating that the all-Canadian route made financial sense, and this meant that Sudbury, like all the other northern municipalities, had to sign franchise agreements with NONG.

Sudbury, NONG, and Trans-Canada Pipe Lines needed each other – badly – and NONG was not shy about making this point. As Grey pointed out in an April 1955 letter to Landreville, it was absolutely essential for communities like Sudbury to pass bylaws providing for agreements between them and gas companies for the distribution of gas. Such bylaws, Grey wrote, would be strong evidence of the interest of the northern municipalities in the northern route and of their desire for natural gas, and would assist Trans-Canada Pipe Lines in raising the capital it required from an increasingly sceptical market. Landreville thanked Grey politely, and promised to bring the issue up when City Council next met.

At that time, and on Landreville's recommendation, the decision was taken to leave the matter in abeyance.[12] While a Labour Progressive Party member of City Council predictably attempted to persuade his colleagues that a municipally owned system would serve Sudbury's interests best, most council members, Landreville included, felt that public ownership was not practical or possible, given Sudbury's debt load, not to mention the admonition from the attorney general. In any event, more study was required, and INCO's intentions had to be ascertained.

Grey stepped up his lobbying activities. There was, he claimed, some urgency in the matter: 'There can be no doubt,' Grey wrote, 'that there are interests who are strongly advocating that the line go south of Lake Superior and through the United States. NONG has always strongly advocated and is continuing to fight for an All-Canadian line and by the Northern route.' In Grey's opinion, it lay within Sudbury's power to ensure that result: 'The strongest evidence that can be offered of the interest of the Northern Municipalities in the Northern route and their desire to have natural gas available would be the passing of a by-law authorizing a franchise agreement.' Such a bylaw – and Grey conveniently included a draft – 'would be a valuable contribution to the support necessary to bring about satisfactory financing arrangements for the pipe line.'[13]

Quite properly, Landreville forwarded copies of Grey's letter to members of the Sudbury City Council, and they discussed the issue when they met on 20 April 1955. Landreville and his Council were in no hurry, however. They made it clear that Sudbury would not act until INCO had made up its mind. Once INCO made a deal with a distributor, Sudbury would, too, and more likely than not with the same company. In fact, both INCO and Sudbury were waiting for each other to act. Neither wanted to award a franchise first. Relations between the two were not good. Part of the explanation was INCO's fear that Sudbury would annex Copper Cliff, and with it, INCO's major facility, and add it to its tax base.

Although both INCO and Sudbury were extremely important to NONG, each presented problems in terms of construction and short-term financial gain.[14] If the northern route was chosen, a long lateral line from North Bay would have to be built, at NONG's expense. And, of the two, NONG was particularly interested in INCO. 'International Nickel, as far as we were concerned,' C. Spencer Clark recalled, 'was sort of the strawberry on top of the frosting of the cake, for the simple reason that, in financial circles, it had more glamour than all of the rest of our operation put together.' Still, NONG's financial forecasts indicated that it would take some years before the company actually began to earn a profit on INCO sales: 'INCO, with its enormous buying power and its fine handling facilities, was purchasing West Virginian coal from the United States at a very cheap price, and in order for us to replace that, our price had to be such that there was very little margin in it for us.'[15] As for Sudbury, despite its large number of potential residential users, installation would be expensive because the homes were spread out over difficult terrain. However, it made financial sense for NONG to supply both INCO and Sudbury, and to achieve some economies of scale. In any event, it was understood that the OFB and Trans-Canada Pipe Lines would not countenance an industrial deal that left Sudbury residents without natural gas.[16]

Sudbury City Council was entitled to delay its franchise decision, but there were risks. Most notably, the all-Canadian route might be lost; or a decision might be made, in the absence of northern support, to build the pipeline along the southern route, bypassing much of the north, though Sudbury would still be served. The pressure to obtain the northern route continued. In July 1955 delegates from twelve northern municipalities, including Sudbury, met with Prime Minister Louis St Laurent and C.D. Howe. They had one request: that the government insist that any pipeline bringing gas from Alberta follow the northern route. No commitments were made, but St Laurent and Howe went out of their way to advise the delegates that they were extremely interested in 'the welfare of all Canadians.' For his part, Howe made it clear that it was not necessary for any municipality to enter into an agreement with any gas company. That could wait.[17]

NONG, however, continued its lobbying efforts, and in December 1955 Grey travelled to Sudbury. By this time the company had secured territorial rights and gas distributing franchises from virtually every community of any size in northern Ontario. Landreville was impressed and told Grey as much. He also indicated that NONG would undoubtedly receive the consideration it 'assuredly merits' when the time arrived for Sudbury City Council to proceed with the natural gas question.[18] This was not the answer Grey was looking for, and he called in reinforcements.

In early February 1956 the vice-president of Trans-Canada Pipe Lines wrote to Landreville. While the company maintained a 'strictly neutral position with respect to competitors for franchise rights in a given area,' A.P. Craig pointed out to Landreville that NONG was his company's preferred choice. NONG had already signed up nineteen northern municipalities and, except at the Lakehead, had eliminated the competition. Craig concluded that it would 'be most helpful to Trans-Canada if the City of Sudbury will make its choice of distributor ... as soon as is practicable.'[19]

Landreville was not unsympathetic. He simply wished to wait for INCO to make up its mind, and as soon as it did the city of Sudbury would almost certainly follow suit.[20] By 1956 NONG was the only company actively seeking the Sudbury franchise; the other contenders had fallen by the wayside. Since public ownership had been ruled out, Sudbury would have to join sooner or later with NONG if the city was to have natural gas.

In the meantime, negotiations between NONG and INCO continued. On 21 February 1956 Landreville reported to City Council that these discussions had, apparently, bogged down. The suggested contract term was not long enough, nor, he advised, was the price right. Landreville again urged council to wait and see.[21] On learning of these developments, Farris decided that his personal intervention was required. He travelled north and, for the first time, met Landreville. He told the mayor that it was his understanding that INCO would sign as soon as Sudbury did. Landreville needed better assurances than that, and the two men got in Landreville's car and drove over to Copper Cliff, where Farris's information was confirmed.[22] Earlier lobbying efforts with INCO in New York had paid off.

With the INCO negotiations on track, Farris turned his attention to securing the Sudbury franchise. Landreville was obviously a key player, and, fortunately for NONG, he and Farris got along extremely well. Only a day apart in age, they liked each other, and in short order their business relationship turned into a social one. There were dinner parties on Elm Street and visits to Landreville's place at the lake. The two men kept in close touch as Farris closely monitored City Council's consideration of his franchise application.

When Landreville was told at the end of April that NONG and INCO had reached a tentative agreement, he arranged for the franchising matter to be brought before an early May 1956 meeting of the city's Board of Control – the executive committee, in effect, of City Council. There was clearly a sense that the time had come for Sudbury to act.

Thanks to NONG's concerted lobbying efforts and those of the communities in the north, Trans-Canada Pipe Lines had become convinced that there were reasons to reappraise its planned route. The Board of Transport Commissioners agreed, and the choice of the northern route was announced. The deal was not done yet, however. Trans-Canada Pipe Lines could not raise the money it needed to finance construction of an all-Canadian route. Although the northern route was now believed to be more favourable from the construction, operation, maintenance, and marketing points of view, the overall cost of the project remained extremely high. In the long term, Trans-Canada Pipe Lines and NONG's projections might be right; but in the short term, the pipeline would not generate sufficient sales to attract the private capital necessary to finance construction.

When it became clear that private enterprise would not raise the required sums, the governing Liberals reversed an earlier decision not to provide a bond guarantee. They created a crown corporation, with the financial participation of the province of Ontario, to finance the uneconomical section of the northern route from the Ontario-Manitoba border to Kapuskasing. This section, just over 1100 kilometres long, would be built and owned by the government and leased to Trans-Canada Pipe Lines until it was in a position to buy it outright. The Cooperative Commonwealth Federation (CCF), of course, favoured public ownership of the entire trans-Canada line, while the Tories were opposed to any public money spent in support of 'American' enterprise.

The decision to create a crown corporation, Northern Ontario Pipe Line Limited, to build the uneconomical section of the northern route led to the confrontation that came to be known in 1956 as the pipeline debate. That debate, long mythologized in Canadian history, was in many respects a microcosm of the Canadian experience. Most, if not all, themes of Canadian history were canvassed in Parliament over the course of a particularly rancorous and unpleasant spring session. The atmosphere was further poisoned by the Liberal government's decision, pointless as it turned out, to limit the discussion by invoking closure and forcing a parliamentary vote.

At issue was a long-serving government's repudiation of parliamentary rights. But the debate was concerned with more than opposition perceptions, real and imagined, about the abuse of parliamentary power by a government that had lost moral authority to act. It was also about the building of a national link, and the impact of that link on north-south continentalism and east-west nationalism. The debate highlighted the conflicts between western producers and eastern consumers, between the federal government and the provinces, and raised the problem of public versus private enterprise and the compromise of a temporary crown corporation.[23] Underlying the discussion was a growing fear about the power of Americans – economic, political, and cultural – in Canadian life.

In the end, though, the debate was about getting an important job done and building a pipeline across Canada, one that was subject to Canadian law and completely under Canadian control, regardless of who actually owned the shares. After all, Canadians did not own a majority of the shares of the Canadian Pacific Railway: they never had and probably never would. The CPR was, however, a Canadian company through and through and wholly subject to Canadian laws and Canadian control. The same would be true of Trans-Canada Pipe Lines. The selling of shares to Americans and other foreigners was not, as some critics claimed, a betrayal of Canadian interests and resources. In the same way that 'British money' built the CPR, the fact that 'American dollars' were used, in part, to finance the trans-Canada pipeline was, in the overall scheme of things, unimportant. The establishment of a crown corporation was, as Howe said when he first supported the bill in the House, 'a limited and prudent intervention by government.' In May 1956, when he introduced closure, he echoed these remarks.[24]

There were other reasons to invoke closure. Unless the financing was put into place, Trans-Canada Pipe Lines would lose an earlier acquired right to purchase scarce supplies of 85-centimetre American- and British-made pipe. Another year would have passed, and with an election expected some time in 1957, further delays might sound the death-knell for the all-Canadian route. Moreover, if for some reason the all-Canadian route was lost, there was no guarantee that Ontario and Quebec could continue to purchase natural gas from the United States, taking into account the vagaries of the highly competitive American market and the uncertainty posed by the need for regulatory approval for American gas exports. There was absolutely no doubt, insofar as the Americans were concerned, that they would place their gas needs first. Should energy come into short supply, the tap to Canada would quickly be turned off, as it had been on several occasions during the Second World War. Canadians needed their own supply of natural gas, and key Liberals believed that the time for talking had long passed. The pipeline had already been delayed far too long, and if the 1956 construction season was not to be lost, something had to be done.

Closure did not, however, achieve its intended purpose, at least not right away. The pipeline debate dragged on for three weeks, as member after member rose on points of privilege or order and proceeded to debate the merits of the bill. CCF parliamentarians insisted that public ownership was the only way to go. They would not be confused by the facts. At the other end of the ideological spectrum, the Conservatives maintained their blind faith in the ability of private enterprise to see that the job got done, notwithstanding the proof to the contrary, and they expressed opposition to the expenditure of any government funds. At the same time they objected to raising funds in American capital markets, claiming that this would be a sellout to 'Texas buccaneers.'

The Liberals, as usual, were somewhere between these two extremes. Their main objective was seeing the project through to completion, and they were secure in the knowledge that they enjoyed widespread public support. Indeed, even the Tories at Queen's Park in Toronto were fully behind the scheme, so much so that the Ontario legislature had unanimously approved a $35 million contribution to the uneconomical part of the northern route. Ultimately, the debate came to an end, the government prevailed in Parliament, and Howe's bill was passed.

As St Laurent told the House of Commons, it had long been the policy of the government of Canada to preserve energy and power produced in Canada for Canadians. Building the trans-Canada pipeline was an integral part of that policy. While it might make some short-term sense to export Canadian gas south at Emerson, Manitoba, and import American gas across the Niagara River for markets in Ontario and Quebec, the result might be that Canada became both obliged to sell natural gas to the United States and dependent on American imports.[25] Canadians were already concerned enough about the growing influence of Americans in their economic life.[26] The east-west pattern of communication and transportation, ever since the fur trade, had fostered a separate national identity. The trans-Canada pipeline would form one more of these important links, tying western resources to the markets of central Canada.[27]

Trans-Canada Pipe Lines was the company with the plans, the organization, and the pipe. St Laurent declared that the line should be built, that it would be built, and that future generations of Canadians would be glad it was built.[28] Howe remained stalwart in support of the scheme. 'There is a price on Canadian nationhood,' he told the House of Commons, and 'if we always looked for the cheapest way of doing things here in Canada, there might have been another state in the United States but there very likely would have been no Canada.' The people of Canada, the American-born Howe concluded, 'have been very jealous about accepting any monetary advantage that would in any way jeopardize the control by Canada over her own resources.'[29] The creation of Northern Ontario Pipe Line Limited, he stated, would protect Canadian sovereignty by financing the uneconomical part of the northern route. It also made fiscal sense, since the money was loaned to Trans-Canada Pipe Lines and the legislation provided for Canadian taxpayers to make a small profit from their investment.

The opposition, the *Financial Post* observed in a 2 June 1956 editorial, was 'unconvincing and unconstructive.' The governing Liberals may have been 'ham-handed' in invoking closure, but the 'case for speed is clear.' Establishing Northern Ontario Pipe Line Limited was not a sellout. Claims to that effect were 'wildly extravagant and ill-founded.'[30] Eventually the closure debate ground to a halt, and the bill establishing the corporation was passed. On 7 June 1956 it was given royal assent. The federal government provided the company with $80 million in financing. Ontario had also pledged $35 million. This money was neither a subsidy to, nor an interference with, private enterprise; it was a means of putting Alberta gas into central Canada as soon as possible. Ottawa had no intention of holding on to Northern Ontario Pipe Line for long.[31]

As it happened, this is exactly what took place. By the summer of 1963 Trans-Canada Pipe Lines had bought the pipeline from the Canadian government, which received its investment back, together with interim rental payments and interest. Passage of the act, meanwhile, sent an important message to Wall Street. With the federal and Ontario governments backing the scheme, the remaining private financing quickly fell into place. All that now remained, from NONG's point of view, was for Sudbury to sign on.

When Sudbury City Council met in early May 1956, the result of its deliberations was preordained. Following discussion about the proposed agreement with NONG, Councillor Grace Hartman, who had a promising union career in her future, and Councillor Joseph Fabbro, who would succeed Landreville as mayor, moved that the Board of Control recommend to council first and second reading of the bylaw granting the gas franchise to NONG. The vote carried, and Landreville telegraphed Howe, advising him that the citizens and industry of Sudbury were most anxious for the gas line to proceed.[32] Howe was delighted to learn about the vote, and observed that it improved the feasibility of the project from Trans-Canada Pipe Line's point of view. He urged Sudbury to sign the contract with NONG without delay.[33]

Landreville also wrote to Farris informing him of the latest developments. 'I may presume this move on our part will not displease you,' he noted with understatement.[34] Farris replied that the timing of his telegram to Howe could not have been better: 'Certification of gas loads of this size is what is necessary to put the all-Canadian line over, and Mr. Howe must be greatly appreciative of your action. Needless to say, NONG is equally so.' Farris planned to visit Sudbury soon and, referring to some earlier correspondence from Landreville, added, 'as you say, we have important things to discuss.'[35]

Giving the bylaw authorizing the franchise agreement first and second reading was easy enough. That took place on 22 May 1956. Slightly more difficult was the matter of dispensing with a requirement that Sudbury citizens vote on the proposed contract. Landreville told council that it was necessary to take immediate action; the Ontario Fuel Board was about to go into summer recess. Accordingly, the suggestion was made to drop the required citywide vote and, on the motion of Councillors Hartman and Fabbro, City Council asked for permission from the OFB to do so.[36] The board held a hearing on this issue in Sudbury on 7 June 1956 and, four days later, gave its permission. There was nothing unusual about this procedure. In no case was the granting of a franchise to NONG or to any other company actually put to the electorate anywhere in the north.

It was expected that third reading would take place on 19 June 1956, followed by an Ontario Fuel Board hearing two days later. This schedule was not followed, however, when city solicitor Kelly wrote to Landreville and the council members raising a number of concerns about signing a contract with NONG. He had more questions than answers about the proposed deal – about rates, the term of the franchise, and service. Until these questions were answered, Kelly suggested that nothing be done.[37]

City Council discussed Kelly's concerns when it next met on 19 June. Farris was there and he urged council to move quickly. If it did not, he suggested, gas might be delayed in coming to Sudbury. Council decided, however, to hold third reading over to another meeting.[38] The Board of Control convened the following day, Landreville again suggesting quick action. Indeed, it was a matter of some urgency, he said, not just to northern Ontario but to the entire pipeline project.[39] And it was true. The Sudbury load, including both the city and INCO, was considered essential by Trans-Canada Pipe Lines, the Ontario Fuel Board, and NONG. But Sudbury was the last remaining municipality to sign, and NONG both needed and wanted Sudbury on board. From an investor's point of view, it was essential that NONG hold Sudbury's franchise rights.

A Sudbury City Council delegation travelled to Toronto on 21 June 1956 for the previously scheduled meeting of the Ontario Fuel Board. Farris testified first about the viability of the project. He told the OFB that there would be one standard rate for the Northern Zone, whatever the installation expenditures. He also said that the gas would be less expensive in the Northern Zone than in the Central Zone, but more expensive than in the Western Zone. How, Farris was asked, could this be so? He replied that NONG anticipated favourable load distribution for its valley and regular gas in the Northern Zone, resulting in lower rates. Farris also told the OFB that there would be a public offering of stock, and that users in northern Ontario would be given the first opportunity to subscribe.

Farris's testimony was followed by the evidence of other NONG directors, who testified about their engineering and financial plans and why they all made sense. The OFB was advised that NONG intended to employ Canadian labour and to use Canadian materials, and the point was made that the Sudbury franchise was critical to the success of the entire undertaking. For his part, the chairman of the Fuel Board indicated that he believed it to be a very good deal, and pointed out that the Northern Zone was getting a fair rate. Arthur Crozier advised those in attendance that, while the board was not trying to force Sudbury to sign with NONG, he did want to indicate 'the seriousness of our consideration.' Crozier could not understand why Sudbury City Council was taking so long 'when they had given the By-law first and second reading and had received copies of the Contract.' There was nothing left to resolve except 'minor details which could be dealt with at the completion of the agreement.'[40]

That afternoon, in an informal session, Crozier warned the participants about the consequences of delay. Trans-Canada Pipe Lines would be in Winnipeg by the end of 1957, and if northern Ontario was not on side, there was every prospect of the pressure groups diverting the route south through the United States. If that happened, the northern route would be lost. Crozier also pointed out that the OFB carefully regulated rates – and profits – and that Sudbury could, if it wished, buy one or more shares in NONG and in that way keep abreast of the company's activities. There was no prospect that Sudbury could undertake the service itself, even if it were so inclined; the financing costs were too great. It would, in any event, be required to buy its gas from Trans-Canada Pipe Lines, or quite possibly NONG, depending on who built and owned the lateral off the main route. This would not be economical. A stand-alone city franchise would not benefit from opportunities to dispose of valley gas over a much larger distribution system. There really was only one choice: going along with NONG.

The trip was sobering, and informative. P.H. Murphy, the city clerk-comptroller, prepared a full report. 'The Hearing,' he wrote, 'was most interesting and beneficial and the opinion of your Delegates was that the trip was very fruitful in that we gleaned a lot of information and had a lot of points cleared up. We were also advised that the Northern Ontario Gas Company would pay for the expenses of this trip.'[41]

Crozier later travelled to Sudbury and appeared before City Council on 3 July 1956 to explain the jurisdiction of his board. One reason he appeared was to help Landreville overcome the difficulties he was experiencing with Kelly.[42] Crozier made it clear that the NONG deal made good sense and that Sudbury had reached a better agreement than some of the other northern municipalities. The OFB had to approve any contract entered into by a municipality, and OFB officials worked closely with city employees in Sudbury in the negotiation and redrafting of the contract. So, when Crozier indicated that he supported NONG, that mattered. Some further negotiations with NONG ensued, and Kelly and Farris, who were present at this meeting of City Council, agreed on some changes to the legal text. More discussion followed, and on 17 July 1956 Sudbury City Council convened to give bylaw 56-58, authorizing the mayor and city clerk to enter into a franchise agreement with NONG, third and final reading.

Even at this late stage, Sudbury displayed a characteristically independent streak. City Council would not be rushed. Some of the legal fine print still had to be worked out, and the city solicitor and some councillors insisted that NONG would have to create a subsidiary company to hold the Sudbury franchise, even though there was no apparent benefit to such a course.[43] Nevertheless, certain undertakings were sought and obtained.[44] Some municipal politicians even tried to rewrite the deal. One controller asked about obtaining price guarantees, and once again it was explained that rates would not be set by NONG but by the OFB. The franchise agreement said as much, and it also gave Sudbury the right, ten years after the system was installed, of purchasing it from NONG at fair market price. Most of the other municipalities did not have that right for twenty years. Moreover, the franchise itself was for a period of only twenty years, at which time the terms and conditions were subject to renegotiation as a condition of renewal. Clearly, the franchise agreement was a good bargain, the best that any municipality had received in the north.[45]

Farris had again made the trip north, and over the course of the session he answered questions and dealt with concerns. Landreville asked the city clerk what he thought of the deal, and Murphy replied that 'in his estimation Mr. Kelly had done a good job and he felt that it covered all of the municipal requirements ... he felt the franchise was a fair one.'[46] Finally, the bylaw was put to a vote. It passed 7 to 3; Landreville did not vote, as it was customary for the mayor to vote only to break a tie. The next day the agreement conferring the franchise was signed on behalf of the city. On 20 July 1956 the agreement was returned to Sudbury with NONG's endorsement. A certificate of 'public convenience and necessity' was instantly issued by the OFB after a hearing in Toronto, during which Landreville cross-examined NONG witnesses on the commitments they had made. Kelly, having earlier pronounced himself satisfied with the deal, made a last-ditch and unsuccessful attempt to defer the OFB approval. All that was left was the deal with INCO.[47]

After Sudbury City Council's final vote on the franchise, Farris and Landreville had gone out for a late supper. They had much to celebrate and to discuss. When Farris had testified before the OFB the previous month, he had announced NONG's intention to give northern Ontario residents the first opportunity to subscribe for NONG shares. Landreville was attracted to the idea, and after the OFB proceedings he approached Farris and expressed his interest in purchasing shares of his own.[48] Farris had been giving this matter some thought, and when the two men went out to celebrate the franchise agreement, they discussed Landreville's future with NONG. As Farris later recalled:

He was most impressed with our company and its future. I think he advised me his term of office was shortly expiring and he would not be standing for office again. I think he initiated it but I wouldn't be too sure of that, of the desirability, from his point of view, of being associated with a new utility such as ours and my agreeing we would need a lot of people in our organization, each with certain talents, each able to contribute something to a company that, up to now, had practically no employees and ... we were just at that time changing the capital of the company and going to make a rights offering on the new company of $2.50 a share and it is quite logical ... in response to his inquiry as to his ability to participate in the stock of the company, that I would tell him, yes, when that association took place that he could and would be allowed to buy shares at this price.[49]

The next day Farris returned to Toronto, and a NONG directors' meeting was purportedly held. Among the issues said to be discussed was the future relationship with Landreville. Three days after Sudbury finally approved the deal, Farris wrote to the mayor:

You have recently expressed an interest in our company indicating that when free to do so you would like to assist us in some capacity, particularly with reference to representing us as we face the many problems ahead in the Sudbury area and Northern Ontario generally. You have indicated your faith and interest in us by expressing also a desire to purchase stock in our company. We greatly appreciate this twofold approbation of us by you.

At a directors' meeting held the 18th of July following a shareholders' meeting on the 17th, your participation in our company was discussed. The shareholders' meeting had approved a change in capital whereby the authorized capital was increased to 2,000,000 shares and the outstanding shares split five for one to bring the total issued shares to approximately 660,000. The directors resolved to offer existing shareholders the right to subscribe for 40,000 additional shares of the 'new' stock at a price of $2.50 per share.

At the same time it was resolved to offer you 10,000 shares at the same price of $2.50 per share. This offer is firm until July 18th, 1957. Should you wish to purchase portions of these shares at different times that will be in order.

At your convenience and when you are free to do so we would welcome the opportunity to discuss our relationship for the future in greater detail.[50]

Landreville responded at the end of the month:

I have your very kind letter of July 20th at hand.

I fully appreciate the advantages of the offer you outlined to me and I fully intend to exercise this option before July 18th, 1957.

There is the additional question of the personal interest I will devote to your Company in Northern Ontario. While all the management questions may be at a problematic stage in your Company, I would like to assure you of my interest in promoting the welfare of your Company in the time to come.

My present Office, as Mayor, does not permit me to a definite commital but in the course of the months following January next, I feel sure we may sit down and see if your Company and I have something which we could exchange to our mutual benefit.[51]

In the summer of 1956, $2.50 a share was probably a fair price for the NONG shares. That began to change, and by December 1956 there was active public interest in the shares, now valued at around $10 each, and the price rose to a high of $28 each just prior to the public issue in June 1957. By 27 February 1957, the future and profitability of NONG was assured, and this was reflected in its share price. On that day, the Metropolitan Life Insurance Company agreed to buy $90 million of Trans-Canada Pipe Lines' mortgage bonds. The public and private financing for the trans-Canada route was completely in place. That meant that NONG was no longer a speculative venture with paper assets, but had become a company with a tangible commodity to sell.

Landreville was not the only politician to benefit from NONG's largesse. A number of municipal politicians were given gifts of NONG shares. In accordance with its stated policy, NONG also made an early offer to residents of franchise areas. Farris approached Landreville's successor as mayor, Joseph Fabbro, asking him to provide NONG with names of persons interested in participating in the public offering, which consisted of one debenture and one share with an initial price of $30. Fabbro was happy to comply and presented Farris with a list of preferred customers. Although demand was in excess of supply, he allocated the largest number of units – 1650 – to himself. Various City Council members and clerk-comptroller Murphy were allotted much smaller amounts, ranging between 100 and 150 units each. After these arrangements were made, the units were offered to the public, and the offering was an unqualified success. Unit holders who immediately sold took easy profits, the units rapidly reaching a market price substantially above the offering price.[52] Similar arrangements were made with other northern mayors, who drew up subscription lists that were forwarded to NONG.

Altogether, 400,000 common shares were offered for sale, which netted NONG more than $11 million. A further $8 million in subordinate debentures were also sold, and commitments were obtained from both Canadian and American institutional lenders for $12 million of mortgage bonds. A majority of NONG shares were held by Canadians. By the spring of 1958 Farris's dream was almost realized. The construction program was ahead of schedule and below budget. The basic industrial sales program was complete and, more importantly, the projections indicated greater potential revenue than originally forecast.

NONG began preparations for an aggressive, full-blown sales campaign once the gas lines were installed. Local dealers were trained in the sale, service, and proper installation of gas appliances and gas-fired equipment. A NONG information bus equipped with demonstration material began travelling from one community to the next, staging informational meetings for the general public. A company-sponsored finance plan was expected to bolster residential sales. Appliance dealers who wished to avail themselves of the plan, and who conformed to company and OFB requirements, were designated as 'Authorized Blue Flame Dealers.' A twenty-four-hour service department was in preparation. Standards exceeding legal requirements were established to ensure the safety of all service lines, installations, and appliances. Other promotional activities such as the 'Gasarama,' a fair with the arrival of natural gas as its theme, were planned for the larger centres.

Gas was coming to the north, and in the process so was prosperity, it seemed. An army of construction crews arrived with money to spend – some 5000 workers at one time. Hotel and restaurant owners profited, and so did local building and cement supply companies. In more than half the communities it crossed, Trans-Canada Pipe Lines became the largest taxpayer. 'The arrival of this low-cost, versatile fuel, available for the first time to energy-hungry industries and communities,' NONG's annual report observed, 'and at a price significantly lower than in Southern Ontario, promises to initiate an era of growth the extent of which time alone can fully assess.'[53] For the first time, compared with competitors in the south, northern industries operated at an energy price advantage. Instead of simply being a colony of Toronto, there was every reason to believe that the north would become an economic power in its own right.

All the signs pointed in this direction. The population of the north was growing. New industries were being established, and it was expected that the market for established ones, such as pulp and paper, would continue to increase. NONG might also expand: the uranium mines at Blind River and Elliot Lake, the Steep Rock–Atikokan iron ore development, and the gold and copper mining areas of Rouyn, Noranda, and Val d'Or in northern Quebec held out the promise and prospect of much new business. NONG was sponsoring research in the use of natural gas, and new applications and possibilities were being discovered every day. By the end of 1958 NONG would be delivering gas to thirty-four communities located between the Manitoba-Ontario border and Orillia, with a population of more than 300,000.[54] The future appeared unlimited.

Just one year later, Crozier told the Borden Commission on Natural Energy, appointed by John Diefenbaker in 1957 in the wake of the Conservative Party's election victory and the now infamous pipeline debate, that prospective markets for natural gas in Ontario were expected to increase fourteenfold in the next thirty years. Moreover, the trans-Canada pipeline really was an important national link. As Ontario's premier

Leslie Frost observed, 'natural gas has brought headaches and heartaches, but the use of gas cannot be overlooked.' Frost, who had served as Ontario's minister of mines during the Second World War, knew that the province had suffered an energy shortage in the war years, and that the natural gas pipeline promised an end to any such future threat. It would have been 'deplorable,' Frost continued, 'if western Canadian gas had been lost to the United States.'[55] The trans-Canada pipeline precluded that result, and NONG was an important part of the project's overall success.

And so, too, was Leo Landreville. One of Sudbury's most successful lawyers and businessmen, Landreville was at the pinnacle of his professional life. In August he was chosen to represent Canada at a conference of North and South American mayors held in Panama City. He was planning to retire from municipal politics, and he was looking forward to a promising and rewarding future with NONG. However, on 13 September 1956 he was appointed to the Supreme Court of Ontario, one of the last judicial appointments Louis St Laurent's government would make before its defeat in the general election the next year. An appointment to the bench is the dream of many lawyers, for service as a judge brings with it great status and prestige. Judicial appointments are highly sought; supplicants usually take many steps to make their desire known. Political connections help, and justice ministers generally bestow this particular reward on partisans of appropriate political stripe. Landreville's elevation had been rumoured for weeks.[56] He was sworn in early the following month.

He had to tell Farris, of course, and an opportunity arose at a Chamber of Commerce dinner in North Bay. Landreville, one of the guests of honour, broke the news to Farris and Clark. He reminded them that he had promised to join NONG – that was the whole basis upon which the stock option had been granted – but both men urged him to accept the appointment. They also told him that the stock option was his no matter what decision he made.[57] 'After the dilemma of whether to have my appendix out or not, the dilemma of remaining a bachelor and happy or get married – this was the biggest dilemma!' Landreville wrote to Farris. 'I feel that given three or four years and with my ambition, I would have squeezed you out of the Presidency of your Company – now I have chosen to be put on the shelf of this all-inspiring, unapproachable, staid class of people called Judges – what a decision! However, right or wrong, I will stick to it and do the best I can ... I want to assure you,' he continued, 'that my interest in your Company, outwardly aloof, will, nevertheless, remain

active. I am keeping your letter of July 20th carefully in my file.'[58] Farris
sent a gracious reply. 'I know that your decision was not an easy one,' he
wrote, 'and those of us who have learned to appreciate your many facets
will understand what a difficult decision it was. There can be no question
as to the wisdom of the appointment and I hope that time will show that
there was equal wisdom in its acceptance.'[59] Landreville reconfirmed that
he wished to retain the NONG option, and Farris, ever generous, again
indicated that that would be fine.[60]

Landreville was Franco-Ontario's new representative on the bench.
The tradition of a French-speaking superior court judge at Osgoode Hall
began in October 1936 when E.R.E. Chevrier, a well-known and highly
regarded Ottawa lawyer, was appointed to the bench. His appointment
was generally well received, although the reaction of the *Fortnightly Law
Journal* was typical. 'We shall watch with interest,' the *Journal* announced,
"the experiment of appointing a French-Canadian to the Ontario Bench.
We note that in the recent Benchers' election, another French-Canadian
did not make much of a showing, which would seem to indicate that the
profession is not enamoured of such an encroachment in a traditional
Anglo-Saxon Province. We have no desire to raise any racial controversy.
But there can be no doubt that there is a very heavy burden upon Mr.
Chevrier if the experiment is to prove a success.'[61] The editorial concluded with the observation that Chevrier's appointment brought forward the question whether the profession should be given a greater role
in the selection of judges, as well as the right to veto any appointment not
meeting with its approval. That, the tenor of the editorial suggested,
undoubtedly would have left Chevrier in Ottawa.

Chevrier was promoted to the Court of Appeal in 1953, the 'experiment' evidently having proven a success. Franco-Ontario's new representative on the Superior Court bench was Arthur M. LeBel. When Chevrier
died in late August 1956, LeBel took his spot on the Court of Appeal, and
a superior court vacancy for a Franco-Ontarian was created. Federal Justice Minister Stuart Garson, on Lester Pearson's strong recommendation,
appointed Landreville to the vacancy.

It took Landreville some time to settle his affairs, and there was also the
little matter of the stock option. It turned out quite well for Landreville. In
early 1957, at Farris's request, the Continental Investment Company,
known as Convesto, 'purchased' 14,000 shares from NONG for $2.50
each, 'on behalf of clients.'[62] Convesto sent NONG a cheque for $35,000.
The distribution was authorized by a 17 January 1957 meeting of
NONG's Board of Directors in New York City. These shares were, on Far-

ris's instructions, then allotted to various persons, including Landreville, who received 10,000 shares in February 1957 at the agreed-upon option price of $2.50 each. 'Some time ago,' a 12 February letter to Landreville from John McGraw, the head of Convesto, a well-known Vancouver brokerage, stated, 'we were instructed by Mr. Ralph K. Farris to purchase for your account 10,000 shares of NONG at $2.50 per share. We have as of this date sold 2,500 shares for your account at $10 per share which clears off the debit balance of your account. You will find enclosed 7,500 shares of NONG with stock receipt attached, which we ask you to sign and return to this office at your convenience.'[63]

Normally, in a transaction of this kind, Landreville would have been required to purchase the stock himself by making a payment directly to NONG. The option had been granted by the corporation, and the payment should have been made to its treasury. Without a doubt, Landreville had the financial means to buy his shares outright and could easily have done so if asked. However, there are many ways of organizing corporate affairs, and there was nothing necessarily wrong with this one. Very simply, Landreville was given 7500 NONG shares for free. Moreover, the transaction was not recorded in the usual way. Convesto, atypically, made its commission by keeping the difference between its purchase price of 2500 of Landreville's shares at $10 a share and the selling price on the open market, which was then upwards of $13 a share.

The sale was also interesting for a number of other reasons. It was recorded by journal voucher and, other than a single ledger entry in Convesto's records, nothing in NONG's books indicated that Landreville was the beneficiary of the transaction. NONG's accounts never indicated that he owned shares. It was not unheard of to structure a transaction this way, but why had Farris not followed the usual course? It was almost as if the sale – and the profits – were being deliberately concealed.

In any event, the remaining shares were sent to Landreville in 'street form' – his name did not appear on the certificates. Beginning in February 1957, Landreville sold the stock in a rapidly rising market. Ultimately, he pocketed $117,000, without ever having to invest one cent. He had reason to be grateful, and he wrote to Convesto on his Osgoode Hall stationery expressing his thanks and adding for good measure: 'Should I be of any assistance to your firm for the promotion or betterment of this company in Ontario, please do not hesitate to contact me.'[64]

Landreville put the money to good use. He improved his Mexican home, bought his wife some new jewellery, and increased his real estate investments. In February 1957 Landreville and Farris met in New York to celebrate their birthdays, and a grateful Landreville thanked his friend for the delivery of the shares.[65] Although he was wealthy, the additional money came in handy. He welcomed the supplement to his salary now that he was a judge. The annual stipend of $18,000 a year was only about a third of what he had earned from the private practice of law.

Although Landreville was not the only northern mayor to receive free NONG shares, he made the most money, by far. That fact, and the manner in which the transaction was recorded on the Convesto books, would raise suspicions about exactly what services Landreville had performed to merit such generous treatment from Farris and NONG. Farris also arranged for three other northern mayors and one city solicitor to receive free shares, but on a much reduced scale. These transactions were also handled in a slightly different way. An account was opened at Convesto in the name of Gordon Kelly McLean, still employed by Farris as his executive assistant, and 800 NONG shares were deposited into that account. Immediately, 200 shares were sold to clear the account. Convesto then mailed the remaining shares to Toronto, again in street form, where McLean gave lots of 150 shares each to Gravenhurst mayor Wanda Miller, Bracebridge mayor Glen Coates, Orillia mayor Wilbur Cramp, and Orillia city solicitor W.L. Moore.[66]

Landreville enjoyed his new career. He had not been learned in the law as a lawyer, nor did he, as a judge, develop any area of law or gain any particular expertise. However, unlike some Supreme Court judges of that day, he was not automatically biased against plaintiffs whose last names ended with a vowel. He had served all sorts of clients in the north, and he ran a surprisingly orderly court. He was courteous to both plaintiffs and defendants, and lawyers felt that they received a full and fair hearing, whether they won or lost.[67] In addition, Landreville did not suffer from 'judgeitis.' While this disorder manifested itself in different ways, the afflicted shared a number of characteristics. Soon after they were appointed to the bench, they forgot what it was like to be counsel. They were now of a breed apart, one of Her Majesty's justices, and had little concern or patience for the problems of the bar. Landreville was different. When he travelled to the county towns on the Ontario Supreme Court circuit, he understood that Toronto was not the centre of the universe and that the administration of justice was important everywhere in the province.

Landreville was, in short, a decent man and an all-round good judge who quickly grasped the facts. He carried a heavy workload and did a good job. In his eleven-year judicial career, only eighty-one of his decisions were appealed. The appeals were dismissed in forty-two cases, allowed in twenty-five, and partially allowed in eight. New trials were ordered in six cases. Two of the appeals proceeded to the Supreme Court of Canada, and in one of these cases, Landreville's original verdict was restored.[68] This appeal record was no better or worse than that of his peers. Still, many of his colleagues at Osgoode Hall could not get over what they saw as his flamboyant manner and extravagant lifestyle. Landreville paid them little attention. He loved life and, whenever he could, he got away to enjoy Landra Villa. Everything was going well for him, until the police came calling.

3

Scandal

Money was being made from natural gas – lots of it. Ontario's minister of mines, Phil Kelly, the accountant who rose from town councillor in the paper-making community of Smooth Rock Falls, made the most. He was among the charter investors in NONG. His shares were held in an Alberta company, Kelmac Oils, which was established by his nephew, Gordon Kelly McLean.[1] Kelmac was, of course, a contraction of the Kelly and McLean names. Kelly's total investment of approximately $5000 had, by early 1957, grown to half a million dollars. His nephew, as it turned out, did almost as well.

Kelly's cabinet colleagues Colonel William Griesinger, MPP for Windsor-Sandwich, and Clare Mapledoram also both bought shares at bargain prices; Griesinger in October 1956, Mapledoram in August 1956.[2] Mapledoram represented Fort William, and in that capacity was aware of some of the early meetings leading to the establishment of Twin City Gas. He was interested in seeing natural gas come to his riding and in acquiring, as he did, both NONG and Twin City shares.[3] NONG purchased a 50 per cent interest in Twin City in 1956. Two years later it took the company over.

Kelly was not averse to reaching across party lines, and the future Liberal Party leader John Wintermeyer joined the gravy train in the fall of 1956.[4] The only problem was that Kelly, Griesinger, and Mapledoram had been ordered by Premier Leslie Frost when the northern pipeline was before the Ontario legislature the previous year not to invest in pipeline stock – and that included natural gas stock – and to sell whatever shares they might already have acquired.[5] Wintermeyer, as his party's finance critic, also should have been concerned about conflict of interest, real or perceived, in the pipeline development. In addition, Kelly had been specifically told on several occasions that it was not appropriate for the minister of mines to dispense 'hot tips,' but he continued to do so and also failed to disclose his holdings or to dispose of them.[6] Similarly, Griesinger and Mapledoram ignored the instructions and, like Wintermeyer, kept quiet about their ownership of NONG shares. In fact, Mapledoram tried to conceal his share purchase; he arranged with Kelly for his shares to be registered in the name of his brother-in-law.[7]

Soon enough Kelly's profiteering came to the attention of Frost, and on 8 July 1957 he was summoned to a meeting at the premier's office.[8] When he arrived, he was told he had to go. While it was later reported that a typed resignation letter was waiting for him, that was not so. He wrote out his letter in longhand, resigning, he claimed, because of pressing business commitments.[9] It took an unusually long time for the real circumstances of Kelly's resignation to become known (he remained, briefly, a member of the legislature, representing Cochrane North). Eventually, the leader of the Ontario CCF, Donald C. MacDonald, found out, and early in March 1958 he raised the matter in the legislature.

After referring to newspaper reports indicating that millions of dollars had been made by insiders who had acquired NONG stock for pennies a share, MacDonald went on to add that it was an 'open secret around Queen's Park, and Northern Ontario, that one of the hon. Ministers in this cabinet was involved in the pipe line profiteering. In fact, so much so, that eventually the hon. Prime Minister had a show down with him and he was dismissed.' The premier rejected the suggestion: 'I did no such thing,' he angrily retorted. MacDonald demanded a royal commission.

Frost was not pleased and, instead of admitting the truth, he accused MacDonald of impropriety, calling him a 'master of insinuation and innuendo.' Kelly's resignation, Frost claimed, 'had nothing whatever to do with the Northern Ontario Natural Gas Company, nor any other gas company. It had to do with the fact that he wanted to engage in other types of business which were not consistent with his being a member of this government.'[10] Moreover, Kelly had fixed his sights on the federal house. Kelly was, Frost claimed as the debate continued from one day to the next, an honourable member and an honourable man. It was time for MacDonald to learn that men and women in public life were not dishonest and were not subject to bribery and corruption. If MacDonald had just asked him why Kelly had resigned, he would have given him the answer.

The implication was obvious: MacDonald was slinging mud, and none of it had stuck. Frost warned MacDonald to start acting like a 'gentleman,' or he would not go far in public life.[11] MacDonald had other ideas.

Following weeks of effort, the CCF leader had managed to obtain a copy of NONG's prospectus. And when he did, he found out that a handful of people, including a mysterious 'Mr. MacLean,' had, before the public offering, obtained tens of thousands of shares, or in McLean's case more than one hundred thousand shares, often for less than one cent each. MacDonald's review of the prospectus left him convinced that, through various stock splits and the exercise of option rights, the promoters of the company had effectively concealed just who owned how much. Not only were MacDonald's socialist sensibilities outraged, but he suspected that a large number of shares had been given to publicly elected officials in return for their political support. This was political corruption, he charged, and he began to press the government for the details.[12] But the premier was not willing to oblige.

Frost told MacDonald to get any further information he required from the Ontario Securities Commission. He also treated him to a lesson in market capitalism. 'Investors,' Frost pointed out, 'had the right to decline to purchase the shares, and to assess the amounts of these shares as being excessive.' A proper reading of the prospectus indicated that all the original shares, at the time of filing, were accounted for. There were no missing shares. There was no under-the-table distribution of shares. No member of the government was involved in misconduct. There was simply no basis for any allegations of untoward conduct, according to Premier Frost. In response to a request from Liberal leader Farquhar Oliver for an inquiry into the whole matter, Frost advised the legislature that none of his cabinet ministers held, or had held, pipeline shares. The allegations were simply wrong. Frost knew they were wrong because he had 'a canvass made of every hon. member of the cabinet.' Frost could, therefore, 'assure the hon. members that I know what I am talking about. I know that no shares were held, and I would say that we have been very meticulous in our dealings in that regard.'[13] It looked, to casual observers, as if MacDonald had got it all wrong.

From his Smooth Rock Falls home, Kelly challenged the CCF leader to 'step outside' the legislature and its cloak of parliamentary immunity. 'If he does,' Kelly asserted, 'he'll face an immediate libel suit.'[14] James Maloney, a lawyer and the Conservative representative from South Renfrew, also challenged MacDonald in the legislature to repeat his comments outside the House and offered his legal services to Kelly. MacDonald, white faced and angry, accepted both challenges and repeated the charge. Within a matter of days, after more denials and following yet another statement from the premier that no one in the cabinet owned NONG shares, Kelly more or less admitted the truth of MacDonald's charge.[15] Too many people knew about his ownership of NONG shares. In a public statement, Kelly confirmed that 'one of the main reasons for his resignation was his family connections with the pipeline deals.'[16]

MacDonald renewed his demand that the government investigate allegations of misconduct by members of the provincial cabinet. He had some proof, and his conclusion that there was something seriously wrong in the way NONG dealt with elected officials appeared to have some merit. Indeed, MacDonald suspected that other provincial cabinet ministers, not to mention municipal politicians, might be involved. The premier disagreed. No member of his government, Frost stated on 12 March 1958, 'directly or indirectly, holds any stock in any of these companies whatever.'[17] MacDonald's calls for an inquiry went nowhere, at least for the time being.

After Kelly resigned, Frost had every reason to believe that the story would evaporate. It did, but only for a short while. Before long, a report in the *Toronto Star* revealed that MacDonald's claims of corruption in high places were not limited to an isolated event. An enterprising reporter, Blaik Kirby, had purchased one NONG share and exercised his right to examine the shareholders' list. Prominent among the NONG stockholders was Colonel William Griesinger, the minister of public works, not to mention the names of numerous elected officials in northern Ontario towns.

Kelly now provided further details about his involvement with NONG. It was true, he said, that he and his family had made a great deal of money from his investment, and that his original stake had not been large. He had put up the money when the venture was risky and capital was required. The fact that he was a minister at the time was, in his view, irrelevant. He had, he insisted, done nothing wrong, morally, ethically, or legally.[18]

Even if that were true, important questions remained. Why had Kelly denied MacDonald's charges when he first made them in the legislature, and why had he sought to conceal his ownership of NONG shares by having them registered in his nephew's name? McLean later insisted that he never told Farris or anyone else in NONG that his uncle, the mines minister, actually owned some of the shares.[19] Kelly corroborated the story. Even though he knew Farris and had regularly met with him in the years leading up to the public offering to discuss NONG, he claimed that he did not once mention the fact that he owned half his nephew's shares. He had, however, told countless colleagues and friends, a large number of whom he let in on the deal.[20] Uncle and nephew had got their story straight. But could either be believed?

The premier had earlier assured the legislature that no other cabinet minister was involved, but a reporter had easily discovered that one of the pillars of his administration was a shareholder of record. Griesinger's shareholding, Frost announced, was a 'surprise.' When he was reached for comment, the minister of public works exonerated the premier. Yes, he had been told not to buy pipeline shares and to dispose of any he already owned. He had not done so, preferring to hold on to his shares, which he sold close to the market peak, earning more than $10,000 in profit.[21] Now he would pay the price. Frost demanded, and Griesinger submitted, his letter of resignation.

The *Star* story also revealed the ownership interests of the new Liberal leader. John Wintermeyer, who would later run unsuccessfully in an election campaign in which he promised to reveal 'a scandal a day,' had bought NONG shares for as little as fourteen cents each. Nevertheless, he now falsely claimed that he had lost money on the deal when he disposed of his shares some time after assuming the party leadership.[22] Wintermeyer was also quick to point out that there was an important distinction to be made between the activities of a private member of the legislature like himself and a member of the cabinet. There was nothing illegal and immoral in what he had done, Wintermeyer later claimed, adding, 'If I had had anything to hide, I would not have bought the stocks in my own name as I did.'[23]

Wintermeyer did not lose money when he sold his shares; all the early insiders profited. And it is far from clear, at least insofar as NONG is concerned, whether anything the Liberal leader said can be believed. After all, he had sat mute in the legislature while the premier asserted that no one in cabinet owned pipeline shares. Wintermeyer knew better: Kelly had sold him some.

Kelly, increasingly upset about the allegations being made against him, was determined to restore his 'good name.' In a generally self-serving press release issued in the middle of May, at the very time that Frost was campaigning in Kelly's former riding on behalf of a local Tory seeking the seat in a by-election, he provided further details about his involvement with NONG. According to Kelly, he bought the NONG shares in 1954. Two years later, the pipeline bill came before the legislature. 'It was at this point,' he claimed, 'that my duties as a minister clashed with my interests as a private individual and I accordingly resigned.'[24] This story was quite different from the account Frost claimed to have received. It was also a lie. The bill authorizing Ontario's participation – to the extent of $35 million – in financing the northern route received approval in principle in the fall of 1955 and third and final reading on 6 March 1956, more than a year before he was called to Frost's office. This was not the first falsehood Kelly had told in his bid to establish that he had done nothing wrong, and it would not be the last.

After the Griesinger and Wintermeyer revelations, the demands for an investigation were becoming harder to resist. Two cabinet ministers and the leader of the Liberal Party were known to have bought shares of NONG, and to have purchased them at advantageous prices. The cabinet ministers had bought and retained their shares in defiance of Frost's directive to avoid any conflict of interest. The possibility of a conflict was real: after all, the Ontario legislature had approved a $35 million contribution to the financing of the uneconomical part of the northern route, and that financing, although never required for entirely unrelated reasons, was at the time critical to the success of the entire scheme. NONG was obviously an immediate beneficiary of this largesse. Both Trans-Canada and NONG were in business in part because the credit of the people of Ontario was pledged to make the pipeline possible. Mapledoram and Griesinger bought their shares after the pipeline bill was passed. The conclusion was nevertheless inescapable that the NONG stock offers to them, to Wintermeyer, and to others were made, at least in part, to ensure a continuing favourable political climate at Queen's Park.

The premier, however, had no intention of allowing some judge or royal commissioner to pass judgment on the truthfulness of his statements. Where public honour and integrity were concerned, Frost knew that he had the support of most of the electorate, and he announced that the 'jury of the people' would soon have the opportunity to indicate whether they believed him or Kelly.[25] From a political perspective, Frost's decision made sense. With an election expected in a matter of months, the last thing the government wanted was a detailed investigation of ministerial involvement with NONG.

The scandal, however, would not go away. If something was to be done, it was the responsibility of Attorney General Archibald Kelso Roberts, a mining lawyer from Cobalt who represented Toronto's St Patrick riding. First elected to the legislature in 1943, he was appointed attorney general by Frost in 1955. In early May 1958, Roberts ordered an Ontario

Securities Commission investigation of NONG stock sales. At the same time, the premier announced that he would be conducting his own investigation into the controversy. 'I don't intend to sit back and let the Attorney General's department and the OSC do it all,' he said. Frost wanted to know whether NONG stock was issued to municipal officials in northern Ontario communities 'for the purpose of influencing them.'[26] He had heard some rumours to that effect, and he now asked that appropriate inquiries be made.

In the meantime, the OSC investigation got under way. Three men were assigned to the task: Gordon W. Ford, QC, a well-known Toronto barrister from a distinguished family; Harry Slocomb Bray, senior solicitor at the OSC; and W.H. Chisholm, senior OSC auditor. It was not exactly the independent public inquiry that MacDonald and the *Toronto Star* had in mind, but it was better than nothing, which was the alternative.[27] The OSC reported to the attorney general, and he was entitled under the Securities Act to direct it to investigate and inquire. Roberts would have been best advised to put the investigation in the hands of outsiders. He had been concerned for some time about the manner in which NONG conducted its affairs, particularly its share capitalization and financing arrangements, and in June 1957 he had written to the premier setting out, in considerable detail, the exact nature of his concerns.[28] Now he had just appointed some of the same officials who had failed to regulate NONG properly in the first place to investigate it. It was not exactly like asking the fox to guard the chicken coop, but it came close. However, at least one of the investigators, Ford, came from outside the OSC.

The investigators established a number of goals. First, to consider whether there had been any infractions of the Securities Act, the Corporations Act, or the Criminal Code. Second, to determine if there was any evidence of bribery or corruption among elected members of the legislature, or of elected or appointed members of municipal councils with which NONG had dealt. Third, to find out if any elected official, who was dealing with NONG before its public issue of 4 June 1957, had owned shares. And fourth, to establish if there was evidence of any irregularity or impropriety on the part of NONG with reference to the issue or trading of NONG shares.[29]

The investigators presented an interim report of their findings on 2 July 1958.[30] Two days later, a press conference was held in the Cabinet Council Room at Queen's Park. Leslie Frost spoke first. The premier, his face grave with concern, announced that he had accepted the resignation of yet another cabinet minister, Clare Mapledoram. Mapledoram, who had arranged with Kelly for the purchase of stock in his brother-in-law's name, had immediately offered to step down in the aftermath of Griesinger's resignation and the appointment of the OSC investigation. Mapledoram, it turned out, had not just bought shares in August 1956, but had compounded his mistake by adding to his portfolio in May 1957. Now, on 4 July 1958, the premier announced that he had accepted Mapledoram's resignation, like that of Griesinger, 'with great regret.' Mapledoram, Frost claimed, was guilty of 'indiscretions,' and he added that he had always found the minister of lands and forests an 'honest, reputable gentleman' and he found him so still.[31] Mapledoram claimed, somewhat improbably, not to have seen the premier's directive that ministers should not own pipeline stock because of 'absence from his office,' or to have simply 'overlooked it.'[32]

When Frost finished, Roberts made an announcement. Charges would be brought against Ralph Farris, C. Spencer Clark, and NONG. The attorney general released a summary of the interim OSC report, which stated that there was no basis for a finding of bribery, corruption, or impropriety at either the municipal or the provincial level in regard to NONG's obtaining of franchises, or with respect to its distribution of shares.[33] 'No evidence,' Roberts reported, 'has been adduced in the investigation which would indicate that any shares were sold by the company to any elected representative or official of the government of Ontario, or any municipality.' The investigation had been 'thorough and meticulous,' and there was no proof of 'influence being exerted affecting any decision of the provincial or municipal authorities in relation to [NONG].'[34] Interjecting as Roberts spoke, the premier went out of his way to stress this point. The government had cleaned house, charges would be brought against Farris, Clark, and NONG, and as far as Frost and Roberts were concerned, the matter was finished.

Even the Liberal *Toronto Star* was inclined to agree. While it would have preferred a full judicial inquiry, the *Star* pronounced itself satisfied, as the 'government's three-man inquiry seems to have been thorough and unwavering.'[35] The Conservative *Telegram* pointed to Frost's actions in this case as an example of the 'high standards set by the Premier for colleagues charged with the responsibility of directing the public affairs of this province.' According to the *Telegram*, the amounts involved were 'trifling,' and it was 'understandable' that Griesinger and Mapledoram would take a 'flyer' on the advice of a 'friend and cabinet colleague.' Besides, the *Telegram* concluded, there was no evidence that either minister had even benefited from the transactions.[36]

Several days after the government press conference, the OSC provided details about the charges that had been laid. NONG was charged with failing to make proper disclosures in its prospectus, for trading in NONG shares without filing a prospectus, and for failing to keep proper books. Farris and Clark were charged with failing to make proper disclosures in the prospectus, with unlawful primary distribution of shares, and with not acting in the best interests of the company by issuing 14,000 shares at $2.50 per share to Convesto at a time when those shares were selling for a much higher amount.

Farris and Clark had, in their evidence in the OSC investigation, claimed the protection of the Canada and Ontario Evidence Acts, which anyone testifying under subpoena in any proceeding is entitled to do. Their testimony, therefore, could not be used against them in a court of law. Moreover, there was a limitations provision in the Securities Act. It provided that some proceedings, and this was one of them, could not begin more than one year after the facts on which they were based first came to the knowledge of the Ontario Securities Commission. The OSC had known that NONG shares had been sold at advantageous prices to 'insiders' for more than a year. NONG made no secret of that fact when it filed its prospectus before the commencement of public trading. It was thus decided that the charge of acting against the best interest of NONG not be pursued, a conclusion supported by the fact that the evidence presently available would not 'support the laying of such charges.'[37] A leading Toronto barrister and long-time Law Society treasurer, Cyril F.H. Carson, QC, was retained as special counsel to the attorney general to prosecute the case, and he agreed with this conclusion. The charge was announced to the press, but not pursued.[38] Kelly and McLean might also have been charged for unlawful primary distribution of shares, since both men had sold shares. However, the sales had been to family and friends, and both men had claimed the protection of the Canada and Ontario Evidence Acts, so this charge too, while recommended in the OSC report, was dropped.[39]

Undoubtedly, the laying of some charges redirected much of the political heat away from the government and to the accused. Still, there was the matter of the interim OSC report. While a summary had been released by the attorney general, the report itself was withheld, and MacDonald and others, having pressed for an inquiry in the first place, insisted that it be released. On what basis, MacDonald wanted to know, had the investigators concluded that there was no evidence of corruption at the municipal and provincial levels of government? Exactly how deeply had they dug, and on what evidence were their conclusions reached? Was it a cover-up or an exhaustive investigation? These questions, and others, could only be answered if the report was released. The government refused, and that refusal was justified, at least temporarily.

When charges were laid as a result of recommendations made in an OSC report, neither it nor the evidence gathered to prepare it was, in the normal course of events, admissible at trial. In OSC investigations, witnesses were compelled to testify. Individuals facing criminal charges, in contrast, had a right to remain silent. Many of those witnesses who did testify, under subpoena, took the protection of both the Canada and Ontario Evidence Acts. By claiming this protection, anything they said could not be used against them in a court of law. The transcripts of the OSC hearings, which were all held behind closed doors, could not be relied on in court, nor could they be released to the press – at least not until all charges laid as a result of the OSC investigation and report were finally disposed of, either by acquittal or by a finding of guilt. There would then be a further delay waiting out the expiry time provided for the filing of an appeal.

The charges against Farris, Clark, and NONG proceeded to a hearing in the fall of 1958 before Magistrate Thomas Elmore. John J. Robinette, QC, was retained for the defence. He was already a legal legend, and probably Canada's most accomplished defence lawyer. The gold medallist in his 1929 Osgoode Hall graduating class, Robinette achieved pre-eminence in a number of celebrated criminal trials, including his appeal of Evelyn Dick's conviction in the Torso Murder Case and his successful defence of her on re-trial. Instead of going to the gallows, Dick served only eleven years in jail for the murder of her baby son. Robinette also acted as a special prosecutor in the Gouzenko spy trials, and he specialized in appellate advocacy, appearing frequently before the Ontario Court of Appeal and the Supreme Court of Canada. A bencher, and future treasurer of the Law Society of Upper Canada, Robinette knew everyone and was widely admired. Modest, gentlemanly, reserved, but always friendly and polite, he was the lawyer to go to if you were in trouble, needed the best, and had the money to pay for it. Farris, Clark, and NONG had made a good choice.[40] In representing them before Elmore, Robinette was beginning an extended involvement in a scandal that would soon come to centre around Leo Landreville – the Osgoode Hall judge.

The case was heard in September 1958. Farris, Clark, and NONG had traded in NONG's shares before receiving OSC approval to do so. But as Robinette pointed out in his final argument, it would come as a 'great shock to every corporation lawyer in the City of Toronto if the view were taken you could not issue shares to people in the early stages of the organization and formation of a company for the purpose of raising capital to carry it through to the financing stage. Practically every company does that sort of thing.'[41] Farris, Clark, and NONG had not traded shares to the public, and Robinette urged an acquittal on that count.

Carson had a different interpretation of events. His study of the records led him to conclude that the stock splits and share sales were not to raise capital for the company, but to 'facilitate distribution among more people.'[42] It was a stock promotion scheme, no more and no less, to ensure easy profits for company insiders and their friends. The evidence seemed to support this suggestion. On 25 October 1955 there were only 1063 shares outstanding, held by some fifty-seven persons, of whom only fifteen could be regarded as true insiders. As a result of two share splits, the number of shares increased exponentially and, because there were no restrictions placed on the sale of these shares, NONG had 1328 shareholders on record by the time public trading in NONG stock commenced. If this was not a public distribution of shares, Carson asked, what was?[43]

In November 1958 Elmore issued his decision: acquittal on all counts except for the charge of making a primary distribution of securities between 1954 and 1957 without first filing a prospectus. After announcing the verdict, he invited defence lawyer Robinette to make submissions on sentence. Robinette suggested a token fine, given that no one had been hurt by the unlawful distribution of shares; indeed, he pointed out, none of the early purchasers of NONG shares had filed a complaint. A penalty would, however, be imposed. 'Well,' Elmore observed tongue in cheek, 'I suppose it will be rather demeaning to the accused if they were not fined a substantial amount.' 'They will not mind,' Robinette replied.[44] Elmore fined NONG $150, and Clark and Farris were given a choice between one month in jail or a fine of $500 each. They paid the fine.

The fines reflected the insignificant nature of the statutory breach. In the halcyon days of boiler-room sales and rampant stock fraud, Farris, Clark, and NONG had, it seemed, acted at worst like some over-anxious boy scouts. And while the OSC had never mentioned it, countless reputable brokers had actively assisted in the sale of NONG shares while knowing that such shares had not been approved for sale by the OSC.

The period for appeal did not expire until the end of 1958, and before then the government, even if it had been so inclined, was precluded from releasing either the preliminary or the final OSC reports. Legal niceties are difficult to communicate in the press, and they stand in the way of a good story. The truth of the matter was that the government was prevented for a considerable time from releasing the report – the final report was submitted on 29 August 1958 – and it could hardly be held accountable for that. By the beginning of 1959, however, that claim no longer held water.

Public interest in the affair continued to grow, encouraged by regular reports of the fabulous sums that had been made and tales of a secret report that the government was said to be scared to release. Farris did not help matters much when he claimed not to know McLean, and added that he did not consider a profit of $700,000 on a $5000 investment 'excessive.'[45] These profits were fantastic at a time when the average weekly wage in the construction trades in Toronto was $84.21, new ranch bungalows in Scarborough cost $15,000, a package of cigarettes retailed for 33 cents, Eaton's sold suits for $69.50, and four Firestone tires could be had for $39.80 plus 50 cents each for installation. They were also beyond the imagination of most Canadians.

In the meantime, Landreville and Farris remained friends. On his return from Mexico in November 1958, Landreville learned that Farris had been fined. 'Of course,' he wrote, 'now that you are an ex-convict and because of my loughty [sic] position I will not be able to publicly appear with you!!!' He sent his old friend a Mexican shirt, 'in view of the fact you lost yours,' and invited him over for dinner. Farris accepted the shirt and promised to call Landreville when he was next in town 'so that we can meet "privately."'[46] It was all in good fun, of course, but the scandal had hardly begun.

Kelly, increasingly isolated but desperate for public attention now that he had turned his back on the Tories and thrown in his lot with the Social Credit Party of Ontario, added fuel to the fire when he told reporters in February 1959 that an examination of NONG's record of shareholders would lead to 'some very interesting stuff.'[47] He deliberately piqued further interest when he claimed that other highly placed individuals were involved. 'If I stood in that House today,' he told the *Toronto Star*, 'I could bat a few of them off their chairs.'[48] This was a lie. Kelly had testified under oath on 18 June 1957 that Griesinger, Mapledoram, and Wintermeyer were the only provincial politicians who had bought shares.[49] For good measure, Kelly added that he initially denied owning NONG shares in order to 'protect the Conservative party.'[50] This claim was ludicrous. Certainly, as Frost pointed out, this was a 'most peculiar way to protect the Conservative party.'[51] Kelly's greed had not only destroyed his own career but threatened his political party as well.

The threat was deliberate, Frost later came to believe.[52] Kelly claimed to be free of blame, however. His priest, Kelly told the press, 'had absolved him ... at confession,' and he 'felt no pangs of conscience for supplying his fellow cabinet ministers with stock.'[53] It would be appropriate, he suggested, for Frost to 'apologize' to him.[54] Kelly added that he would welcome a public inquiry.[55] In the legislature, MacDonald again demanded that the government come clean and release the report. Even Wintermeyer was finally forced to take a public stand in supporting this demand.

Frost demurred. According to the premier, who continued to defend Griesinger and Mapledoram, his 'great personal friends,' there was absolutely no need to give way.[56] A 'meticulous examination' had been made of the stock transfers and original stock issues, 'everything was followed through,' and the process was careful and complete. 'May I say,' Frost stated on 6 February 1959, 'that the report made fully discloses those whose names appeared in this matter, and who held stock, and every possible lead was investigated.'[57]

The premier was either misinformed or lying. It was absolutely clear that every possible lead had not been pursued. The investigators did not have the jurisdiction to compel out-of-province evidence, but there was nothing stopping them from going west to interview John McGraw. They decided against doing so even though McGraw had indicated to them that he would answer their questions if they came to see him in British Columbia. As a result, they were unable to trace the transactions that went through the Convesto account, notwithstanding the fact that one transaction in particular had attracted their attention. In January 1957 NONG had sold Convesto 14,000 shares for $2.50 each when the shares were trading at a much higher amount. Who had reaped the benefit of this sale? The Kelly press interview raised more questions than answers. Moreover, if, as Frost claimed, the report was exhaustive, it could surely speak for itself. If there was nothing to hide, why not release it?

That was the conclusion that Frost and Roberts had gradually begun to reach. After Kelly's revelations, the continued withholding of the report could only lead to allegations that the government was engaged in a cover-up. It had been known for some months that, in addition to the three cabinet ministers, A.D. McKenzie, president of the Ontario Progressive Conservative Association, had, for a time, been on the NONG payroll. McKenzie was Frost's closest adviser. The two met regularly, often daily, to discuss party business and public business. McKenzie was *the* key player in the provincial Tory party, and Frost did not make a move without consulting him first. The details of McKenzie's retainer arrangement were now revealed. McKenzie, approached at the suggestion of Phil Kelly,[58] had drawn an annual retainer of $6000 from NONG; he had been hired to advise the company because of his 'intimate knowledge of the Ontario situation both from the legal aspect and the personal.'[59] He later abandoned the lucrative assignment, which included some handsome stock options, when the Ontario legislature became embroiled in the financing arrangements of the uneconomical part of the northern route. Considering his early role in the affairs of the company – and why he was hired, and what he was hired to do was never properly explained – McKenzie would almost certainly have known that mines minister Kelly was a major shareholder.[60] Had he failed to mention this to the premier? Or even worse, had this been disclosed despite what Frost had always claimed? And why had he really been retained?[61]

And what about Frost? It was conceivable that he might not have known about Kelly's early involvement with NONG, but it seems much less likely that he was not aware of the involvement of Griesinger, Mapledoram, and McKenzie, three of his closest colleagues. Conservative cabinet ministers met regularly for breakfast at the Royal York Hotel, and the NONG play was a frequent topic of conversation.[62] When Frost rose in the legislature in March 1958 and angrily refuted MacDonald's charges that Kelly had resigned because of his involvement in NONG, was he telling the truth? And if he was, how come Griesinger and Mapledoram, who knew the truth, failed to alert their leader that he was misleading the House? When all the evidence is considered, there is little doubt that Frost knew that some of his colleagues owned some shares, but he had no intention of taking action unless forced to do so. He would continue dissembling in the legislature until he was left with no choice but to tell the truth. When he did, consummate politician that he was, he would turn the situation around by making it look as if he was the one who had been betrayed and was now cleaning house.

In the meantime, Donald MacDonald would simply not give up. He renewed his call for a royal commission. Frost defended McKenzie – 'a great friend of mine' – and refused the demand.[63] The release of the OSC report was another matter, and on 9 February 1959 the premier again rose in the legislature. He began his remarks by repudiating Kelly's comments as reported in the press. They were completely inconsistent with the evidence Kelly gave when he testified under oath in the 1958 OSC investigation, Frost advised the House. Since he had quoted from the transcript, there could be no further claim that the evidence was confidential. The attorney general spoke next, and announced the government's intention to table the evidence and the report. Three days later, on 12 February 1959, Roberts tabled both.

The report added little that was new. It traced in some detail NONG's share capitalization from incorporation in Ontario in 1954 to the public offering in June 1957. An original issue of 500 shares had, by new issues and splits, grown to 400,000 shares when the stock, along with debentures, was first offered to the public in June 1957. OSC investigator Chisholm had followed each of the original shares and could account for just about all of them – with one important exception: the 14,000 shares sold to Convesto at $2.50 each in January 1957. The OSC investigators had no idea what happened to those shares. They did know that the market for NONG shares was particularly active between December 1956 and May and June 1957, and that the shares rose rapidly and steadily in price from about $10 in December 1956 to a high of about $28 just prior to the public offering.

The early insiders not only knew when to buy, but when to sell. A handful of men had reaped a financial windfall. Farris initially invested $300 in the company and ended up with 37,500 shares. He sold 22,500 shares between December 1956 and May 1957 for $318,000, and retained another 15,000 shares. Gordon Kelly McLean and Phil Kelly purchased 105,750 shares for a total consideration of $5425. The two men later cashed out for approximately half a million dollars each. Other prominent citizens, including some leading Ontario Tories such as Beverley Matthews, QC, whose firm, McCarthy & McCarthy, performed NONG's legal work, were known to have earned extremely handsome returns. This money was all tax free. There was no tax on capital gains.

The government had put a lot of stock in the report, particularly that it found no evidence of wrongdoing. One way of assessing these findings, and thus the government's reliance on the report, is by examining the investigation and determining whether it really had, as the attorney general later claimed, left no stone unturned. There is no doubt that NONG, and some of its officers, had engaged in unauthorized trading of stock before its sale had been approved. In the regulatory climate of that day, these were insignificant offences, affirmed by the minor penalties imposed on Farris, Clark, and NONG. What really mattered was why NONG had provided 14,000 shares to Convesto at a wildly discounted rate, and who had benefited from that sale of shares.

The OSC had asked John McGraw, the head of Convesto and a former president of the Vancouver Stock Exchange, to come to testify, but he declined the invitation to travel to Ontario. The commission had no legal right to subpoena his attendance, but why was someone not sent to Vancouver to talk to him?[64] Ralph Farris did appear at the OSC hearing, and he was questioned about the sale of the 14,000 NONG shares.[65] 'Are you aware,' he was asked, 'of the disposition of those 14,000 shares issued and allotted to Convesto under date of January 17, 1957?' No, he lied, he was not.[66] Farris told the OSC that NONG sold 14,000 shares to Convesto because Convesto was a good company and friendly to NONG, and because it had earlier asked for the shares 'on behalf of clients.' Shares were sold pursuant to an arrangement reached the previous fall – one Farris had unfortunately failed to document – because NONG needed more funds.[67] Farris was asked whether the shares were allotted to Convesto as a principal, or for distribution to clients. He testified they were allotted to Convesto as a purchaser, and he claimed to have no knowledge about the 'clients' referred to in the Convesto application.

According to Farris, NONG never issued shares to individuals through Convesto acting as a nominee. To the question 'Have you at any time sold, directly or indirectly, any shares of Northern Ontario to or for the benefit of any Provincial Cabinet Minister of Ontario?' he replied, 'No I have not.' He gave the same answer when asked whether NONG had sold shares, directly or indirectly, to any MP, MPP, or any member of a municipal council with which NONG was in negotiation for a franchise agreement, including Leo Landreville, whose name was specifically mentioned. 'No,' Farris said under oath, 'I have not.'

Farris was asked if he was aware, at any time before the municipalities granted franchises to NONG, whether there was any arrangement to sell shares to municipal officials. 'No,' he said, there was not. He was then asked a blanket question. 'Have you at any time, apart from selling, given any shares of NONG Limited to any Provincial or Dominion Cabinet Minister, any Provincial Member of Parliament, any Dominion Member of Parliament or any elected or nominated official of any municipality with whom your company was dealing?' The answer, once again, was 'No, I have not.'[68] In a sense, in answering this question, Farris was telling the truth. Landreville was given an option to buy shares after the Sudbury franchise agreements were completed, and Farris would continue to deny knowledge of any gifts of shares to the Bracebridge, Gravenhurst, and Orillia mayors.

Gordon Kelly McLean also testified. His evidence was directed primarily to the role he played in the promotion of NONG; in addition, he provided the OSC investigators with details about the shares held and traded by himself and his uncle, the minister of mines. He did not mention owning any other shares or distributing them on behalf of NONG to anyone else. C. Spencer Clark denied any knowledge of the distribution in January and February 1957 of the 14,000 Convesto shares.[69] Phil Kelly, whose genius inspired the whole deal, testified that, other than himself, Griesinger, Mapledoram, and Wintermeyer, no other politicians, federal, provincial, or municipal, bought shares through him, or, to his knowledge, received a benefit of shares.

When Attorney General Roberts tabled the report and the evidence, he told the legislature that he was convinced that everything had been disclosed and was above board. There was no indication anywhere, beyond what appeared in the report, 'that any cheap stock was made available by the company to any other person.' It was true enough that various speculators, all of whom the report identified, had obtained stock for less than those who purchased in the public offering, 'but whatever they may have done with their stock, the company itself does not appear to have, in the period under review, issued any stock to any undisclosed person.' The early insiders were interested in themselves; they were not, Roberts believed, 'interested in handing out stock to bribe anyone or to give them gifts.'

Nothing sinister had happened to the 14,000 shares, according to the attorney general. While McGraw did not testify, and while the OSC investigators did not follow through on his invitation that they travel west, Roberts was convinced that the transfer of 14,000 shares at a price of $2.50 each was completely legitimate, although somewhat questionable. 'In my view,' he said, 'it is a very unwise thing for directors to authorize shares to be issued at prices well below the market at the time.' Such a course, while often done for justifiable reasons, could be 'misunderstood.'[70] To be sure, it was difficult for most people to understand why NONG would have sold Convesto 14,000 shares for $2.50 each when they were actively trading for a much higher amount, but, Roberts asserted, there was no evidence of any bribery or corruption at any level of government. Roberts knew of 'no stone left unturned.' It was time, he claimed, for the legislature to get on with constructive business. Instead of pursuing the one clue that suggested impropriety, he asserted that it did not establish evidence of wrongdoing. On that basis, he took the position that the matter should be closed, despite his concerns since June 1957 about improprieties in the trading in NONG shares.[71]

MacDonald saw things differently. Did the attorney general know, he asked immediately after Roberts tabled the evidence and the report, what happened to those 14,000 shares? Roberts assumed they were sold in the ordinary way. He could, however, 'assure the hon. member that the name of at least one person, I think he is thinking about, is referred to in the sworn testimony of several of these people, where it is denied positively.'[72] It was almost out. Twice, in the past week, MacDonald had asked, 'Was a block of stock made available to the Sudbury area at the early stages when the franchise was under consideration, and if so to whom?'[73] The answer to that question was no, and the CCF leader was invited to pass over to the authorities the name of anyone he believed to be involved in impropriety. That was before the evidence and the report were made public. Now both had been tabled in the legislature, and Mac-Donald returned to the question. Everyone knew exactly whom he had in mind. Several years would pass, however, before MacDonald started naming names.

Formal debate on the report began on 18 March 1959. Kelso Roberts spoke first. He again reviewed the OSC report, and warned, given the findings in that report, against 'any attempt being made on the part of anyone to infer wrongdoing, by innuendo, by suggestion, or by anything else than positive and absolute evidence, on the part of any hon. member alleging anything which he himself is prepared to stake his own reputation, his own seat, on.' It was a bit garbled, but the attorney general's message was clear: Put up or shut up. The time had come, Roberts concluded, finally to dispose of this matter, as everything relevant to it had been 'put before the House or before the Courts.'[74]

Wintermeyer, as leader of the opposition, was entitled to speak first. He concerned himself with McKenzie's involvement with NONG, focusing on the gentle treatment McKenzie had received when he was called to testify before the OSC. It was true enough that his examiners never really probed what he gave in return for his $6000 per year retainer from NONG, not to mention his extremely lucrative stock option. Wintermeyer demanded a royal commission to clear the air once and for all. Mac-Donald naturally echoed that request, but, first, he had a number of observations to make.

The CCF leader had carefully studied both the report and the 1500-page transcript of evidence that accompanied it. From his Second World War experience in naval intelligence, MacDonald knew that puzzles like NONG could be completed only one piece at a time, and that where no pieces were found, where there were gaps, he had to do some ordinary detective work. He had done that work; now he had documents to fill in the gaps, and he was in a position to make a real contribution to the debate.[75]

Through a painstaking study of the transcripts, MacDonald had identified numerous inconsistencies in the evidence of key witnesses, particularly Kelly, McLean, and Farris. If these men were not telling the truth about some things, their evidence, and the conclusions drawn from it, were in doubt. MacDonald also raised a number of concerns about the large number of high-ranking Tories retained by NONG to assist it as it went about its business in Ontario. The conclusion was inescapable, at least to him, that McKenzie and others had been hired, and given attractive stock options, in order to guarantee a favourable climate at Queen's Park. After making that observation, MacDonald moved to one of his major areas of concern: the disposition of the 14,000 Convesto shares, and allegations of corruption in Ontario's north.

It was 'remarkable,' MacDonald began, that 14,000 shares would be sold for $2.50 each at a time when the market price for those same shares was in the $10–$14 range. If those shares had been sold immediately, someone would have benefited by more than $100,000, and MacDonald had a good idea who. After noting that the Sudbury franchise was of paramount importance to NONG, and that Farris personally handled the negotiations for that deal, MacDonald suggested that the government extend its investigation to find out whether Farris had used shares to 'sweeten up' elected officials.[76]

Roberts rejected the suggestion. There was no evidence, he told the legislature, that the Honourable Leo Landreville had, in any way, 'improper connections' with NONG at any time.[77] The attorney general, not MacDonald, first identified Landreville as the mysterious 'someone,' but went on to rule him out. No one then had the details of Landreville's involvement with NONG. No one knew about the option granted to him or about the correspondence that he and Farris had exchanged. No one knew about the fabulous windfall that the Sudbury mayor had received, or that other mayors and municipal officials had also been given gifts of stock. No one knew because, Roberts explained, there was nothing to know.

'I say,' the attorney general told the legislature, 'that, as far as promotional stock is concerned, it has been accounted for in every way that it would be possible to account for it ... I stake my own reputation on that statement.'[78] MacDonald could not believe what he had just heard. He knew that at least 14,000 shares had disappeared into a nominee account in January 1957, sold by NONG at way below market price. How could Roberts possibly claim, and in the process put his seat on the line, that the promotional stock had been accounted for? 'I warn him,' MacDonald stated in reply, 'he will be sorry before this is over.' The attorney general was unconcerned. It was MacDonald, he predicted, who would not be sitting in the legislature after the impending election.

The premier shared this view, and when MacDonald finally finished, Leslie Frost let him have it. MacDonald was 'wallowing in the gutter.' He should 'close his trap,' and stop sitting in the House 'chittering like a pig in a trough.' Just looking at MacDonald made Frost want to 'laugh.' MacDonald was 'yammering away' and had gone down 'into the sewer and covered himself with it.' Instead of doing his job, the CCF leader was running 'around the province making cowardly insinuations and half-truths and using twisted evidence and things of that sort.' He was a 'character assassin.' He had 'smeared' honest politicians and was 'beneath contempt.' Single-handedly, MacDonald had vilified and degraded 'the dignity of the House.'

'Character' and 'honour in public life' meant nothing to the CCF leader, according to the premier. His allegations about NONG were nothing but a 'tissue of distortions.' It was 'ridiculous' to suggest that the OSC should have gone beyond the transfer of the 14,000 shares to the Convesto account. The evidence indicated, 'beyond a doubt that the transactions with this company were in the ordinary course of business and there was nothing in them, directly or indirectly, which could affect the honour of this House or any hon. member thereof.' There was no connection between any of the sales and public business. They were personal transactions between friends. Griesinger and Mapledoram were 'honourable and decent men' and MacDonald should be ashamed for 'rubbing salt in their wounds.'

Echoing the attorney general's earlier remarks, Frost told the legislature that the 'matter has been thoroughly, fairly and impartially investigated and the full facts have been given to the people.' There had been no bribery or corruption at any level of government. The integrity and honour of public officials had been vindicated. 'I think that we can view with gratification,' the premier concluded, 'the fact that in this very wide investigation there has not been a tittle of evidence that there were evidences of bribery or corruption at any level of provincial or municipal government. This is a very great statement to be able to make, and I think that the time has come to stop throwing mud at public men and public officials and devote ourselves entirely to the pressing needs of this great province which we serve.'[79] The legislature then adjourned.

Leslie Frost was, by nature, an even-tempered man. But on 18 March 1959 he lost his temper for the first and last time in the legislature. Frost came to regret his outburst, particularly when he returned to the Royal York that evening and faced the real leader of the opposition. His wife, Gertrude, had been watching from the gallery. She 'angrily ordered him to apologize.'[80] And the next day, he did. He told MacDonald when the legislature reconvened on 19 March that he was 'extremely irritated' and had been 'provoked.' Nevertheless, he was 'very sorry if I made references ... which might not have been in accordance with parliamentary procedure.' Frost then went on to say, however, that what MacDonald had done was 'highly reprehensible' and was not 'consonant with the conduct of gentlemen.'[81] MacDonald was unable to get a word in, and the legislature moved on to other business.

The fact of the matter was that MacDonald was right, and Frost and Roberts were wrong. The investigation was not 'thorough and complete.' It was not 'meticulous.' It was a sham. Important stones had been left 'unturned.' There was more than a wisp of smoke, but who would find the fire?

4

The Police Come Calling

Four years passed after the OSC issued its report. 'The Convesto account, like the gas pipeline, seemed buried.'[1] There were rumours, but not much more. Donald MacDonald continued to raise the matter occasionally in the legislature, and the *Toronto Star* kept on the story. A leading official in Sudbury was said to be involved, but, without proof, MacDonald had no intention of naming Landreville, even though parliamentary privilege would have protected him had he done so. 'Who Is Mystery Man of Gas Scandal?' the *Star* asked. But for the time being, there were no answers.

In 1962 that changed. As a result of a tip, the RCMP began an investigation into the activities of J. Stewart Smith, British Columbia's superintendent of brokers. Smith, who soon fled to New Zealand, was believed to have used his position to improve himself financially.[2] In the process of investigating Smith, the RCMP became interested in Landreville. Both men had benefited from the distribution of the 14,000 NONG shares: Smith with 800 shares, and Landreville with 10,000. What intrigued the police was the unusual manner in which the sale of the shares was recorded in the Convesto books. The circumstances suggested that the 'transactions were artificial and merely a means of disguising gifts to ... Landreville.'[3] Soon enough, the authorities in Toronto were made aware that there was more to the story than Farris and the others had originally led them to believe.

Everyone knew that NONG had, in early 1957, sold Convesto 14,000 shares at $2.50 each. The story was that Convesto had bought the shares for itself, but a review of the books indicated otherwise. The RCMP realized that something was amiss, and a few calculations showed that there really was something to hide. If Landreville had sold his stock the day he received it, he would have made a $105,000 profit without investing one cent. If he had held on to his stock for just two months, he would have profited to the tune of $187,500. This was a matter, Superintendent C.W.J. Goldsmith, wrote, 'which may in due course be of interest to the Department of Justice.'[4] Ultimately, the investigation against Smith was closed because of lack of evidence. The investigation of Leo Landreville, however, was about to begin.

First, the police came calling. Officer A.R. Bates from the Vancouver RCMP came to Toronto in September 1962 to ask Landreville some questions. Bates was accompanied by the chief superintendent for 'O' Division, R.W. Wonnacott. The two men wanted to know about Convesto and certain shares that Landreville had acquired. The investigation, Justice Landreville was advised, was being conducted at the request of the attorney general of British Columbia.[5] In the course of that investigation, Landreville's name had come up. Before the interview began on 11 September 1962, Landreville was cautioned. He did not have to answer any questions, but if he chose to do so, any answers he gave could be used against him in court.

The meeting did not go well. Landreville told the police he had ordered the shares through a Sudbury broker. Which broker, they asked? Landreville did not recall. Suspicions were aroused by this answer and by Landreville's request to turn on his tape recorder, so he would not be 'misquoted.' Landreville, rambling, volunteered that the Department of National Revenue was investigating him, and the two RCMP officers knew that further probing was required.[6] The interview ended with Landreville asking to see whatever questions they wished to ask in advance, so he could carefully consider his answers to them.

The next day, the questions were provided. How did you order the shares? How did you pay for them? Do you know Farris? What was your involvement as mayor in granting NONG the gas franchise? There were other questions as well, and it was agreed that Landreville would meet with the police again, after he considered his position. When he did, the promised answers were not forthcoming. Instead, Landreville told the Mounties that the whole matter had been investigated some years previously and that the Ontario Securities Commission had recently reopened its investigation into the matter. Indeed, when Attorney General Kelso Roberts heard about the new evidence, he immediately launched another probe.[7] By the middle of September it was open knowledge, after Roberts mentioned the investigation in a speech. Landreville told the police that it was on the instructions of the attorney general of the day that Sudbury and other cities had signed with NONG. Dana Porter was, he added, now chief justice of Ontario.

Even though Landreville indicated on 12 September 1962 that he would not answer any more questions, and his decision was politely accepted by the RCMP officers, he continued to talk. He told them that he had spent sixteen years in government service, and that he intended to continue to do what he could for his country. He described the background to the NONG negotiations, insisting that he got the best deal possible for Sudbury and not denying that he 'exercised his influence to enable NONG to obtain the franchise for the City of Sudbury.'[8] He advised Bates and Wonnacott that he and others had been offered NONG shares for $2.50 each, and that he had purchased some shares from a broker in Sudbury at this price.[9] It was a good thing too, he added. Had he and others not bought the shares when they did, they would have been placed on the New York market and 'Americans' would have ended up owning the company. Landreville then showed the police to the door.

Soon enough, reports of the reopened OSC inquiry reached the press, although Landreville's name, for a time, stayed out of the news. Four investigators were said to be 'scouring over the evidence,' and dozens of subpoenas were issued. Although OSC investigations were conducted in secret, with the proceedings closed to the public and the press, nothing stops leaks, and the press was filled with speculation. The Toronto *Telegram* announced that a 'prominent Ontario figure' would be named in the OSC report, which was expected in a 'matter of weeks.' Conservative Party circles were 'buzzing over the possibility that a political bombshell will be exploded when the report is made public.'[10] This investigation, unlike the one conducted in 1958, would not be completed quickly. It extended over a matter of months, though intelligence that Landreville had been subpoenaed did not take long to seep out.

At first appearance, there was really nothing extraordinary about the fact that Landreville was asked to testify. Every member of the 1956 Sudbury City Council received a summons in the mail. The others were, however, called merely to give evidence; the subpoena Landreville received indicated that the purpose of the investigation was to examine allegations made against NONG, Farris, McGraw, McLean, and him. Roberts now wanted more information about those 14,000 shares. Not long after the inquiry got under way, on 25 October 1962, the cabinet was shuffled.

Roberts was moved to Lands and Forests, and Frederick McIntosh Cass, a lawyer from eastern Ontario first elected to the legislature in 1955, left Municipal Affairs to become attorney general. Cass was now responsible for the investigation and, unlike 1958, this time the OSC would leave no stone unturned.

When the investigation moved to Sudbury, the *Sudbury Star* kept its readers informed about the witnesses called to testify in a closed room down at the local court-house. The details did not, however, emerge until the following spring (as witnesses who testified in these proceedings were specifically warned at the conclusion of their evidence not to disclose any of their evidence to anyone, unless the OSC gave its permission in advance). By then Frost had retired, replaced by a new man, John Robarts, from London, Ontario. In April 1963 Kelso Roberts, still angry over being demoted from the attorney general's job, rose in the legislature. It was probably the end of the session, Roberts observed, and an appropriate moment for review and reflection. He was proud of his record of service and of the accomplishments of the government, but there was one matter he wished to refer to before the legislature prorogued: the 1958 OSC investigation of NONG. 'I now firmly believe,' he announced to a shocked and silent assembly, that 'the Legislature of 1959 was misled by the acceptance then of certain sworn statements concerning the disposition of some 14,000 shares of NONG stock in January 1957.'[11] Donald MacDonald, who had kept up his questions in the legislature, could not resist interrupting Roberts's address with the remark, 'I told you so at the time.' The former attorney general, who years earlier had staked his reputation and his seat on the thoroughness of the investigation, was now convinced 'that the bulk, if not all of the 14,000 shares were disposed of to Convesto ... at a price several times below the market price, not as principals at all, which is what had been sworn to, but as agents for named persons, named by the president of the gas company.' Roberts's statement was an admission of failure, or worse.

Roberts advised the legislature that one person in particular had benefited, and that person was, 'at certain relevant times, an elected official of a municipality doing business with the gas company, i.e. granting a franchise to the gas company to distribute natural gas in its area.' Roberts concluded his remarks by informing the legislature that he had raised these concerns with the new attorney general.[12]

Roberts's increasingly erratic behaviour and reputation as an 'outsider and loner' in government had led to the portfolio switch.[13] Even so, no one expected him to get up in the legislature and effectively take his own government to task, especially with a provincial election expected in a matter of months. The next day, he was attacked from all sides. Attorney General Cass, barely concealing his anger, told the legislature that an OSC investigation, initiated as a result of information provided by the attorney general of British Columbia, was continuing and that the report was not expected for several months. He undertook, once the report was completed, to inform the legislature of its findings. Liberal MPP Vernon Singer followed, railing against Roberts for his obvious violation of his cabinet secrecy oath. The legislature then recessed for the afternoon, but when it reconvened that evening, Donald MacDonald led the charge.

MacDonald accused Roberts of both a 'cover-up' and a 'leak.' He alleged that Roberts knew in 1958 that false statements had been given and that the investigation that year had not, in fact, been designed to 'clean up the mess,' but 'to sweep all this under the mat.' Red-faced with anger, Roberts denied the charge. It was incredible, MacDonald continued, that a minister of the Crown would come into the legislature and preview the OSC report in all but naming names. Not that he needed to identify the individual involved; 'anybody who has even a bit of background information with regard to what went on in NONG knows that he is talking about one person only.' 'Why does the honourable member not name him?' taunted Lloyd Leatherby, the Conservative member from Simcoe East. MacDonald obliged: 'Justice Landreville,' he shot back.[14]

MacDonald was not finished. Although subjected to a running stream of interjections and heckling as he spoke, he did not let up. He accused Roberts of playing politics, and claimed that if the legislature was misled in 1958 and 1959, Roberts deserved much of the blame. MacDonald quoted generously from the earlier debates in which both Roberts and Frost had defended the earlier report and its finding that nothing was amiss. The government had reopened the investigation and was looking into the very areas MacDonald had insisted, years earlier, required further investigation. MacDonald had claimed that Farris was a liar in 1959; Roberts had confirmed this was so in 1963. MacDonald had claimed that the Convesto explanation did not make sense; Roberts had confirmed that the company was not the buyer but a nominee. MacDonald had suggested there was evidence that Landreville was corrupt; Roberts now acknowledged this might be true. With his limited resources, MacDonald had got the story right years earlier.

The next day, Landreville was front-page news. 'Landreville named in NONG Dispute' was the lead story in the *Globe and Mail*. A *Toronto Star* editorial called on the government to 'clear up the NONG stench.'[15] Landreville was, of course, asked about the charges. He claimed that he paid 'cold hard cash' for his NONG shares, but declined to give further details. 'I love politics, and I'm itching to get into it,' he told the press, but he could not do so as his position did not allow him to 'meddle in politics.'[16] He also claimed that the Securities Act prohibited him from speaking about the case until the investigators had completed their report.[17] Needless to say, the Supreme Court justice was extremely displeased by this turn of events. In fact, when he heard about the investigation in September 1962, around the same time that he was interviewed by the RCMP, Landreville had done what he could to nip it in the bud. He wrote to the premier and asked for an interview, in camera, to advise him of certain matters. 'My subject matter,' he wrote,'would be to impart some information concerning NONG Ltd. in its relations to the Attorney General's Office and the Securities Commission, which is out of their respective domains.'[18] A similar letter was sent to Attorney General Cass.

These interventions were unwise. They made it appear that Landreville had something to hide, or that he intended some other use for the information he had in mind, a point Cass made when he replied to Landreville's request: 'While I would not understand what information there might be that you may be able to impart to me which would not come within the purview of the present inquiry by the Ontario Securities Commission, I can assure you that I am most anxious to follow every line of inquiry which may be open to me or to my officials in connection with this long-standing and involved matter.'[19] Cass agreed to a meeting, but advised Landreville that it would not be in camera, and that one of his senior officials would also be there. Cornered, Landreville lacked judgment. Asking for a meeting with the attorney general when he knew that Cass might have to lay charges against him was extremely unwise.

The new inquiry, under OSC counsel H.S. Bray, QC, a veteran of the 1958 investigation, had begun on 13 August 1962. Landreville was not the only former municipal politician of interest to Bray and his rapidly increasing staff of investigators. The activities of Bracebridge mayor Glen S. Coates, Gravenhurst mayor Wanda Miller, and Orillia mayor Wilbur M. Cramp, along with Orillia city solicitor William L. Moore, were also under review. Bray's mandate was to review the disposition of 14,000 shares of NONG stock allocated to Convesto at $2.50 per share in January 1957 and, in the process of doing so, to consider whether the trading of those shares violated either the Securities Act or the Criminal Code. Bray was also asked to report on whether there was any evidence of bribery, corruption, irregularity, or impropriety on the part of any elected or appointed official in relation to the granting and approval of municipal gas franchises to NONG, directly or indirectly stemming from trading in NONG securities. By and large, it was a repeat of the 1958 investigation, except that this time the authorities had a good idea of what had transpired. All they needed was proof.

British Columbia securities officials cooperated. So too did the Americans, including the regulators of the Securities and Exchange Commission and agents of the Federal Bureau of Investigation. Bray and his team travelled throughout Ontario and gathered voluminous records. They also heard evidence from dozens of witnesses, except Gordon Kelly McLean, now living in Victoria, who refused an invitation to appear. McLean did, however, tell one of the OSC investigators that he delivered shares on NONG's behalf to Mayors Coates, Miller, and Cramp, and Orillia city solicitor Moore.[20]

John McGraw agreed to appear. His evidence made it absolutely clear that Farris was a liar who had deliberately sought to mislead the OSC in 1958. McGraw left little doubt that Convesto 'purchased' the 14,000 shares in January 1957 in name only. The purchase was at Farris's request, and the names of the beneficiaries of the purchase were provided by Farris.[21] McGraw told the OSC investigators that no commission was charged, to Landreville or anyone else, because Convesto was performing a service to Farris. In fact, Convesto did indirectly make money on the transaction. By buying the shares from the beneficiaries at $10 each and immediately selling them at the higher market price, Convesto was able to pocket the difference. Farris looked after all his friends, and McGraw was one of them. After all Farris's instructions had been given effect, a number of shares were left over: 350 of them went to a McGraw family investment corporation, and the remainder were directed to a separate Convesto account and distributed to several political parties and charities.[22]

OSC investigators interviewed virtually every city councillor who had served with Landreville, and many other individuals, some of whom were only remotely connected to the affair. In October 1962 Landreville was given an opportunity to tell his story. The Supreme Court judge arrived at the OSC hearing with counsel in tow, P.B.C. Pepper, QC, a well-known Toronto barrister with expertise in securities law.[23] Landreville denied the suggestion that the NONG stock option had anything to do with its getting the Sudbury gas franchise. The only reason he had been granted the investment was because he and Farris had become friends. Moreover, Landreville explained, he was committed to stepping down as mayor at the end of 1956, and they both realized that Landreville could be of use to NONG when he returned to the private practice of law.

'I had a substantial law office,' he told Bray, 'and it became apparent that the company would require a multitude of documents, easements would be signed – it was obvious that the company needed a firm of solicitors in Northern Ontario. That, in the ensuing years, would prove lucrative and if I had stock in the company I could voice, with some influence, my desires much more than if I had no stock.'[24] He insisted that he and Farris did not discuss that possibility, and Landreville's desire to purchase stock, until after Sudbury City Council had decided in favour of NONG.

'It would,' Landreville testified, 'have been a departure of my whole conduct of life to stoop and try to pry stock out of Mr. Farris and it would have been beyond Mr. Farris's stature to offer me stock' before the franchise deal was completed.[25] He also pointed out that while he expressed an interest in acquiring NONG stock after City Council had given the franchise agreement second reading, he did not learn that he had been granted an option until after third reading.[26] He had, however, received and accepted the option before travelling to Toronto to represent Sudbury at the final hearing of the OFB, at which time he cross-examined witnesses, including Farris, on the terms of the franchise deal.[27] There was no conflict there, Landreville explained, because, by this time, the franchise arrangements with NONG were a *fait accompli*. For good measure, but probably to poor effect, Landreville told the OSC investigators that he had done nothing illegal or wrong, and that he would do it all again.[28] Landreville reported that anyone could have approached NONG to buy stock, and that he should hardly be faulted for having the foresight to do so.

Not many people, Bray retorted, were in Landreville's position and not many made $117,000 without laying out any money of their own. To this question, Landreville's lawyer objected. The amount of money made, Pepper said, was really not the point. The point was whether Landreville had solicited or accepted a bribe. On this point, Landreville was absolutely clear. He had become a friend of Farris, and he was still his friend. He did approach Farris for stock, and he had a future relationship with NONG in mind. Yet 'there was not one mention of the gas franchise, not one mention; there was not one mention of even the smallest favour that I would be binding myself to give to him in exchange for shares.'

Landreville insisted that his dealings with NONG were completely legitimate. He claimed that he had told his former law partner, Judge J.M.

Cooper, before the final vote that he had arranged for the purchase of these shares; he also thought that he might have mentioned doing so to one or more members of Sudbury City Council. Landreville agreed that he did not disclose the matter to members of council in any formal way, but insisted that he never kept it secret or dealt with it covertly.[29] Cooper, when asked, had no recollection of this conversation. No one but Landreville did. Landreville also contended that, in July 1956, Farris told him to communicate with Convesto when he was ready to acquire the shares, which he did in the late fall of 1956. Landreville could not provide any answers when he was asked why he did not obtain the shares from NONG, given that it was that company which granted him the option. In January 1957, according to Landreville, someone from Convesto – he could not recall who – telephoned him and advised him that the market price for NONG shares had reached $10.00 per share. With Convesto holding 10,000 shares in Landreville's account, it was suggested that he sell 2500 shares to pay off the balance owing. Landreville simply agreed with this suggestion.

At the conclusion of his evidence, Landreville pleaded with Bray to make a formal finding in his report. 'I am conscious of my position,' he said, 'and I am conscious of the reflection on the Bench ... And my position on the Bench, is a most uncomfortable one until this matter is settled. I can hardly sentence a man before me for theft when he looks at me and implies I am one, too, except they haven't found me guilty.' Bray interjected and claimed that his job was to find facts, not to determine innocence or guilt. This, Landreville replied, was unacceptable. 'If you find that I have been, that there has been misconduct on my part in municipal office, and I say, "Serious misconduct," of course you shall say so and will point it out but if you find that there has been no misconduct, I would obviously appreciate it be clear and not in ambiguous language so that the general public will understand.'[30] Landreville, it appeared, truly believed that he had done nothing wrong. He never wavered in his assertion that any objective examination of the facts would prove it.

Several weeks after Landreville appeared, Farris was called in, also under subpoena. He was represented by Joseph Sedgwick, QC, another leading lawyer and current Law Society treasurer. Sedgwick, known most of all for his 'silver tongue,' first gained public notice when, as a young lawyer working in the attorney general's office, he reviewed all the contracts entered into on behalf of the Dionne quintuplets. He had also served as a prosecutor in the 1930s trial of Communist Party boss Tim Buck; after returning to private practice, he successfully defended

Eric Adams, of the Foreign Exchange Control Board, who was charged with spying for the Soviets. Sedgwick was not only an accomplished orator but he was also a zealous advocate, and he immediately advised Bray that Farris was claiming the protection of the Canada Evidence Act for each question asked and each answer given. The evidence he gave could thus not be used against him in a criminal trial. Even so, as in 1958, Farris was obliged to tell the truth, and failure to do so would constitute perjury, itself a serious criminal offence.

The OSC was no longer groping in the dark. It knew, for instance, that Landreville had received an option to purchase 10,000 shares. It knew, from McGraw, that Convesto had not bought any shares, but had merely distributed shares on Farris's behalf. And it knew that McLean had given shares away to three mayors and one city solicitor after Farris instructed him to do so. Farris was questioned about his 20 July 1956 letter to Landreville giving him an option to purchase shares. He had no recollection of writing that letter or of the circumstances surrounding it.[31] This option was, in the circumstances, unique. First, it was not recorded in company minute books. Second, no other NONG director, with the possible exception of C. Spencer Clark, was aware of its existence. Other shareholders had been given the right, on 25 July 1956, to purchase one share of NONG stock at $2.50 per share for every fifteen shares already held, but they were given only one month to exercise that right and were required to pay for their shares by certified cheque. Landreville had been given a year to exercise his option.[32] This was all very odd, but Farris had an explanation. He assumed the date of the option letter was wrong, and pointed out that he was busy running around the north at this time. He had no recollection of Landreville's 30 July reply.

NONG was a new company with few permanent employees, Farris explained. 'Sometimes the minutes were put in shape and put in order a long time after the meetings themselves were held ... and I think this was to be expected in a company that had little, if any, office organization and whose principals were running all over the country and had, practically, no place of business.'[33] Farris would not agree with the suggestion that he signed the letter knowing it was not true, since no directors' meeting had taken place. All he could suggest was that the letter was dated incorrectly.[34]

The date on the letter was clearly accurate, and the fact that Landreville replied several days later accepting the 'option' proved that was so. More important than when it was mailed was why it was mailed. 'What was the possible consideration at this point for NONG granting Mr. Landreville the right to acquire 10,000 shares of its treasury stock at $2.50 per share?' Bray asked.[35] Farris insisted that the option arrangement had nothing to do with the Sudbury franchise. It was, he said, an arrangement entered into on the understanding that Landreville would, when he stepped down as mayor, join NONG in one capacity or another.[36] Landreville was, Farris explained, a lawyer, bilingual, knowledgeable about the north, and a man of ability. He was just the kind of man Farris wanted for his company, and the stock offer reflected that fact. Landreville did not get the option as an inducement or a reward; according to Farris no one did. All the franchise negotiations were conducted on a public level, and, in any event, NONG did not and would not behave in this way.[37]

Landreville had gone to the bench instead of joining NONG, and Farris testified that soon after Landreville was appointed he inquired whether he could still purchase the stock. Farris did not feel any obligation to him, but agreed to honour the request because NONG needed the money.[38] A number of other people had expressed interest in acquiring NONG shares, and it simply made sense to consolidate these requests. Around this time, NONG sold 14,000 shares for $2.50 each to its New York investment banker, Lehman Brothers. It seemed logical to make a similar arrangement with Convesto.

NONG was not 'taking care' of Landreville or anyone else, Farris insisted to Bray. When these arrangements were made in the fall of 1956 there was not a great market for NONG stock. That demand for shares 'happened late in December, from nowhere, it just developed.'[39] Commitments were made at one price, and by the time the deliveries came the price was higher. Had the stock been sold when the arrangements were first made there would not, Farris suggested, have been any fuss, because there would not have been any immediate profits. Unfortunately, he said, there were difficulties in arranging a meeting of NONG's Board of Directors. As soon as this was done, the stock was sold to Convesto, which in turn distributed it to those individuals who had requested it, as well as to several others.

Attempting to establish that the Convesto account really belonged to Farris, Bray asked a number of questions about that account. He also wanted to know who was in charge. It was McGraw, Farris testified. According to his version of events, he told McGraw that there was a growing market for these shares, and provided him with the names of people, including Landreville, who had expressed an interest in the company. He did so to assure him that he could resell the NONG shares. Other than providing him with this information, Farris claimed he had nothing to do with the disposition of the shares.[40] The Convesto account belonged to Convesto. The fact that Convesto did not charge a commission on the sale of the shares and that Farris enjoyed the benefit of the profits being distributed to charities and political parties in his name did not, he insisted, alter that fundamental fact.[41]

'I don't think you will find anything binding between McGraw, or any other director, which required him to do one thing or required him to do another,' Farris testified. 'I think I gave him assurance he could sell the stock and not lose money by telling him who I knew wanted to buy stock. I never forced him to buy stock or forced Mr. McGraw to sell to them. I think it was mutually desirable on both of their parts.'[42] With respect to Convesto's letter applying for shares 'on behalf of clients,' that was, Farris insisted, standard industry practice. Convesto was a principal, no matter what the application letter said.

Farris explained that McGraw's letter to Landreville and the other beneficiaries, beginning, 'As instructed by R.K. Farris ...' was 'pretty loose language.' He had merely been responsible for bringing a buyer and a seller together. McGraw should have indicated to the prospective purchasers that he was writing 'at the suggestion of' R.K. Farris.[43]

Farris testified that he had no idea that Gordon Kelly McLean had ended up with 800 of the 14,000 shares sold to Convesto. He assumed, however, that McLean got the shares to distribute to friends. He did not know that municipal politicians had benefited, and he told Bray that he did not 'believe it.' When Bray spelled out the details, Farris claimed that it was news to him. McLean, Farris emphasized, was not acting under his instructions. 'In buying them or in any action he took with regard to those shares, he did it without my knowledge whatsoever.' Farris had met Mayors Miller, Coates, and Cramp only once, and had played only a minor role in the Bracebridge, Gravenhurst, and Orillia negotiations. He testified that these franchises were acquired more out of a matter of pride than anything else. NONG liked the idea of outdoing Consumers Gas on its own doorstep, even if it meant that it had to sell these communities, all three of which were located in southern Ontario, natural gas at the northern rate.[44]

Farris was adamant that no gifts were offered to any public officials to secure their support for NONG's franchise bids. Many public officials, as well as the residents of northern Ontario who were to be served by NONG, were given an early opportunity to purchase shares before the general public had its chance. Farris and NONG did not publicize this opportunity. Rather, meetings were held in selected communities and an attempt was made to ascertain the requirement for shares. That information, in the form of a list of names and the amount of stock that each person was to receive, was later forwarded to the underwriters.[45]

In Sudbury, Landreville's successor, Mayor Joseph Fabbro, had provided Farris with a list. Fabbro received the largest number of shares, followed by his wife, the new city solicitor, the city engineer, the clerk-comptroller, and various other notables including the local members of provincial parliament, the presiding county court judge, and the publisher of the *Sudbury Star*.[46] In the trade, such privileged persons are referred to as 'sacred cows.' If the issue is oversubscribed, they are effectively guaranteed after they obtain the stock they wish, that they will be able to sell it at a profit. Fabbro, as it happened, held on to his stock for too long and, following the initial flurry of excitement, it dropped below the purchase price. Arrangements were made for him to jettison his holdings without suffering a loss.[47] NONG looked after its friends.

Farris never denied that he made sure there was sufficient stock available for distribution in the franchise area. While he claimed that he had no control on how the underwriters went about their work, he also ensured that sufficient stock was available for some of his Vancouver associates, including the registrar of companies and the deputy superintendent of brokers, who, like Landreville, had their stock registered in Convesto's name. As Farris's testimony progressed from morning to night, it became clear that he had a significant role in the distribution of NONG stock and that a considerable amount of it passed through his personal Convesto account.[48]

At the end of his second day of questioning, Bray asked Farris why he had lied in 1958 about the disposition of the 14,000 Convesto shares. 'I put it to you, Mr. Farris,' Bray said, 'that in your previous evidence, the whole tenor of it ... led the listener to believe Convesto were buying as a principal with no thought of re-sale?' Farris denied the suggestion, saying he did not think he would ever make a statement of that kind. While his evidence may have been interpreted that way, that was not what was intended. Bray tried again. 'Why,' he asked Farris, "was there no mention made by yourself on this previous evidence that you anticipated and expected that other people would have the benefit of some or all of these 14,000 shares at $2.50?' That question, Farris stated, was never asked. 'Are you suggesting,' Bray asked, that 'you did not know that was the purport of the questions put to you at that time?' That was exactly what Farris was suggesting. He did not 'know what the purport of your questions or Mr. Ford's question were at that time.' He presumed that it had to do with trading in securities before registration, because that was the subject of the charge against him. The deal with Convesto was a simple one. It bought shares as an investor, and what it did with those shares was its business.[49]

Farris was reminded of his evidence in 1958. He denied at that time any knowledge of the disposition of the 14,000 shares. Four years later he claimed that he was not aware of what happened to those shares. To be aware, he would have had to 'trace the stock register into Continental and out.' 'Are you suggesting,' an incredulous Bray asked Farris, that 'you took the questions to mean particular share certificates?' Yes, came the response.[50]

In 1958 Farris had also been asked whether he had, at any time, sold any NONG shares directly or indirectly to any elected member of any municipal council with whom NONG was negotiating for a franchise. Farris then claimed that he had not. In 1962 he was asked whether this was a candid answer, given that Landreville had been able, thanks to Farris, to purchase stock. Farris insisted he had told the truth. It was, he told Bray, a candid answer to a question 'so pointed as to time.' Bray, disbelieving, asked how such a broad question could be misinterpreted. How could Farris claim that he answered it honestly? Sedgwick interjected. The question reads, 'Have you sold stock to any municipal politician with whom NONG were in negotiations?' When NONG granted Landreville the option, the franchise negotiations were effectively completed.[51]

Farris was obviously a liar. His evidence and that of the other witnesses more than established as much. There was no doubt whatsoever that McGraw had opened the Convesto account on Farris's orders and had distributed the stock as instructed. Farris had sold shares to his friends for a fraction of their current value. There remained the open question whether he had bribed or sought to bribe an elected official.

When J. Chester Grey, the NONG official in charge of many of the franchise negotiations, appeared before the OSC, he had an interesting story to tell about his dealings with Orillia mayor Wilbur Cramp. A lot of 'wining and dining' was involved, and at some point before the franchise agreement was reached, Cramp told Grey that NONG looked like a good deal. 'Now,' Grey testified before the OSC, 'just to what he was alluding, I don't know.' In fact, Grey had a good idea. On one occasion he bought Cramp a bottle of Crown Royal. But Cramp was not satisfied with this gift, and purportedly told Grey that 'it's going to cost lots more than a bottle of liquor to get the franchise.' Another NONG official testified that when Farris heard of this remark, he said 'to hell with him.'[52]

Eventually, Orillia City Council had to decide between two rival bids, and it did so with a promise from NONG that it would supply gas at the northern and lower rate, even though Orillia was in southern Ontario. That rate was announced at a meeting to which the mayors of Brace-bridge and Gravenhurst were also invited. In contrast, Consumers Gas, NONG's rival, had not even submitted a written proposal. Accordingly, NONG won the day. As it turned out, before the NONG franchise received OFB approval, Consumers Gas returned with a rival and more competitive bid, this time for all three municipalities. In December 1956, however, the OFB approved all three franchise arrangements with NONG.

While Gordon Kelly McLean did not testify before the OSC, he did tell an OSC investigator that, sometime after February 1957, he divided 600 of the 800 shares allocated to him to Mayors Coates and Miller, and 300 shares to Orillia city solicitor Moore, who gave half to Mayor Cramp.[53] Cramp, in his evidence, rejected any suggestion that the shares were an inducement or a bribe: he had paid for his shares, he claimed, adding that he handed over some cash to a NONG official whose name he could not recall at a party held at the King Edward Hotel. He denied receiving any shares from Moore, who also said he paid for his shares. He was unable to provide any proof of payment.[54]

The OSC also looked into NONG's relations with Coates and Miller, and, other than their receipt of 150 NONG shares each after the franchises had been approved, there was no evidence that either mayor had done anything out of the ordinary in support of NONG's application for a franchise. NONG was, after all, the only applicant in both cases.

NONG was not, however, the only applicant for the Port Arthur and Fort William franchises. It competed with Twin City, which was success-ful in both cities. Ultimately, NONG prevailed by buying Twin City. As part of its review, the OSC looked at how Twin City initially succeeded in obtaining franchise rights for Port Arthur and Fort William, and it learned that it, like NONG, encouraged local support through a generous pre-public offering of shares to citizens and politicians in a position to promote the welfare of the company. After Farris took over, some other interesting arrangements were made. On 3 May 1957, for example, NONG sent a former Port Arthur alderman named D.H. Coghlan a cheque for $2500. Coghlan told the OSC that this cheque was an advance on some insurance commissions he hoped to make by selling policies to Twin City Gas. He never did sell Twin City any insurance, and used the money for living expenses while working full-time on the 1957 re-election campaign of the local member of parliament, C.D. Howe.[55] Obviously, Howe's survival was in NONG's interests.

Given the matters under review, and the much wider scope of the inquiry in 1963, it took the Securities Commission some time to complete its investigation and prepare its report. In the meantime, the rumours and allegations took on a life of their own. It was only a matter of time, it was reported in the press, before charges would be filed. Landreville, and his lawyer P.B.C. Pepper, began to press Attorney General Cass for the release of the OSC report. Pepper pointed out that the rumours and insinuations were making it difficult for Landreville to perform his judicial functions.[56] Cass replied sympathetically, but until the report was completed and ready for release, there was nothing that he could do.[57]

In February 1963 Pepper asked Cass for an interview. His purpose was to find out about the status of the OSC report, and he advised Cass that Landreville did not know about his inquiry.[58] Pepper later reported that the interview had gone well, but he still did not know when the report would be released.

On 22 July 1963 Bray submitted a 286-page report. Notwithstanding his undertaking to provide the public with a copy of that report as soon as it became available, Cass failed to do so. Farris had once again claimed the protection of the Canada and Ontario Evidence Acts, so anything he said could not be used against him in a subsequent trial. Just as in 1958, neither the report nor the evidence could be released if criminal proceedings were pending. The attorney general sought and obtained an opinion from a leading criminal counsel, A.E. Shepherd, QC, as to what charges, if any, should be laid. Shepherd opined on 20 August 1963 that there was sufficient evidence in the OSC report to support criminal charges against Farris,[59] and two days later he was charged with two counts of perjury in his evidence during the 1958 and 1962 OSC investigations. If convicted, he faced a maximum sentence of fourteen years in jail.

5

Trials and Tribulations

Ralph Farris had a peculiar view of the world for a businessman: he did not believe in competition. It made no sense, he observed, for two companies to try to sell the same product to the same consumers. 'That kind of competition,' he remarked, 'breeds ulcers and creates old men very fast.' Farris had a different approach. He preferred to circumvent competition by specializing in the sale of products and ideas that no one else happened to be selling at the time. And he believed that extraordinary profits rightfully belonged to men who took extraordinary risks. His profit of 200,000 per cent in NONG was not 'excessive'; indeed, Farris felt it might not even be sufficient, given the risks he took.[1]

Though Farris disliked ordinary competition in business life, he was, by nature, a competitive man. With some of his profits from the sale of NONG shares, he bought a 14-metre racing sloop, *Hawk*, which he moored at the Royal Vancouver Yacht Club. Farris loved to race. 'When a race is on,' he observed, 'you want to win it. I guess it is the same way in any competitive situation. When I'm fighting at a franchise hearing, I hate my opponent just as hard as I can hate him.'[2] An intense, driven man, Farris was one of Canada's first jet-age executives. He would leave his fashionable Shaughnessy home, drive his Corvette or Jaguar to Vancouver airport, climb aboard a first-class flight for Toronto, and land five hours later at Malton Airport. His Toronto residence was a suite at the Lord Simcoe Hotel, the city's newest hostelry. Across the street was NONG's University Avenue headquarters, with its view of

Queen's Park. There, more likely than not, the politicians were talking about him.

Farris was certainly the subject of conversation one morning in early September 1963 when, soon after arriving in town, he was arrested by the police and taken into custody, charged with having committed perjury on two separate occasions: first, before the Ontario Securities Commission Inquiry in 1958, when he denied any knowledge of the disposition by Convesto, in January 1957, of 14,000 shares of NONG stock; and second, when he testified before the OSC investigators in 1962 that he had nothing to do with the distribution of free NONG shares to a number of northern mayors. Farris was immediately released on bail of $10,000 – paid for with ten new $1000 bills.

A preliminary inquiry took place before Magistrate Joseph Addison in late 1963 and early 1964. Addison was a popular Toronto judge. Called to the bar in 1937, he was appointed one of Toronto's first Jewish magistrates by Kelso Roberts in 1958. He was a tough but fair-minded judge, never afraid to express colourful views from the bench, often in informal ways. Joseph Sedgwick, QC, continued to act for Farris; R.P. Milligan presented the case for the Crown. On 21 January 1964 Addison concluded that there was more than enough evidence to commit the accused for trial, and Farris elected trial before a judge and jury. The case began in April 1964, before Mr Justice Dalton Wells. A future chief justice of the High Court, Wells looked very much the judge with his big shock of white hair. The trial turned out to be a long one. Sedgwick challenged twenty prospective jurors until he found twelve men he was satisfied with.

The Crown was now represented by special prosecutor Harvey McCulloch, QC, a hard-nosed Hamilton lawyer. It was required to prove beyond a reasonable doubt that Farris had lied while under oath. The court reporters from the 1958 and 1962 investigations were called, and they testified that their transcripts of his evidence were both accurate and complete. Harry Bray testified next, and he told the judge and jury about the conduct of both the 1958 and 1962 investigations. Officer Bates described the investigation and his meeting with Farris in June 1962. At that time, Bates asked Farris about the 14,000 shares, and he admitted directing the distribution of some of those shares to Landreville, McLean, and J. Stewart Smith. Bates also described how Farris told him that Landreville, a friend, had asked if he could purchase stock in October 1956. Farris said he could, but for some reason the stock could not be released until 1957, at which time Farris made the necessary arrangements with McGraw. Under questioning by Sedgwick, Bates agreed that Farris fully cooperated in the investigation; Farris even left him alone with some files when he went off for an appointment.[3]

Gordon Kelly McLean also testified – under the protection of the Canada and Ontario Evidence Acts. He told the court that Farris met him at NONG's Toronto office and gave him an envelope containing NONG shares along with a list of persons who were to receive 150 shares each: Miller, Coates, Cramp, and Moore. According to McLean, this was the only task of this kind that Farris ever gave him, and he claimed, somewhat improbably, that he had no idea why the shares were being given away. J. Chester Grey, NONG's point man for the early franchise negotiations, offered a partial, and for the first time public, explanation: the shares were undoubtedly a bribe. When he was negotiating the Orillia agreement, Mayor Wilbur Cramp had made it clear that it might 'cost us something to get a franchise in Orillia.'[4] Farris listened, Grey claimed, but said nothing when he reported the conversation to him.

Grey did not fare well on cross-examination. An American resident in Arizona, Grey had forgotten to bring with him any of the documents he claimed supported his account. His evidence may have provided a motive for bribery, but other evidence already adduced indicated that neither Farris nor NONG was really interested in extending the franchise south of North Bay. None of the communities to the south, given the almost complete absence of industry, would provide much opportunity for the sale of valley gas.

From the defence point of view, McLean was the important witness to attack. If his evidence was believed, Farris was finished. Sedgwick proved, in cross-examination, that McLean's memory for detail was somewhat lacking. The evidence led established that McLean received the shares from Convesto, and that they were sent by mail. Farris had never, as McLean earlier claimed, handed over the shares along with a distribution list. More likely than not, Farris was not even in town when McLean received the shares from McGraw; there was correspondence indicating that on the day McLean claimed to have received the shares, Farris was in Vancouver. In addition, McLean's memory of the actual distribution of the shares differed, in some significant respects, from the recollections of the recipients. Still, McLean's testimony was potentially extremely damaging. Farris had earlier disavowed any knowledge of these shares or their disposition.

No one took issue with the fact that the three mayors and the city solicitor had received the shares. The individual allotments were given in street form, and none of the recipients was asked to pay for the stock.

Eventually Coates, who earned a salary of $600 a year, sold his shares for more than $3000. Miller's timing was not as good; she netted only $1761. Coates told the court that McLean advised him that the shares were compensation for the work and inconvenience he had been put to by NONG's application for the Bracebridge franchise; he protested that he had done nothing but his duty, and then pocketed the shares. William Moore, a lawyer in private practice who also acted as Orillia's town solicitor, gave fifty of his shares to his partner, kept the rest, and informed Mayor Cramp that the value of the stock was used to offset the town's account.[5] Cramp got the remaining 150 shares. He testified that they arrived one day in the mail. He claimed that he had some recollection of paying for them, but insisted, Grey's suggestion notwithstanding, that he had never suggested that a bribe would be necessary to secure the Orillia franchise. Cramp, who also advised the court that the shares came long after the franchise had been approved, took them to the bank and used them as collateral for a loan. Eventually he sold them for $10 each.[6]

As interesting as this evidence was, the mayors of Bracebridge, Orillia, and Gravenhurst were small pickings, and the amounts involved were nominal, to say the least. There were bigger fish to fry, and the spotlight was soon on one man, and not the one sitting in the prisoner's dock. Attention was focused on the Honourable Leo Landreville, one of Her Majesty's justices of the Supreme Court of Ontario.

On 14 April 1964 Landreville took the stand. 'I have been waiting for two years. I have kept silence for two years. I have been harassed for two years,' he began.[7] He spoke for more than three hours, virtually without interruption, and he frequently referred to the minutes of Sudbury City Council and other documents he had brought. He told about meeting Farris, and becoming impressed with him and his company. He relayed to the jury the process Sudbury followed in granting the franchise to NONG. He pointed out that the decision to grant NONG the franchise had effectively been made years earlier when the provincial government instructed the northern municipalities to choose one distribution company, and that all those municipalities then chose NONG.

Landreville insisted that he never did anything wrong by expressing an interest in acquiring NONG shares or in joining the company. He also made it absolutely clear that, while he supported NONG's application, he did not do so on the basis of any inducement, promised or received. When the matter finally went to a vote, Landreville abstained. Sudbury City Council, he hastened to point out, granted NONG the franchise by a vote of seven to three.

Landreville's interest in NONG was reciprocal, and it only made sense, if he was to become involved in the company, that he be given an opportunity to buy some stock. The stock option he received was hardly, in the summer of 1956, a great deal. NONG had no assets, and Trans-Canada had not yet laid a foot of pipe. There was nothing wrong, Landreville pointed out, with NONG deciding to grant him this option, given their understanding of his future role. Landreville testified that he would have been 'highly offended if Mr. Farris had even given me the slightest indication there would be some reward to me, and I would have had neither truck nor trade with him from that moment on.' That never happened, and in 1956 Landreville was proud to be associated with Farris 'and I am still proud to be associated with him today.'[8]

John McGraw followed Landreville to the witness stand. At that point, the full details of the 1957 share distribution finally emerged publicly. When the OSC invited him to give evidence in 1958, he had declined. His evidence during the 1962–63 investigation was in camera, and the OSC had not released either a transcript or the completed report. Now, McGraw was testifying at a criminal trial. His evidence made it absolutely clear that Farris, in 1958 and in 1962, had lied while under oath.

The Vancouver broker had a simple story to tell. In October or November 1956 Farris approached McGraw and asked Convesto to apply for some NONG stock. McGraw understood that this distribution was to be a finalization of the original NONG financing, and that Farris would let him know the names of the recipients and the number of their shares. Nothing happened until January 1957, when Farris instructed Convesto to apply for 14,000 shares at $2.50 each. Convesto then sent NONG a cheque for $35,000, the cost of the 14,000 shares.

McGraw told Wells and the jury that when Landreville was offered 10,000 shares at $2.50 each in the summer of 1956, the price was a fair one. Indeed, throughout the summer and early fall the price for the shares hardly moved. NONG had no assets other than the franchise agreements. He also told the court that it was on Farris's orders that his company sold 2500 of the 10,000 shares allocated to Landreville, clearing his account. He then delivered the remaining 7500 shares to the judge in street form.

According to McGraw, not only did Farris instruct him in the disposition of Landreville's stock, but he also instructed him in the disposition of the remaining shares. Eight hundred of these shares were deposited to Gordon Kelly McLean's account, and 200 shares were promptly sold clearing it. In addition, J. Stewart Smith was given 800 shares; David Levy of New York, an investment banker employed by NONG's New York underwriter and a friend of Farris, was given 800 shares; Gene Graff, who was employed on the original NONG feasibility study, was given 200 shares; and 350 shares went to Glacier Investments Limited, a McGraw family company.[9] All told, 12,950 shares were sold or given away, and in most cases the method followed was the same. A sufficient number of shares was sold to clear the account, and street certificates were delivered to the recipients.

One thousand and fifty shares were left in the account after the initial distribution was completed, and McGraw asked Farris what to do. They were ultimately sold, providing the account with a $20,000 profit which, on Farris's orders, was divided between several political parties – there were federal elections in 1957 and 1958 – and a number of charities. Only $1000 was directed back to Farris. No commissions were charged on any of these transactions, although Convesto profited handsomely by taking advantage of the price spread between the amount it bought the shares for from the designated beneficiaries and the amount it obtained when it sold the shares on the open market. In the circumstances, the beneficiaries had little cause for complaint.

After the Crown presented its case, Sedgwick announced that the defence would not be calling any evidence and launched a blistering ninety-minute attack on the prosecution. Sedgwick argued that the two OSC investigations had no business looking into the distribution of the 14,000 shares, since that distribution did not constitute trading. He also took the position that there was no evidence establishing that Farris knew what happened to the 14,000 shares after they left NONG. He was not 'aware of the disposition of those 14,000 shares allotted to Convesto under date of January 17th, 1957.'[10] What evidence there was established that Landreville dealt directly with Convesto, and this, Sedgwick submitted, refuted the suggestion that Farris was somehow involved.

With respect to the other count, the defence argued that the evidence of Gordon Kelly McLean should not be believed. Farris, Sedgwick submitted, could not have handed the 600 shares over to McLean on the day McLean claimed he did because there was a letter written by Farris which indicated he was in Vancouver that day. Sedgwick suggested that the perjury charge should be against McLean; it was McLean, Sedgwick alleged, not Farris, who should be sitting in the prisoner's dock.

For his part, Crown attorney McCulloch argued that the Crown had discharged its burden of proof, and that Farris committed perjury when he denied knowing the 'disposition of those 14,000 shares.' After all, Farris not only arranged for their delivery to Convesto but oversaw their distribution and the allocation of both the proceeds of the sales and the surplus shares before the closing of the account. McCulloch also took the position that McLean should be believed. The evidence established that Farris ordered McLean to distribute the 600 shares. This proved that Farris committed perjury when he testified in 1962 that he had no knowledge of these events.

Wells was obviously not impressed with the Crown's case. In his address to the jury, he observed that the Crown had used tactics of 'McCarthyism' against Farris and had gone further than necessary in the ten-day trial by clouding the perjury charges with allegations of widespread municipal corruption. The charge before the jury was perjury, and he cautioned the twelve men to keep that fundamental fact in mind. Their job was to consider the evidence of perjury, not of guilt by association. 'Don't let that fetid atmosphere of municipal corruption influence your thinking,' he warned the jurors.[11]

The Supreme Court of Ontario judge also made some observations about the evidence. In his view, it was far from clear that the Crown had proved its case. Certainly, he suggested, there was a possibility that Farris was telling the truth when he testified he was not aware of the 'disposition' of the 14,000 shares. More than one interpretation was involved in that question, and Farris may have thought he was being asked if he knew the fate of the actual share certificates themselves. Mr Justice Wells told the jury that he would have difficulty accepting John McGraw's version of events, and he suggested that Chester Grey's evidence was 'too remote and unreliable' to offer the Crown's case much support. McLean's evidence that Farris instructed him to distribute the 600 shares was also problematic. 'McLean,' the judge said, 'is an extraordinary witness.' Not only was he an ex-convict but a 'rolling stone and one that had not gathered much moss: It may be the moss was washed off by the excessive use of alcohol,' making note of the fact that McLean was a reformed alcoholic.[12] In Wells's opinion, McLean had probably distributed the shares to Coates, Miller, Cramp, and Moore 'as a generous gesture ... and then got frightened and made up this story which he stuck to.'[13]

McLean did have a generous streak. He had, after all, arranged for ten members of his family to buy NONG shares. Generosity was clearly a family trait. His uncle had also arranged to share the spoils with some of his friends, even crossing party lines to do so. At base, Wells did not believe McLean's version of events, and he pointed to the evidence establishing that Farris was in Vancouver at the time McLean claimed to have met him in Toronto and received instructions to distribute the NONG shares. The judge left the jury with little doubt as to its proper course. Even if McLean's evidence was accepted, the jury would have no choice but to acquit on the second count because his evidence had not received the corroboration necessary, in law, to support a perjury charge. Grey's testimony, while supporting the assertion that a bribe had been solicited, did not corroborate the claim that one had been given.

The judge had all but said that the Crown had failed to prove its case. Jurors, however, are apt to have minds of their own. They knew what the word 'disposition' meant, and they concluded that Farris was perfectly aware of the fate of the 14,000 shares. He had concealed the facts from the OSC in order to derail its investigation. The perjury charge on the 600 shares was obviously more difficult to decide. For all his faults, McLean was probably telling the truth. However, the evidence adduced was not compelling, there was no corroboration, and there was a 'reasonable doubt' about his guilt on that score. The Crown had not proved that case. When the jurors returned to the courtroom on 24 April 1964 they had reached their verdict: guilty on the first count, not guilty on the second. Farris, who had throughout the trial seemed attentive but tired, sunken-eyed, and at times sad while sitting in the prisoner's dock, now appeared visibly shocked. He had every reason to believe he was on his way to jail.

The verdict was not perverse, and Wells had to accept it. Like it or not, Farris was found to have committed a crime. Sedgwick suggested that a suspended sentence would be appropriate in the circumstances, perhaps accompanied by a large fine. McCulloch disagreed. Farris had to go to jail. Asked if he had anything to say before sentence was imposed, Farris said simply, 'No, My Lord.' In imposing the sentence, Wells made a number of unorthodox, indeed extraordinary, comments. He stated for the record, having already been told that the verdict would be appealed, that there was nothing about the questions the OSC investigators asked that would bring the matter of the 14,000 shares to Farris's attention. He thought the perjury was of a 'minor nature,' and observed there was nothing in any of the evidence before him that would substantiate charges of corruption in Farris's dealings with municipal officials in Ontario.[14] On 24 August 1964 Farris was sentenced to nine months in jail. He was released on $10,000 bail pending appeal.

Attorney General Arthur Wishart was asked to comment on the case, but all he would say was that further charges were under consideration. He would not release the long-awaited OSC report until after Farris's appeal had been decided. As long as that case was before the courts, it would be improper, Wishart said, to make the report public.[15]

Sedgwick got to work on the appeal and enlisted the assistance of one of Canada's leading appellate advocates and future Law Society treasurer, G. Arthur Martin, QC. The Crown meanwhile appealed the acquittal on the second count. Soon enough, the case came before a panel of the Ontario Court of Appeal. The Crown's appeal was disposed of first and was dismissed. That left the perjury conviction on the first count, and the appellant's argument was relatively straightforward. The evidence at trial established that when Convesto acquired the 14,000 shares, it received street certificates in a variety of denominations. These denominations were not attributed to any of the ultimate recipients; rather, they were kept like cash in a box, and distributed to each purchaser as the sale occurred. The lawyers therefore argued that when Farris 'stated that he was unaware of the disposition of the 14,000 shares in question, his answer was literally true, for the actual shares, as represented by the share certificates delivered to Convesto, were not those eventually distributed to parties among whom Convesto was directed to distribute, and while this was done by Convesto according to the custom of brokers, the accused was entitled to believe that he was being asked about the distribution of the share certificates only.'[16] In January 1965 a three-member panel of the Ontario Court of Appeal rejected this argument.

Speaking for the Court, Mr Justice George McGillivray looked at the particular question in context, and when he did it was obvious that Farris must have known he was being asked if he realized who had received some of those 14,000 shares. That fact was established in McGraw's evidence, and had been corroborated by Bates, who testified that Farris told him that Landreville was one of the recipients of the shares. Corroboration of this nature was necessary because the Criminal Code provided that no one could be convicted of perjury on the evidence of only one witness. The evidence of that witness had to be corroborated by other evidence implicating the accused. The Court of Appeal ruled that the evidence of McGraw and Bates met this legal test. 'The net result of Bates' testimony,' McGillivray stated, 'is that it corroborates that of McGraw to the effect that the 14,000 shares were dealt with and distributed pursuant to instructions received from the accused.'[17]

Of that, as the jury found, there was little doubt. 'I must conclude from the whole of the evidence in this case,' McGillivray wrote in the court's reasons for decision, 'that there was no confusion in the mind of the accused when he answered the question and that he knew it was the equities represented by the shares about which he was questioned and not the share certificates; and, as a consequence, that he knew his answer to be false. He was not asked about the disposition of certain share-certificates, but about shares and, as a man with a wide business experience, he must have known the manner in which street certificates were handled by a firm like "Convesto."' Had Farris controlled a number of similar accounts, McGillivray observed, there would be reason to understand his plea of ignorance of the share disposition. But this was not the case. This account was 'unique and one about which he could readily have given the details.' Farris did not, choosing to lie instead. McGillivray was, accordingly, 'compelled to hold that the evidence in this case supports the conviction and establishes that the accused was aware of what he was being asked.' Farris's answer, therefore, was 'false and intended to mislead.'[18] McGillivray was not a leading legal authority, but this time his judgment was right. Sedgwick sought leave to appeal to the Supreme Court of Canada, but his application was refused.

Farris resigned from the presidency of NONG and was, in January 1965, taken away to jail. Said to be suffering from pancreatic and prostate cancer, he served five months in a provincial hospital jail before being released on parole.[19] NONG, meanwhile, continued to distribute gas to its customers and profits to its owners.

Landreville had testified at Farris's trial and, quite understandably, anxiously awaited its result. An acquittal on both counts offered the promise of some finality and a return to the relatively cloistered life of a sitting judge. If Farris was not guilty of any crime, what possibly could Landreville have done that was wrong? When Farris was convicted in April 1964, Landreville was extremely concerned that he might be charged next, and he took steps to avoid that fate.

In early June 1964 Landreville wrote to the federal minister of justice, Guy Favreau, and asked him to hold a public inquiry, possibly to be chaired by a retired judge of the Supreme Court of Canada. This inquiry, Landreville suggested, could be convened in Sudbury, with the mandate of determining whether there had been any conflict of interest, bribery, undue influence, or corruption in Sudbury City Council's award of the franchise to deliver natural gas. Landreville pointed out that the 'reputation of one of your Justices is at stake,' and that the only alternative to a public inquiry was the laying of a criminal charge. 'Of course,' Landreville continued, 'the simple fact of being charged with any offence, even if intended to give me a forum to prove my innocence, does irreparable and conclusive harm.' Favreau replied that he was studying the matter, and hoped to give Landreville a definite reply in the near future.[20]

Soon, Landreville got an answer, but not the one he was looking for.

One month after hearing that Favreau was studying his request for an inquiry, Landreville received shattering news. On 27 July 1964 Ontario Attorney General Wishart advised Landreville's lawyer, P.B.C. Pepper, QC, that Landreville would be criminally charged.[21] Privately, Landreville 'begged' Wishart not to charge him. The two men were old friends from the north, and Wishart had entertained Landreville in his home. The politician rejected the request. 'Leo,' he said, 'I can't help it, you are going to have to be prosecuted.'[22]

The behaviour of municipal politicians was governed by the Ontario Municipal Act, which required only that shareholders of companies holding municipal office not vote on any question affecting that company.[23] The courts had intervened, to a limited extent, by disallowing the votes of municipal politicians who participated in matters in which they had a pecuniary interest.[24] Landreville had not violated the Municipal Act, or breached this rule. When Sudbury City Council finally approved the NONG deal, he was not a NONG shareholder and, in any event, he did not vote. The Municipal Act was amended in 1961 to provide that councillors must declare pecuniary interests, direct or indirect, in any matter that came before them.[25] Even if this standard had been applied to Landreville, it would have been open to him to argue that when Sudbury City Council finally gave the franchise third and final reading, he did not have any present interest in NONG. All he had done was express an interest in purchasing NONG stock, and he did not exercise the subsequently obtained option to do so until long after City Council had finally approved the deal. As a result, Landreville could only be charged under the Criminal Code, and would be, notwithstanding real reservations within the Attorney General's department about the likelihood of success.[26]

Pepper was called to a private meeting with Wishart and advised exactly what charges were to be laid against Landreville. Pepper urged Wishart to reconsider. He pointed out that merely laying a charge, rather than holding a public inquiry, would do his client irreparable harm and would likely lead to Landreville's resignation. According to Pepper, Wishart looked 'aghast but said nothing,' and gave the impression that 'pressure had been brought upon him.' Afterwards, Pepper encouraged Landreville to look on the bright side. He was confident that Landreville would be acquitted. 'I do recognize the inconvenience, embarrassment and harm that the laying of the charges does to you. But at the same time,' he added, 'after three long years of harassment I frankly cannot disguise a feeling of relief; I have an idea that you may feel the same.'[27]

Landreville, who was summering at 'Landra Villa,' returned to Sudbury, where the charges had been preferred. He was charged with municipal corruption and conspiracy.[28] The allegations were straightforward: he was alleged to have accepted a bribe while mayor of Sudbury in return for assisting NONG in obtaining the Sudbury franchise. He was also charged with conspiring with Farris to commit an illegal act – the offer and acceptance of a bribe for awarding NONG the Sudbury gas rights.[29] If convicted on either count, Landreville faced the prospect of up to two years in jail. Mayors Coates, Miller, and Cramp were also charged. Landreville's case proceeded first. He appeared with Pepper in Magistrates' Court in Sudbury on 4 August 1964 and was released on his own recognizance.

The mere laying of the charge probably ended Landreville's usefulness as a judge. In a private memorandum to the chief justice, Landreville had earlier expressed the view that the public and media attention was not only damaging his career as a judge, but was undermining public confidence in the judiciary. Landreville pointed out that as a judge he did not have the opportunity to speak out, nor had he been provided with any forum to present his version of events. Even a judge, he wrote to Chief Justice Dana Porter, is entitled to speedy justice. 'My position on the Bench,' he observed, 'becomes more and more difficult. I am considering asking the Minister of Justice to relieve me of my functions until my character is vindicated, on failure of which I will resign as a Judge.'[30] The day after the charges were laid, Landreville wrote to the minister of justice and asked, given 'recent events,' that he be given a temporary leave of absence, without pay, from his functions as a judge of the Supreme Court of Ontario and the Ontario High Court.[31] In the circumstances, the minister could only accede to this request. It would have been intolerable for Landreville to judge others while he himself was accused of having broken the law, the presumption of innocence notwithstanding. The leave request was granted the following week.

On 29 September 1964 Landreville appeared in Magistrates' Court for the District of Sudbury before Magistrate Albert Marck. He was, on Pepper's suggestion, accompanied by new counsel, the skilful John J. Robinette, QC.[32]

Over the course of the six-day preliminary inquiry – the purpose of which was to determine whether there was sufficient evidence to send Landreville to trial – the Crown adduced considerable evidence about the evolution of NONG and its dealings with the City of Sudbury. If anything, this evidence assisted the defence, for it demonstrated the importance of the joint approach of the northern municipalities to ensure an all-Canadian route and to meet the risk of Trans-Canada Pipe Line choosing the southern route. This testimony also established that the award of the NONG franchise had been both thoroughly and publicly discussed, and that it was not Landreville who decided that Sudbury grant NONG the franchise rights. That decision was effectively made by all the northern municipalities, which jointly determined that public ownership was out of the question and that one private company, NONG, was to be given all northern rights. That decision, furthermore, was made long before Sudbury City Council finally approved the NONG deal. In part, economic considerations dictated this result, but the agreement between the municipalities was an integral part of the lobbying campaign to ensure a northern all-Canadian route.

Nevertheless, Crown Prosecutor Harvey McCulloch argued that there were under-the-table negotiations to provide Landreville with shares in return for delivering a favourable City Council vote. The proof of these negotiations was in their result: Landreville's receipt of 7500 shares that cost him nothing. Robinette argued that the Crown had failed to prove that Landreville was offered or had received a benefit, and even if he had received a benefit, there was no evidence that it was given in consideration of anything. Robinette took the position that Landreville did not participate in the decision to grant the franchise to NONG, and that this decision was virtually preordained.

After hearing the evidence and submissions of the parties, Marck was convinced that no person could conclude anything other than that natural gas was desirable for the north and that NONG was to be given the franchise. Moreover, the magistrate found that the question had been thoroughly studied by Sudbury City Council and publicly debated on numerous occasions. When the bylaw finally came up for third reading, Marck continued, it was not Landreville who pressed for its passage, but Crozier, the chair of the Ontario Fuel Board.

In reaching his conclusion that there was no evidence that Landreville had committed a crime, the magistrate relied on the testimony of a number of former Sudbury city officials who had given evidence, including J.J. Kelly, the former city solicitor, and Patrick H. Murphy, the former city clerk-comptroller. Kelly, the most vocal opponent of the transaction, made it absolutely clear that Landreville acted properly throughout. At no time did Landreville put any pressure on Kelly to disregard his duties. 'I was never made subservient to the Mayor,' he testified in court.[33] Murphy told the court that Howe's 4 May 1956 telegram urging Sudbury to sign with NONG had a significant effect on Landreville, who then demonstrated a desire to expedite negotiations with NONG. Speed did not, however, result in any disadvantage to Sudbury, Murphy recalled. 'We were able to get much better agreements. We picked the meat from all the other agreements and got the best deal.'[34] Landreville himself did not vote on the bylaw, and Murphy insisted that the mayor did nothing to pressure anyone to vote in favour of the proposed agreement. He also agreed, when questioned by Robinette, that while Sudbury may have once considered establishing its own gas distribution network, it quickly concluded that it did not have the money to do so. The cost would have been exorbitant.

Marck concluded on all these facts that Landreville had not committed any criminal act. The stock option was a problem, to be sure. Marck accepted Landreville's explanation that he received the shares as a result of his friendship with Farris, and that when he received the option the shares had a nominal value. 'Throughout the investigations by the Securities Commission, the preliminary hearing of Ralph K. Farris and the subsequent trial of Ralph K. Farris which evidence is all before this court, the accused has given the same explanation – "I became friendly with Ralph Farris and as a result of that friendship was able to purchase some stock which at the time was of nominal value because Northern Ontario Natural Gas at that time was little more than a paper entity with some franchises."'[35]

Referring to the evidence of John McGraw, who made yet another trip east to detail the workings of the special Convesto account, Marck found that it was only because of a 'gas explosion' that the shares increased in price. Marck, who knew something about business and was aware that shares can be allotted and distributed in a number of different ways, found nothing wrong in the manner in which Landreville exercised his option, nor in the way the shares were delivered to him. He noted that a ledger entry was made in Landreville's name in Convesto's books, and that there was nothing devious or circuitous about this arrangement.

The shares were sent to the judge at his office at Osgoode Hall, and the judge wrote to Convesto with some questions about these shares on his official stationery. The shares were then sold through a Toronto brokerage firm, and the monies deposited in the judge's Toronto bank account. These were not, Marck concluded, the actions of a man with something to hide. 'Surely,' he concluded, 'a man of his known intelligence would not act in such a manner if he were guilty of a criminal offence.' For all these reasons, Marck found that a properly charged jury could not find

Landreville guilty and that there was not therefore 'sufficient evidence to place him on ... trial.'[36] The charges were dismissed. Visibly tense while Marck read his decision, Landreville kept his eyes fixed on the counsel table. When the judge read that he found no evidence of any criminal act, Robinette patted Landreville on the back. As soon as the decision was announced, Landreville smiled broadly as he was surrounded by supporters.

Several weeks later, Marck dismissed the same charges against Bracebridge mayor Glen Coates. There was 'not one scintilla of evidence to indicate the accused influenced his council in any way.'[37] No judge, Marck continued, 'would allow these charges to go to a jury.'[38] Moreover, there was no evidence establishing that Coates and Farris had ever met, other than at a public meeting of the Ontario Fuel Board. The likelihood, therefore, that they conspired together was remote. Defence counsel Charles Dubin, QC, a tenacious, highly regarded lawyer and future chief justice of Ontario, then went on to his next assignment, representing another accused, former Gravenhurst mayor Wanda Miller.

Miller did not testify at her preliminary inquiry, but the Crown read into evidence a statement she had provided to the Ontario Securities Commission in 1962. She had then told an OSC investigator that she met McLean for lunch in Toronto at the King Edward Hotel. At that time, he gave her an envelope and told her to keep it in her purse. Some day, he said, it might be worth something. Miller told the investigator that she did not know why McLean gave her the shares, but 'I suspected quite a few things, really.'[39] Crown Attorney Harvey McCulloch argued that Miller received these shares as payment for her support for the NONG franchise application, but he could not prove that this was the case. The law as it then stood did not prohibit receipt of a gift.

Marck also dismissed the charges against Mayor Miller. There was 'not a shred of evidence,' he found, indicating that she attempted to influence Gravenhurst City Council in any way.[40] The evidence he heard established that Miller had left leadership in the gas franchise decision to other members of council, who were unanimous in their support of NONG. This evidence negated any inference that Miller had been bribed. Besides, the magistrate observed, Canadian law 'would not allow the conclusion that mere acceptance of the gift of stock constituted accepting a bribe.'[41] This was an accurate statement of the law. On the other hand, what other possible reason would there have been to give away NONG shares – or to accept them?

There remained the case of Mayor Cramp. In June 1956 Orillia City Council granted the gas franchise to NONG. Eleven months later, some city councillors began to have second thoughts, particularly after receiving a rival bid from Consumers Gas. Cramp strenuously opposed that bid. In his view, NONG was to be preferred, and he advised council that, as a result of his personal representations, the company intended to establish a distribution centre in Orillia creating ten to fifteen jobs. Cramp never mentioned his receipt of NONG shares, and ultimately Orillia stayed with NONG. In September 1964 Marck committed Cramp to trial.

The trial took place the following year before C.E. Bennett, the county court judge of Grey County.[42] Cramp, a feed merchant and bowling alley proprietor, was charged with accepting NONG shares in return for assisting NONG in obtaining the Orillia franchise, and with conspiring with Farris to block the rival Consumers Gas bid. It was clear that Cramp worked hard to ensure that NONG was awarded the franchise, and various council members testified to his aggressive lobbying efforts on NONG's behalf. In handing down his verdict in mid-June 1965, however, Bennett declared Cramp not guilty on the charges of municipal corruption and conspiracy. A defence of 'reasonable doubt' came to Cramp's rescue, the judge said, angrily adding that he 'condemned Cramp's actions' in accepting the free shares. This serious violation offended the 'morality of public office.'[43]

In the meantime, Marck's decision in the Landreville case sowed some seeds of future ambiguity. While he had applied the legal test properly, his use of the term 'insufficient evidence' in dismissing the charges left open the question just how much evidence there was, and whether that evidence should have been put before a jury. Moreover, when a politician is charged with a criminal offence, the appearance of justice is an important consideration. If a close call has to be made, the public interest may be best served by a full trial. The decision was questionable for other reasons as well. Marck never addressed the conspiracy charge, nor did he pay much attention to the timing of the share purchase option, which came immediately after Sudbury City Council had finally, and belatedly, decided to award NONG the Sudbury franchise. Marck also made no reference in his decision to the evidence of J.M. Cooper, Landreville's former law partner and a long-time judge. Cooper testified at the preliminary inquiry that he did not recall Landreville mentioning his share purchase plan to him before the final vote. Landreville, however, had testified before the OSC that he had told Cooper and some of the members of the Board of Control about his plans in this respect. While Cooper testified that Landreville was the soul of 'integrity, honesty and ability,' it was a disturbing discrepancy.[44] Not a single member of council had any recollection of Landreville ever disclosing his intentions or arrangements.

There may not have been positive proof of a conspiracy between Landreville and Farris, but there was certainly some reason to believe that a jury, following a full criminal trial, could conclude on the evidence that the facts were consistent with the commission of that crime.

In large part, the problem was more with the law than with the application of the law to these particular facts. As some commentators pointed out, the law required evidence proving that some kind of benefit was received in exchange for an official act or omission. In England, for example, the applicable legislation declared that any consideration given a government official by anyone signing a contract was 'corrupt' in the absence of proof to the contrary. The British provision recognized the difficulty of establishing why benefits were conferred on public officials, and placed the burden of justifying the receipt of the benefit on the official. As Edward McWhinney of the Faculty of Law of the University of Toronto observed in the aftermath of the Landreville case, 'I think there is a gap in our law and it should be remedied as soon as possible.'[45] Donald MacDonald was more blunt. If there was nothing wrong with a public official making more than $100,000 from a gift of stock from a company to which a city council had given a franchise, 'then the law is an ass.'[46]

As far as Wishart was concerned, however, the matter was finished, and the attorney general's office issued a press release to that effect. Marck, the statement noted, was experienced and competent. Both the Crown and the defence were ably represented, and there had been a full and complete hearing. The attorney general would not prefer a bill of indictment before a grand jury, since that was an extraordinary proceeding reserved for cases where there was some obvious defect or omission. This was not such a case.[47] Wishart also wrote to Landreville, telling him of his pleasure at the decision and informing him that he had privately hoped for this result. He told the judge that it was with 'great reluctance' that the decision to prosecute had been reached, but that he felt the path of duty left him with no other choice. Now that a full and fair trial had taken place, Wishart wrote, 'both of us can feel happy and take satisfaction both from the verdict and from the knowledge that the proper and courageous course was followed from beginning to end.'[48] A somewhat different message was delivered for public consumption. Wishart announced that he would be taking a look at the Criminal Code with a view to requesting some amendments to the provisions respecting municipal corruption.[49] For his part, defence counsel J.J. Robinette told the press that 'never before have I had a case ... in which I was so convinced of the innocence of the accused.'[50]

Publicly, the Department of Justice in Ottawa was of the same view.[51] Landreville met with Guy Favreau in mid-October 1964 and gave the justice minister a copy of Marck's decision. Following up on an earlier request, Landreville suggested that the minister order some kind of public inquiry. Favreau told him that he did not think it would now be necessary and that the matter was closed.[52] The justice minister told the *Toronto Star* that he was 'very pleased' with the decision of the preliminary inquiry,[53] and Landreville was advised that his leave was over.[54]

While the public message from Ottawa was that Landreville could resume his duties as a judge, quite a different message was delivered behind the scenes. On 5 November 1964 Prime Minister Pearson telephoned Judge Cooper, who reported to Landreville exactly what was said. It was time for Landreville to step down. The other judges at Osgoode Hall were not 'too friendly to the position you have taken by returning to the Bench,' and neither was Pearson. The instructions Landreville received were straightforward: resume your duties for the current session, and then tender your resignation. The alternative was the appointment of a commission of inquiry, and the possibility of a finding leaving Landreville with no alternative but to resign 'under a cloud.' Once he had resigned, the government would be in a position to consider 'partial pension rights.'[55] In the circumstances, Pearson had given Landreville some good counsel, but Landreville rejected it. The advice was repeated in newspaper editorials across Canada,[56] and by many of Landreville's closest friends.[57] Those newspapers that did not call for his resignation demanded an inquiry instead.[58]

In the meantime, rumours began to circulate that the Crown attorney had, on Pearson's orders in return for Landreville's long-standing Liberal support, soft-pedalled the charges, and had deliberately failed to bring enough evidence forward to secure a conviction.[59] The story was preposterous, since the administration of criminal justice was in provincial hands, and the government at Queen's Park was Tory, not Grit. Nevertheless, the story took on a life of its own. As it did, opposition politicians, excited by even the hint of scandal, began calling for a public inquiry.

Coincidentally, Landreville was not the only judge in the news. A Quebec superior court justice, Adrien Meunier, a former MP who had resigned from the House of Commons in return for his judicial reward, had been convicted of perjury and sentenced to two years in jail. Pending appeal, Meunier continued to draw his judicial stipend, and would eventually receive a disability pension. Landreville suffered from the comparison. Almost every day the House was in session, someone rose during question period to ask the government when 'something' would be done. John Diefenbaker, the leader of the opposition, led the pack. Beginning in October 1964, Diefenbaker missed few opportunities to criticize the government for its lackadaisical approach. He suggested that a commission of inquiry be established to look into Landreville's behaviour, and he, too, argued from the outset that if Landreville stepped down he should do so without a pension.[60]

The rumours about the conduct of the Landreville prosecution were ridiculous, but much of the criticism of Landreville was understandable. Marck may not have sent Landreville forward to trial, but there were still more questions than answers about his behaviour as mayor. While there was no evidence that Landreville had delayed consideration of NONG's franchise application in order to obtain some special advantage for himself, the circumstances of the delay naturally attracted attention. It was also somewhat odd that in the summer of 1956, Landreville was actively seeking a future position with NONG, but in a matter of months he was accepting an appointment to the bench. Was his elevation a complete surprise, or had it been in the works for a considerable period of time? Moreover, since becoming a judge, he had written very questionable letters on his official stationery and engaged in questionable behaviour – the exercise of the stock option being one example, the manner in which he answered questions about his involvement with NONG another.

Given his conduct, Landreville's critics quite properly raised genuine concerns. Questions were increasingly asked about Landreville and his activities, both before and after he became a judge. The suggestion was repeatedly made that Landreville had lost the respect of both the bench and the bar. A judge, surely, should be above reproach, and there was reason to believe that Landreville failed to meet this test. An inquiry was essential. Without it, Landreville's usefulness as a judge was probably at an end. If it was found that Landreville had done nothing wrong, his judicial career might possibly continue, although there was reason to believe that nothing could now salvage his reputation. If the opposite result was reached, he would have no choice but to resign.

The prevailing sentiment, indeed, was that Landreville's judicial career was finished, that the time had long passed for him to step down. Both the *Toronto Star* and the *Globe and Mail* called on Landreville to resign. His conduct as mayor, the *Star* wrote, was 'questionable' and 'unprofessional.' He had 'fatally impaired his position and authority as judge' and his 'only honourable recourse is to resign.' Quoting the words of Donald MacDonald, the situation was 'a scandal in the administration of justice in this province.'[61] For its part, the *Globe* editorialized that 'a judge must have judgment or he cannot be a judge.' Landreville had shown bad judgment; he was not 'the embodiment of justice' or 'clearly seen as such,' and should therefore either resign or be removed.[62]

Landreville, however, concluded that Marck's decision had vindicated him. He had no intention of resigning. He truly believed that the issue would go away, that the demands would stop, that order and sanity would prevail, that all would be well again. But then the Law Society got involved. It convened a kangaroo court.

6

A Kangaroo Court

The Law Society of Upper Canada is an institution established by statute. Its mandate is to govern Ontario lawyers, and to do so in the public interest. From time to time, Ontario lawyers elect benchers. These benchers meet in convocation, and from their ranks one is elected treasurer – the titular head of all Ontario lawyers, and the holder of a position of great prestige and influence. In early December 1964 J.J. Robinette, QC, Landreville's lawyer, a bencher of the Law Society of Upper Canada, and its former treasurer, was privately advised by the then treasurer, John D. Arnup, that convocation was going to take action – if Landreville did not quickly make such action unnecessary by stepping down. Robinette was also advised that the Canadian Bar Association intended to intervene. At its forthcoming mid-winter meeting, a resolution was to be introduced demanding that Landreville resign. Robinette knew that Landreville had some difficult days ahead; he had heard that the case was attracting political interest. Landreville could expect the issue to be raised again in the Ontario legislature by both the Liberals and the NDP, as the CCF was now known.[1]

Landreville was never the establishment's favourite judge. His high living and ostentatious ways were in direct conflict with the puritan and straitlaced atmosphere prevailing at Osgoode Hall. He was an outsider at a time when the legal establishment was dominated by insiders. He was, furthermore, the Franco-Ontarian judge, and he was expected to know his place. Some had been won over by his engaging personality, but for the majority, Landreville would never measure up to their ideal of a judge. The judges and the benchers of the Law Society not only shared the same views, but also quarters at Osgoode Hall. They were a formidable force of disapproval against Landreville, who was not one of them and who had been caught in some questionable conduct.

'In Ontario as in England,' Arnup told the press after Landreville testified in his preliminary hearing about approaching Farris with a request for employment, 'any form of solicitation of business is regarded as highly unprofessional.'[2] Arnup was technically correct, but Landreville was not the only lawyer, then or now, to approach prospective clients and offer services. What was questionable in Landreville's case was that he did so as mayor, while he was in a position to confer or withhold benefits to the prospective client.

In the aftermath of his preliminary inquiry, the Law Society suggested to Landreville that the time had come for him to step down, 'if only on the basis that no member of the court should ever be in a position where his past conduct, as a lawyer, or as a judge, can be called into question.'[3] Chief Justice G.A. Gale, who succeeded Dana Porter in June 1964, was asked to pass on this message, as was J.J. Robinette. Again, Landreville refused to resign. He had been discharged at a preliminary inquiry; he believed that his reputation was intact, and that he had established his right to return to the bench. While many of the judges and benchers were against him, that was nothing new. What mattered to Landreville was that he believed he was accepted by the bar and the public, and he was convinced that he had many years ahead in which to serve as a productive judge.[4]

Arnup saw things somewhat differently. 'I have been exercising my influence over the past four months,' he wrote Justice Minister Favreau in a personal and confidential letter in February 1965, 'to try to keep the Bar quiet.'[5] The disquiet among many members of the profession was, however, palpable, and they turned to the Law Society.[6] Members of the profession, who had concerns about a judge, had nowhere else to go. The Canadian Bar Association was ineffective in such matters. Nor would it have been appropriate for individual lawyers to complain directly to the chief justice about the conduct of a sitting judge. The Law Society was the natural repository of complaint and action. On two previous occasions, the Law Society had intervened with the chief justice to raise concerns about the conduct of sitting judges.[7]

The message Arnup received from the benchers could not have been more clear: Landreville had to go. Arnup was in an invidious position.

The benchers were pushing him to take action, while he was trying to lessen damage to the reputation of the justice system by keeping the bar quiet. 'Eventually,' Arnup later recalled, 'I could not wait any longer, particularly since I was told point blank by one Bencher that he proposed to make a motion at the next Convocation that the Law Society appoint a committee to look into the matter and then if it saw fit to draw the facts to the attention of the Minister of Justice.'[8] Accordingly, and in response to the growing chorus of demands, he 'let it be known' that he would not object to the matter being raised in convocation.[9] On 15 January 1965 convocation passed a motion calling for the appointment of a special committee to consider and report on what action, if any, should 'be taken by Convocation as a result of Mr. Justice Landreville's decision to continue to sit as a Judge of the Supreme Court of Ontario.'[10]

Five men, all QCs and pillars of the legal establishment, were appointed to the committee: Arthur S. Pattillo, R.F. Wilson, Stanley E. Fennell, G. Edwin Beament, and W. Gibson Gray. Pattillo, a well-known litigator and senior partner at Blake, Cassels & Graydon; Beament, an Ottawa lawyer; and Fennell, a Cornwall counsel, were well-known Tories. Wilson was a senior partner at Day, Wilson, Kelly; and Gray was a future Law Society treasurer and superior court judge. They quickly got to work and by 17 March 1965 their report was complete.

The report began with a sketchy recital of the facts, followed by a number of conclusions. There was no doubt, the committee reported, that on the facts the magistrate 'was correct in dismissing the charges against Landreville,' even though he had solicited legal business from NONG, to be given to him on his retirement as mayor of Sudbury, and had profited to the extent of $117,000 on the sale of the shares.[11] Though the criminal charges were properly dismissed, there were still other issues the committee considered 'unexplained,' giving rise to 'speculation.' Why, the benchers wanted to know, did Landreville speak to Farris about obtaining shares prior to third reading? He could easily have waited if the sale of influence was not involved. Did Farris offer the shares to ensure passage against the potential opposition of city solicitor Kelly and one or two other members of council? Did Farris offer the shares to avoid having to establish a separate company for the Sudbury franchise, given that such an arrangement would have diluted the value of a NONG stock offering? Why was Convesto used as an intermediary in the sale of the shares? In the normal course of events, stock options were fulfilled directly by a company. Was Landreville telling the truth when he said he was contacted by Convesto with the suggestion that he sell 2500 shares to clear his account? Or was John McGraw correct when he said that he sold the 2500 shares and delivered the remaining 7500 to Landreville in street form on Farris's orders? Someone was lying, and the Law Society committee wanted to know who – and why?

The Law Society committee did not have the answers to these questions, an obvious admission since they had been asked entirely in the abstract. Nevertheless, 'inferences could be drawn.' In the committee's view, 'the fact that Landreville was given an opportunity to acquire shares at the same price as the original promoters of the Company and that the option was given immediately following the passing of the third reading of the by-law and for no apparent consideration, and that subsequently without any exercise of such option by Landreville he received 7500 shares free and clear, which he subsequently sold for $117,000, and that when Farris was first questioned about the matter he deliberately lied, supported the inference that the acquisition of shares by Landreville was tainted with impropriety.'[12] This, the committee concluded, was inconsistent with the reputation for probity required of one of Her Majesty's judges for the due administration of justice in the province of Ontario. Having now found Landreville guilty of misconduct, in part because someone else, Ralph Farris, had lied, the committee turned its attention to the punishment Landreville should receive for his, and others', misdeeds.

The committee recommended that convocation pass a motion deploring the 'continuance of Landreville as a judge.' It suggested that copies of its report, along with a copy of convocation's resolution, if passed, be sent to the minister of justice, the chief justice of Ontario, the attorney general of Ontario, and – almost as an afterthought – Leo Landreville. The committee further recommended that the treasurer of the Law Society be given the authorization to release copies of the report to the press. The committee clearly wanted to force Landreville to resign.

On 23 April 1965 convocation considered and adopted the special committee's report. An attempt was made to tone down some of the language, and one of the benchers pointed out that the report was nothing more than 'a public campaign to drive a judge from the Bench.'[13] Convocation, under Arnup's strong guiding hand, was in no mood for dissent, and went on record, as suggested, 'deploring' the fact that Landreville was continuing to sit as a judge. The assembled benchers dutifully directed the secretary of the Law Society to forward a copy of the report to the four men concerned. Landreville was also to be given a copy.[14]

When Landreville received the report several days later, it was the first time he had heard about the workings of this kangaroo court. Assuming that the Law Society had jurisdiction over a judge, which it did not, it might have asked this judge what he had to say about those matters that were 'unexplained.' Perhaps he had an explanation. Perhaps he had answers to the questions. Even if he had neither, that was no excuse for these leaders of the bar, who had sworn in their barristers' oath to uphold the highest standards and traditions of their independent legal profession, to convene what was in effect a secret trial, to conduct a hearing in the absence of the accused, to issue a verdict, and to make plans for the communication of that verdict to the press – all of which they knew, or should have known, was likely to destroy Landreville permanently as a man and as a judge.

Landreville wrote to Law Society secretary W. Earl Smith, asking why a committee and convocation of the Law Society of Upper Canada would not see fit to speak to him before issuing a report so damaging to his reputation. This was a good question, but the Law Society already had some experience in character assassination. This was not the first time that it had, on its own initiative, solicited evidence against an individual and used that evidence in an effort to ruin that person's standing and reputation in the community.[15] However, this was the first time that the Law Society had acted in such a way against a judge.

On learning of the report, Magistrate Marck, on Landreville's suggestion, wrote to the Law Society, and he sent a copy of his letter to the minister of justice. There was, he said, not only a total absence of evidence of corruption, but there was evidence disproving that conclusion. He pointed out that there was unanimous agreement by all northern Ontario municipalities that one company should distribute gas and that NONG should be that company. Sudbury had delayed making a final decision pending the conclusion of an agreement between INCO and NONG. When the essential terms of that agreement had been reached, Sudbury City Council passed the appropriate bylaw. Marck suggested that his decision could not possibly recount all the evidence he heard during the course of the six-day proceeding, but he had considered all this evidence and there was no doubt in his mind about the propriety of the final result. The same could not be said about the conclusions reached by the benchers in their report.[16]

Landreville received a polite reply to his letter, as did Marck.[17] Marck's letter was not, it appears, brought before subsequent meetings of convocation, nor did that body take up his offer to attend before convocation to explain the conclusions he had reached. In the meantime, the report was kept confidential.

After receiving the report, Landreville wrote to the minister of justice and again asked for an inquiry to ascertain the facts. After a lengthy recital of his version of events, Landreville claimed that he was innocent of any wrongdoing, that he wished an inquiry to establish that fact, and that he would not resign. If the government wanted him out, he would have to be formally removed. Landreville, his eye on the press, asked the justice department to make it known that he was the one asking for the inquiry, and he noted that this was the third time he had written to Ottawa with this request.[18] Within a matter of weeks, however, Landreville changed his mind.[19]

In yet another letter to the justice minister, Landreville observed that the issue had been thoroughly aired in numerous investigations: twice by the Securities Commission, at the preliminary inquiry, and during the Farris trial. The Law Society intervention was, Landreville pointed out, completely unfair. He was never given the opportunity to present his version of events, and the report itself was filled with flaws. Despite the various attacks on his standing and reputation, Landreville had returned from his leave of absence and was back at work as a judge. Members of the bar and bench, he reported, were showing him the usual courtesies. The issue had been resolved. All an inquiry would do was reopen the case, with no real benefits to anyone. The predictable result would be negative publicity detrimental to Landreville's reputation.

There was also the question of the independence of the judiciary. Judges should not, he suggested, be put on trial. Parliament had its rights, and they were set out in section 99 of the British North America Act. A public inquiry was inconsistent with judicial independence. If Parliament wished to initiate removal proceedings, so be it. Anything else would be inconsistent with the Constitution and its guarantees. For all these reasons, Landreville urged the justice minister either to begin impeachment proceedings against him, or, once and for all, let the matter drop.[20]

Landreville had made a number of important points in support of his position that calling an inquiry was not only unnecessary, but also inconsistent with the independence of every Canadian judge. Robinette, writing to the justice minister, expressed these views more cogently. He began his remarks by observing that there was a division in the legal community between those who felt that Landreville should step down and those who believed he was entitled to stay. That issue did not concern Robinette. What mattered, he wrote, was the position of Supreme Court judges and the maintenance of their independence.

Under section 99 of The British North America Act 'The Judges of the Superior Courts shall hold office during good behaviour, but shall be removable by the Governor General on address of the Senate and House of Commons.'

Thus, by our constitution the Judges of the Superior Courts enjoy security of tenure and freedom from harassment and they are removable only by the Governor General on address of the Senate and House of Commons.

County and District Judges are in a different position and this seems to be recognized by sections 32 and 33 of The Judges' Act, R.S.C. 1952, chapter 159. Under section 32 a Judge of a County Court may be removed from office by the Governor-in-Council for misbehaviour and under section 33 the Governor-in-Council may issue a commission of inquiry with reference to the conduct of a County or District Court Judge. Sections 32 and 33 of The Judges' Act do not and could not apply to Superior Court Judges in view of the provisions of section 99 of The British North America Act.

Under ... The Inquiries Act, R.S.C. 1952, chapter 154, 'The Governor-in-Council may, whenever he deems it expedient, cause inquiry to be made into and concerning any matter connected with the good government of Canada or the conduct of any part of the public business thereof.'

In my respectful view this section does not authorize the Governor-in-Council to set up an inquiry with reference to the conduct of a Superior Court Judge. Superior Court Judges are not civil servants; they do not participate in the government of Canada and they do not conduct the public business or any part thereof of the government of Canada. They are appointed under section 96 of The British North America Act to administer and enforce the laws not only of Canada but of the province for which they are appointed. The separation of judicial, executive and legislative powers is implicit not only in the English constitution, but in The British North America Act and it would be quite inconsistent with constitutional history and theory to say that a Judge participates in the government of Canada or conducts any part of the public business of Canada.

... The essence of the position is that under our constitution the only person who has any jurisdiction whatsoever over the behaviour of a Superior Court Judge is the Governor General and then only 'on address of the Senate and House of Commons' as stipulated in The British North America Act.[21]

Robinette urged Favreau to uphold the important principles at stake, and suggested that the government either take action in parliament or declare the matter closed.

Everything Robinette said was true. But politics and the law travel different paths, and momentum for an inquiry was building. It did not take long for news of the existence of the Law Society report to be published in the press. The *Toronto Star* broke the story at the end of April 1965, and soon questions were being raised in the House of Commons. New Democratic Party MP Andrew Brewin, a friend of Donald MacDonald, asked the minister of justice in May 1965 what he planned to do about the Law Society report.[22] The minister had the matter 'under consideration.' For its part, the Law Society refused to comment. Pressure mounted. The fact that the report was 'secret' and that the Law Society refused to make it or its conclusions public added to public concern. Eventually the Law Society issued a press release confirming that a confidential report on Landreville had been forwarded to Ottawa.

Accepting the principle that the Law Society had no jurisdiction over any judge, the press release went on to say that the society did have 'a right and a duty, as representing the bar of Ontario, to make known its views upon matters relating to the administration of justice, and to communicate those views to the appropriate official or tribunal having jurisdiction over the particular matter in question.'[23] The Law Society had considered various documents, including the transcripts of evidence from the OSC investigations, the Farris trial, and Landreville's preliminary inquiry, as well as Marck's decision finding that there was 'insufficient evidence' to send Landreville on to trial. Having considered these materials, 'the Benchers concluded that, with respect, the judgment of the learned Magistrate was quite correct, but that after reviewing all of the evidence (only a part of which was relevant to the charge before the Magistrate) they should inform the Minister of Justice of their views concerning the decision of Mr. Justice Landreville to continue to sit on the bench of the Supreme Court of Ontario.'[24]

Even though Arnup had been authorized to release a copy of the report, he refused to do so; he also failed to spell out, in this statement to the press, that Landreville had not been notified of the Law Society's action against him until after the fact. The press release, which was especially destructive because of what it did not say, gave the impression that the Law Society was united in its desire that Landreville be removed. That was not the case. As W.S. Martin, QC, one of the benchers who passed judgment on the committee's report, pointed out to Arnup, twelve benchers voted in favour of the report and seven voted against. Five abstained.[25] Nor was it fair, Martin privately observed to the treasurer, to withhold relevant information that 'may colour the report one way or another.'[26] Obviously, Arnup thought otherwise.

Public interest was understandably piqued by rumours of the Law Society report, and there was a new round of calls for an inquiry. In the

House of Commons, some members sought unsuccessfully to obtain a copy of the Law Society report pursuant to the standing rules. Landreville, who had hoped that the story would soon fade from view, was not pleased by the continuing press and parliamentary attention, and his displeasure deepened when he learned that the worst was not yet over. It had hardly begun.

In early June 1965 Robinette was called to a meeting with Favreau in Ottawa. Robinette was informed that an inquiry would be called, and that the only way to preclude it was for Landreville to resign. The justice minister helpfully provided the text of Landreville's resignation speech. Landreville could, Favreau told Robinette, announce that he had served for one year after being cleared at his preliminary inquiry. 'This,' Favreau continued, 'would be a good occasion for him to make an appropriate statement to the effect that his honour and honesty have been vindicated both through judicial proceedings and also by the comportment of the Bench and the Bar toward him during that year. He could add, notwithstanding this, it seems that there are those who, in the press or elsewhere, will persist on casting further doubts on his ethics and that, consequently, he is resigning out of a sense of duty, to prevent any further embarrassment (slight as it may be) to the judiciary, to his family and friends.' According to Favreau, Robinette liked the idea, and promised to communicate it to his client. Prime Minister Pearson supported the plan.[27]

For the second time in a matter of months, Landreville was told that it was the prime minister's wish that he resign. Landreville again rejected the suggestion, and when he did, the government had no choice but to proceed with an inquiry.

On 29 July 1965 Justice Minister Cardin, who had replaced Favreau on 7 July 1965 – Favreau himself had been the subject of an inquiry – sent the beleaguered judge a telegram advising him that after 'very serious consideration' he had decided that it was in Landreville's interests, as well as those of the administration of justice, that a formal inquiry be held. The relevant facts, Cardin wrote, had to be ascertained in order to ensure that the judicial process was, and was seen to be, 'beyond reproach.'[28] Cardin offered Landreville a few days' grace before announcing his decision in the event that Landreville cared to comment or, presumably, to tender his resignation. Landreville took advantage of the opportunity to set out his views.

In a letter to Cardin, with a copy to Prime Minister Pearson, Landreville repeated his arguments against investigations of the kind proposed by Cardin. He also raised some objections with respect to the applicability of the Inquiries Act to a judge. These comments basically echoed Robinette's earlier submissions, although in a more self-serving way. Landreville asked whether it was appropriate to investigate a judge's activities under the Inquiries Act when the activities in question predated the appointment of the person to the bench and did not relate in any way to the performance of the judicial function. (Landreville had received the stock option prior to his appointment, but exercised it after.) He suggested, given the important principles involved, that the justice minister refer the procedural issue to the Supreme Court of Canada. While waiting for a decision from that court, the government could at any time move in Parliament for his removal from the bench since the British North America Act clearly gave the government the power to initiate proceedings of this kind.

These arguments aside, Landreville pointed out to Cardin that even though he had suggested an inquiry on several occasions in the past, neither Justice Minister Chevrier nor Justice Minister Favreau had considered one necessary or appropriate. As there were no 'new facts,' what could possibly justify an inquiry now? 'Exactly a year ago,' Landreville concluded, 'I entertained the same purported arguments ... from the Ontario Attorney General. It would be in my interests and that of justice to clear the matter up by the laying of charges against me. That opinion was reluctantly accepted ... I suffered the ignominy of baseless charges. The magistrate's judgment and letter not only hold on the facts an absence of evidence, but advise an innocence beyond suspicion. But the judge's image is damaged ... I view a further proceeding as bordering on the abuse of legal process. However favourable the findings, it would deal a fatal blow to the judge's image.'[29] Landreville again asked that the matter be dropped.

Cardin saw things differently. The issue, he wrote Landreville in mid-August 1965, was not whether 'an offence was committed' or there was a need 'to review the decision of the Magistrate.' Rather, the subject matter of the inquiry would be 'whether it is in the interests of the administration of justice, having regard to all the circumstances, that you should hold your present office.' It was to answer this question that the opinion of an 'eminent outside and independent authority' was required.[30] From the government's point of view, proceeding in this way made a great deal of sense. If the commissioner reported that Landreville had done nothing wrong, the case could be easily and finally closed. Cardin defended his approach with another rationale as well: 'judicial independence would be better served if the government's decision to bring an allegation of judicial misconduct before Parliament was based on an independent judicial inquiry.'[31] While Cardin urged Landreville to accede to such an inquiry, he also made known his view that Landreville should resign, remarking at the time that the Law Society report expressed 'some reservations' about Landreville continuing to sit as a judge.[32] Landreville refused. 'Why should I resign?' he asked Cardin, adding, 'I have done nothing wrong.'[33]

Having expressed the view that Landreville should resign, it was incumbent upon the government to take some immediate action to achieve that result. Cardin was in an unenviable position, 'between the devil and the deep blue sea,' as he put it.[34] The British North America Act said that Canada was to enjoy 'a Constitution similar in principle to that of the United Kingdom.' One of the features of the United Kingdom's Constitution at Confederation was the independence of the judiciary. That was established by the Act of Settlement of 1701. The antecedents of that act are important. Before the revolution of 1688 in England, judges of the Superior Courts held office at the pleasure of the Crown. Upright judges who fell into official displeasure were frequently removed. This gave rise to serious complaints and led to a number of attempts, in the seventeenth century, to grant judges some security of tenure and thus minimize the opportunities for official abuse. The Act of Settlement represented the culmination of these reform efforts, and it provided that judges would hold office during good behaviour, but could be removed by consent of both Houses of Parliament. This act fettered the ability of the executive to interfere with the judiciary, first, by establishing the standard of 'good behaviour,' and, second, by requiring the House of Commons and the House of Lords to agree that a particular judge had failed to meet that standard and should, therefore, be removed.

While the Act of Settlement established tenure according to good behaviour rather than royal pleasure, further formal guarantees of judicial independence developed later. Exclusion of judges from cabinet, and therefore from direct executive influence, was not achieved until the early nineteenth century in England. Colonial Canadian judges continued to be allowed on governing councils, and tenure remained according to royal pleasure until the mid-nineteenth century. At Confederation, the British North America Act adopted the language of the Act of Settlement in section 99: 'The Judges of the Superior Courts shall hold Office during good behaviour, but shall be removable by the Governor General on Address of the Senate and House of Commons.' Canadian practice was now fully in line with England, and the new dominion government assumed extensive powers on appointment. Nothing, however, was said in the British North America Act about the manner in which judges could be removed other than that it was to be by 'address.' A standard legal work, Todd's *On Parliamentary Government in England*, however, set out some of the common law rules governing the removal of judges.

'The legal effect of the grant of any office during "good behaviour" is the creation of an estate for life in the office.' Such an estate is terminable only by the grantee's incapacity from mental or physical infirmity, or by his breach of good behaviour ... Misbehaviour includes, firstly, the improper exercise of judicial functions; secondly, wilful neglect of duty or non-attendance; and, thirdly, a conviction for any infamous offence, by which, although it be not connected with the duties of his office, the offender is rendered unfit to exercise any office or public franchise ...

In the case of misconduct outside the duties of his office, the misbehaviour must be established by a previous conviction by a jury. [citations omitted][35]

Clearly, if the common law was applied, Landreville's conduct did not fall within accepted definitions of misconduct. An address in parliament was premature. Nevertheless, something had to be done. Having publicly announced his opinion that Landreville should resign, Cardin had little choice but to initiate some kind of proceeding. Holding an inquiry, in this context, seemed like a good idea.

In reaching this decision, some support could be found in the Judges Act, which provided a different mechanism for the removal of county court judges. A precondition for their removal was an inquiry into allegations of misbehaviour and the issue of a report. On four previous occasions, in 1915, in 1928, and twice in 1932, this procedure was followed.[36] The first case involved complaints against Judge C.R. Fitch of the Rainy River District Court. Following an investigation, an order in council was passed removing Judge Fitch from his post. The second case concerned Harold Maulson, an improvident Manitoba judge with 'an unquenchable thirst.' As his drinking problem worsened, Maulson was frequently found in the company of persons whose prosecutions were pending before him. Moreover, he also began passing worthless cheques. The Law Society demanded Maulson's resignation, and when he refused to comply, the society reported his misconduct to Ottawa. Mr Justice Trueman was assigned to investigate. The allegations were substantiated and Maulson was removed.[37] The third case also involved drunkenness and dishonoured cheques. It concerned Nova Scotia Judge L.H. Martell. The government appointed Mr Justice Chisholm of the Supreme Court of

Nova Scotia to investigate and report. Judge Martell was subsequently removed from office.

The fourth case concerned the controversial Manitoba judge, Lewis St George Stubbs. A committed socialist, Stubbs became particularly embittered about the economic suffering he witnessed during the Depression and, believing that judges should be free to express their views, made his feelings known in inappropriate ways. He refused, for example, to grant letters of administration in the estate of a Winnipeg millionaire. When Judge Stubbs was reversed by the Manitoba Court of Appeal, he called a public meeting to demand that the legislature invalidate the decision of the Court of Appeal. The controversial judge had the public on his side, and a petition was presented in the House of Commons containing the signature of more than 50,000 supporters. After receiving numerous complaints about Stubbs's language and conduct – one complaint was signed by virtually all of Manitoba's Superior Court judges – the government was left with little choice but to act. Mr Justice Frank Ford of the Alberta Court of Appeal was appointed to investigate and his report was published on 31 May 1933. Stubbs was removed by the Governor in Council later that day.[38]

Clear as the Judges Act was about the process to be followed in investigating county court judges, it said nothing about inquiries into allegations of misbehaviour by Supreme Court judges, nor did it provide a mechanism for the holding of an investigation or the preparation of a report. Prior to the Landreville case, no Canadian Superior Court judge had ever been impeached, and while a few, in the nineteenth century, came close, in no instance since Confederation had parliament actually been called upon to pass an address leading to the removal of a judge.[39] In each of these cases, however, the same preliminary procedure was envisaged: an inquiry by a parliamentary committee first, followed by an address. British practice might have provided some precedents, but only one judge, Sir Jonah Barrington, had been removed since the passage of the Act of Settlement. While there was no precedent for a royal commission or other type of public inquiry, there was also no reason why the government could not pursue such a course. And that was, by the fall of 1965, the decision it had reached.

Given that there would be an inquiry, Cardin suggested to Landreville that he give his consent. In the interim, details from the Law Society report began to be leaked to the press. Predictably, public demands followed, some from Tory politicians who may have had an axe to grind, that the whole report be released and that Landreville not be allowed to continue to sit on the bench. When full details of the Law Society report were published on the front page of the *Globe and Mail* on 20 November 1965, Landreville's career on the bench was effectively and permanently destroyed.[40]

On Robinette's advice, Landreville still did not consent to an inquiry. Robinette wrote to Cardin at the end of November 1965 and, raising the same constitutional reasons with Cardin that he had earlier put to Favreau, he urged him to reconsider his approach. Superior Court judges serve under the British North America Act on good behaviour, he pointed out, and are removable only by the governor general on parliamentary address. The Inquiries Act provided for inquiries into 'any matter connected with the good government of Canada or the conduct of any part of the public business.' This provision did not, in Robinette's opinion, authorize an inquiry into the activities of a Superior Court judge. These judges were not civil servants and they did not participate in the government of Canada. Their job under the Canadian Constitution was to administer and enforce the laws of Canada and the province in which they served. It would be inconsistent with constitutional law and doctrine, including the concept of the separation of powers, to describe these activities as being part of the government of Canada. Accordingly, the only person who had any authority over a Superior Court judge was the governor general, and then only following a parliamentary address. That being the case, to order an inquiry would interfere with the independence of the judiciary. It might also be unlawful. The fact that Landreville 'consented' to an inquiry, Robinette wrote, would not cure this fundamental illegality.

Robinette, like Landreville several months earlier, urged Cardin to refer the jurisdictional question to the Supreme Court of Canada, and at the same time obtain a ruling from that court about the meaning to be given to the words 'during good behaviour.' Landreville, Robinette concluded, 'would welcome an opportunity to state his position before a forum having jurisdiction to deal with the matter. Such a forum would be removed from any considerations of political expediency and would be in keeping with the dignity of his position.' This was not only in Landreville's interest, Robinette added, but in the interest of the administration of justice.[41]

Cardin still did not agree, and he expressed the view that the 'good government of Canada' comprised all branches of government, including the judiciary. Accordingly, an investigation of a Superior Court judge under the Inquiries Act was, in his opinion, perfectly lawful. The justice minister also pointed out that Landreville could consent to an inquiry if he wished, and he expressed surprise that Landreville was not doing so, given his oft-stated request for an opportunity to set out his version of events. Cardin rejected Robinette's suggestion that the jurisdictional issue be referred to the Supreme Court. 'I think it would be most undesirable to engage in preliminary legal skirmishes in order to determine a question that does not need to be determined. There is no doubt that Parliament itself has the right and the power to make such an inquiry into the conduct of a judge ... Such an inquiry would be founded on an allegation of impropriety, and I should have thought that the Judge would prefer an "open" inquiry under the Inquiries Act that is not founded on an allegation of impropriety and would be designed simply to ascertain the facts.' In addition, as Cardin noted, there was no way that the Supreme Court could interpret the words 'during good behaviour' in the abstract. 'The most that could be done would be to refer a statement of facts to the court and ask whether on these facts there had been a breach of the condition of judicial office.' In Cardin's judgment, the first task was to determine what had occurred.

The question is not so much whether the Judge has breached the condition of his office, namely, that it be held during good behaviour, but whether he has in the opinion of Parliament conducted himself in such a way as to render himself unfit to hold high judicial office. Under section 99 of the British North America Act, a judge may indeed be removed for 'misbehaviour,' but the power to remove on address extends to any ground and it is open to Parliament to make an address for the removal of a judge on any ground it sees fit, whether it constitutes misbehaviour in office or not.[42]

This conclusion was arguable but those arguments would have to await another case and another day. In the meantime, Landreville was given a choice: consent to an inquiry, and in so doing agree not to frustrate the proceedings by seeking judicial review of the government's right to proceed with that course, or face the prospect of an immediate parliamentary response. Between these two options there was no choice, and Cardin promised that the inquiry would be limited to ascertaining the facts.

As Robinette pointed out to Landreville, there was some chance of preventing an inquiry from degenerating into a media circus. In the forum at parliament that would not be possible because 'political and publicity considerations will dominate the thinking of such a committee.' Members of parliament would, some notable exceptions aside, be more interested in exploring allegations and attracting headlines than in determining what had actually taken place. Besides, Robinette added, if they agreed to an inquiry, there would be an opportunity to exercise some influence in an effort to obtain a 'reasonable commissioner.'[43]

The selection of the commissioner was critical. It had to be someone who commanded widespread public respect. Pearson was aware of the rumours that Landreville had only been acquitted because he was a Liberal; he had received enough correspondence from across the country suggesting as much, and worse, and he was determined to clear the air. There would be a full investigation, not a whitewash. The prime minister urged Landreville and Robinette to accept an inquiry and advised them that the government had decided to appoint Ivan Rand. Robinette knew Rand well from having appeared before him on many occasions in the Supreme Court of Canada. He had an intense admiration for him as a judge, and told Landreville as much. As for Landreville, he had little choice; he capitulated, notwithstanding some misgivings about the commissioner.[44]

Robinette met with Cardin and his deputy, E.A. Driedger, in mid-January 1966 and advised them that Landreville was prepared to agree to an inquiry limited, as Cardin had proposed in his letter of 28 December 1965, to ascertaining the facts.[45] Robinette had prepared draft terms of reference limiting the inquiry to whether Landreville's conduct amounted to misbehaviour. This was fine as far as it went, but the minister of justice believed that the scope should be broader, determining also whether Landreville had proved himself unfit for the proper exercise of his judicial duties. Robinette, following consultation with both Cardin and Landreville, agreed to accept these terms, and wired the minister on 17 January 1966 that the inquiry could proceed.[46]

Later that day, Cardin raised the matter in cabinet. He reported that he had been pressing Landreville to accept a commission of inquiry under the Inquiries Act and that he had agreed. The discussion then turned to the appointment of Ivan Rand: 'Mr. Justice Rand had been mentioned as a Commissioner ... and most Ministers felt that he would be a good choice although he could be expected to be very stern in dealing with the matter under enquiry.'[47]

The son of a railway mechanic, Rand attended Mount Allison University, then Harvard Law School. His legal career began in Medicine Hat. He then returned to Moncton and served for a time as attorney general of New Brunswick, before joining the legal department of Canadian

National Railways, eventually becoming 'commission counsel,' as one of the top law jobs with the corporation was known. In 1943 Prime Minister Mackenzie King appointed Rand to the Supreme Court of Canada, where he distinguished himself for both his judicial and his extrajudicial tasks. Rand was a member of the liberal wing of the court and the author of most of the noted civil liberties opinions of the 1950s.

It was his work outside Ottawa, however, that thrust Rand in the public eye. In 1946 he settled the Ford strike, and the compromise solution he imposed – the Rand formula – was a union security provision that soon became a fixture of Canadian labour law. In 1948 he served as Canada's representative on the United Nations Special Committee on Palestine, and was one of the authors of the majority report that led to the creation of the state of Israel. In 1959, having reached the age of seventy-five, Rand retired from the Supreme Court. He was immediately asked by Ottawa to head a royal commission on coal, and he followed that by becoming the founding dean of the University of Western Ontario's law school.

A tall and craggy man of eighty-one, Rand was a jurist of the old school, stern, firm, fair, and with a mind of his own. While his appointment was announced in January 1966, he had been under consideration to head the Landreville inquiry for some months. Law Society treasurer Arnup had suggested Rand to Justice Minister Favreau in April 1965.[48] Favreau obviously passed the suggestion on to his successor and, in July 1965, Cardin asked Rand if he would take on the task. Rand replied that the task would be an 'unpleasant one.' However, he also told the justice minister that without a compelling reason not to undertake it, he felt as if he had no choice but to accept the assignment.[49] Cabinet duly agreed to the selection of Rand.

Two days later, on 19 January 1966, the appointment of a royal commission under Part I of the Inquiries Act was announced. Paid at the rate of $200 per day, Rand was to inquire into Landreville's dealings with NONG and to advise whether any of his actions, in the course of those dealings, constituted misbehaviour in his official capacity as a judge of the Supreme Court of Ontario, or whether he had, by such dealings, proved himself unfit for the proper exercise of his judicial duties.[50] Landreville would be given yet another opportunity to tell his side of the story.

7

Canadian Gothic Meets the Mambo King

Royal commissions have been part of the Canadian political firmament since before Confederation, and the circumstances leading to them are as varied as the exigencies of political life itself.[1] Sometimes they are appointed to prepare the way for the implementation of some preordained policy. Other times they are established to ascertain in some expert fashion the best or most feasible solution to a problem that the government wishes to address. They are often called to sample public opinion, and they are a useful mechanism for the controlled expression of grievances, real and imagined. There is always the possibility that a commission will be established to delay resolution of some problem until it goes away or the timing for its resolution has improved from a political point of view. Usually, the decision to establish a royal commission incorporates several of these objectives. The range of subjects is broad: from 'half-breeds in N.W.T.' to sexual psychopaths, bilingualism and biculturalism, the status of women, and Canada's economic prospects.

The adjective 'royal' means that the commission is established under the Great Seal of Canada and it can cover any matter connected with the good government of Canada or the conduct of any part of the public business (provincial governments may appoint royal commissions as well). Allegations of misbehaviour by one of Her Majesty's judges more than met this test, despite Robinette's objections to the contrary. By 1966 the government had decided that a royal commission was needed to examine Landreville's dealings with NONG, and to report whether anything done by Landreville in the course of such dealings constituted misbehaviour in his official capacity as a judge, or whether he had, by such dealings, proved himself unfit to continue on the bench. Landreville announced that he was ready for the inquiry to begin so he could vindicate his name, 'twice and for all.'[2]

William George Morrow, senior partner in the Edmonton law firm of Morrow, Hurlburt, Reynolds, Stevenson & Kane, was appointed counsel to the commission. Born in Edmonton on 5 February 1917, Morrow was educated at the University of Alberta law school. He served in the Royal Canadian Navy during the Second World War, and then returned to Edmonton, joined his father's law firm, and earned a reputation as an excellent courtroom lawyer and an active participant in the affairs of the Canadian Bar Association. Morrow, who later became a judge in the Northwest Territories, before being elevated to the Alberta Court of Appeal, immediately contacted Robinette and agreed on procedural details. All witnesses would be commission witnesses, and Morrow would examine them all in chief. If any of those witnesses appeared with counsel, their lawyer could cross-examine them next. Robinette would have the last opportunity to cross-examine. Morrow would make final submissions, as would Robinette.[3]

The commission first met in Vancouver on 14 March 1966. Five witnesses testified over the course of three days: J. Chester Grey was called to the witness stand first. He had given evidence at the Farris trial, and when he appeared before the Rand Commission he had absolutely nothing new to say. C. Spencer Clark followed Grey, and his evidence mirrored his testimony before the OSC in 1962. Gordon Kelly McLean testified next, under subpoena. He claimed the protections of the Canada and British Columbia Evidence Acts for each question asked and each answer given. He repeated the same story he had told at the Farris trial. Edward Dulian, Convesto's accountant, reviewed the ledger books. Among all the witnesses, only one, Ralph Farris, had a new story to tell.

Released on parole on 1 July 1965 after serving five months in jail, this was the first time that Farris had testified publicly since the 14,000 shares attracted regulatory attention eight years earlier. Farris told the Rand Commission that when Landreville bought shares in January 1957, the purchase was not connected to the July 1956 option arrangement. That deal was based on his coming to work for NONG and, when he failed to do so, the option was effectively cancelled. After Landreville became a judge, he indicated to Farris that he was still interested in buying shares; around the same time, NONG sold Convesto some shares, a sale made necessary, Farris explained, because NONG required additional operating funds. Since John McGraw was not enthusiastic about NONG's future prospects, Farris provided him with a list of potential purchasers, of whom Landreville was one. The fact that the option was for 10,000 shares at $2.50 each and that Landreville was later 'sold' the exact number of shares for the same price was merely coincidental. Farris insisted that the $2.50 price, arrived at in the fall of 1956, was, at that time, a fair one.[4] What made the transaction appear questionable, he acknowledged, was the explosion in the share price which began in the last days of 1956 and the first month of 1957 when, as it happened, Landreville and the others finally got the opportunity to execute their earlier purchase agreements.

The only problem with this explanation was that it was at odds with the truth. As Farris knew, Convesto was trading NONG shares in early December for $10 each, and he could find no record of any sale from that period for any lesser amount. There was no way of getting around it: selling 14,000 shares for $2.50 each any time after October 1956 was in effect giving away money, NONG's money. The recipient could immediately cash out with a huge tax-free capital gain. The explanation that NONG needed the money was bogus – if the company was truly cash-starved, it would have sold the shares at the market price, not practically given them away.

NONG's corporate records were a mess. A shareholders meeting, authorizing a further stock split, had purportedly taken place on 16 or 17 July 1956 in Toronto when Farris was in Sudbury. On 17 July Sudbury City Council finally approved the NONG franchise agreement. A NONG directors meeting was purportedly held on the 18th, at which time Landreville's stock option was approved. NONG's minute books did not record this meeting, nor did they record approval of the November 1956–January 1957 sale arrangements with Convesto until some time after those arrangements had been made. Farris did not deny that NONG's record-keeping was lax. He did, however, point out to Rand that NONG was a young company, and, while there were a number of directors, he and Clark basically ran the show.

Sometimes, Farris admitted, directors meetings were never formally held, but were recorded as if they were. 'We might all have been in New York on some business and the lawyer says: "Where were you all together so we can constitute a meeting?"' It was very difficult getting people together, and NONG once held a directors meeting 'in the elevator of the Ritz Hotel in Montreal.'[5] Rand found these goings-on difficult to understand. He was far removed from the realities of business life, and when he had practised law it was largely for a publicly owned company that was subject to constant scrutiny and regulation. His understanding of business, such as it was, had little in common with the practices that were now being described.

Given Rand's mandate, Farris's testimony that the share option, when offered, was completely legitimate was of some significance, although ultimately unbelievable and entirely self-serving. It was important to note, however, that some NONG executives were invited to participate in the capital growth of the company, and Landreville, the story went, intended to join the group. The only distinguishing feature about the arrangements with him was that they were made before he began employment with the company. Even so, they were not concocted, Farris insisted, for the purpose of inducing Landreville to betray his office or his duty to the people of Sudbury for the benefit of NONG.

Unfortunately for Farris, McGraw stuck to his story. When he gave evidence, his account, as at the earlier criminal trial and the preliminary inquiry preceding it, was quite different from Farris's version of events. Once again, McGraw explained that Farris asked him to buy the shares and also arranged for purchasers, each and every one of them. McGraw, however, insisted that $2.50 per share was the market price for NONG stock in November and December 1956, although he had no knowledge of any shares trading at that price. There was no public record of the trades, McGraw explained, because NONG had not yet been approved for public trading. All McGraw knew was that Convesto did not sell any shares at $2.50 each, and the inference was irresistible that $2.50 per share was not the market price. Given the windfall that Landreville and the other beneficiaries of this transaction immediately obtained, it was hard to believe that either McGraw, on this point, or Farris, more generally, was telling the truth.

In virtually every case, when it was time for Robinette to cross-examine one of the commission witnesses, he had few questions to ask. Rand, however, was another matter. While Landreville's lawyer was, by and large, satisfied with the evidence, Rand was brimming with curiosity. He made his scepticism about Landreville's relationship with Farris clear from the outset, and if he found an opportunity to make Landreville look bad, he took it.

The commissioner also signalled at the start that Landreville's character was one of his chief concerns. Over Robinette's objections, he let Morrow lead evidence from McLean about the distribution of free shares to Mayors Miller, Coates, and Cramp, as well as city solicitor Moore. That event, Robinette pointed out, had nothing to do with Leo Landreville and Rand's terms of reference. Rand disagreed. 'The character of these men' made the evidence relevant. Robinette was incredulous. 'Well, I hope you aren't going to decide Mr. Landreville's case on the character of other mayors; I would take very strong objection to that.' Rand quickly recovered. 'I don't mean their character; I mean, the character of the position. They were all mayors, and they all had shares distributed from this same vote of 14,000.'[6] He let the evidence in, prejudicial and irrelevant though it was to the issue of whether Landreville had done anything wrong.

If there were any doubts about what reception Landreville would receive when he gave evidence, they were dispelled by Morrow after the Vancouver part of the proceedings came to an end. Morrow told Robinette that Landreville should be ready to answer questions about the evidence he had given in all the previous proceedings. 'I would suggest,' he wrote on 29 March 1966, 'that you be fully prepared to clear up any inconsistencies that may have arisen in that evidence, and which may become apparent from the evidence that has come before this Inquiry.'[7] That Landreville was in for a rough ride became obvious when the commission reconvened in Sudbury on 21 March 1966.

Every living member of the Sudbury City Council of 1955 and 1956 was called to give evidence. With few exceptions, all this evidence was the same. Sudbury wanted natural gas, NONG was the only company in the running, and by the spring and summer of 1956 there was some urgency, communicated in large part by C.D. Howe, A.R. Crozier, and Ralph Farris, to sign the deal. Indeed, Crozier now testified that it was 'government policy' to 'put pressure' on Sudbury to make up its mind what it was going to do. Moreover, it was apparent to Crozier and the Ontario Fuel Board, as it was to everyone else after the March 1955 meeting of the northern municipalities, that there would be one gas distribution company in northern Ontario and that it would be NONG.[8] Landreville, the evidence established, took virtually no part, public or otherwise, in the decision. He did not press anyone to vote for NONG. A majority of council members were satisfied not only that it was a good deal but that Sudbury had got the best deal.

While everyone knew that Sudbury would sign with NONG, no one knew at the time the franchise agreement was before council that Landreville had asked for an opportunity to buy NONG shares. Most of the council members were later given a chance to buy shares, and they did. They insisted in their testimony before the commission that there was nothing wrong with the purchase. When Robinette, for example, asked

Joseph Fabbro, who succeeded Landreville as mayor and who had voted to delay the passing of the franchise bylaw, whether he viewed the shares he received as a reward, Fabbro smiled and said 'hardly.'[9] NONG was a generous company.

This was not the evidence commission counsel Morrow was looking for, and he made a direct appeal to the people of Sudbury through the press: 'May I say this to any member of the local press who are reporting these proceedings, will they please put this: Should anyone here have any information or wish to give me any information that they think might help me in these proceedings, I am at the President Motel, if they would contact me.'[10] No one did – at least no new witnesses were called as the result. Other than former council members, the only other witness of note was Landreville's former law partner, Judge James Cooper. He had no recollection, contrary to Landreville's version of events, of ever being told by Landreville that he had acquired an option to purchase NONG shares. One thing he could say, however, was that if Landreville said the conversation occurred, then it did. Landreville was that kind of man.

If Landreville had been on trial, the case for the prosecution was, from the Crown's perspective, going badly. Rand, obviously and increasingly frustrated, could not resist interjecting himself into the proceedings, and he relentlessly pursued every allegation of misconduct. When one former Sudbury City Council member testified, for example, that he felt compelled to approve the NONG deal, Rand spent considerable time in trying to find out who exactly caused the witness to react that way. And when this same city councillor reported a disagreement with Landreville on matters entirely unrelated to NONG, the commissioner, without hearing Landreville's version of events, suggested out loud that Landreville was somehow to blame. Rand failed, however, as one of his questions led to another, in his effort to place the dispute at the time that the passage of the bylaw became a matter of some urgency and importance.[11]

On another occasion, Sudbury's engineer testified that Landreville, in the weeks leading to the final vote, accused him, in a meeting held in the mayor's office, of being 'obstructionist' in his demands for further contract modifications as a condition for NONG's being awarded the franchise. In cross-examination, Robinette established that the witness *was* obstructionist. He was making demands that were both unrealistic and unlikely to be approved by the Ontario Fuel Board. However, when Rand got his chance to ask questions, he wanted to know if 'that was the only occasion on which you were subjected to that sort of address.' He also wanted to know if Landreville 'had gone beyond the realm of politeness' in expressing his views. Later, he asked another witness whether Landreville was a 'dominating personality.' The questions were ridiculous, and witness after witness, including Sudbury's former city solicitor John Kelly, indicated as much in their answers.[12]

Although Robinette had consented to the choice of Rand as commissioner, he quickly came to regret it. Rand made no secret of the fact that he despised Landreville. His conduct of the commission, from the first day forward, gave Robinette and Landreville cause for concern. When the hearings began, Rand instructed Morrow to read into the record various newspaper clippings that had been accumulated documenting the NONG affair. This was not evidence, and it was clear from Rand's questions that he was focusing on matters not directly relevant to his mandate so he could obtain evidence to support a preordained result.

Landreville did not help himself. A strange incident occurred at the end of the hearings in Toronto. Landreville, the story went, approached Officer A.R. Bates and another member of the RCMP in the anteroom of the Exchequer Court and remarked, 'Bates, that's the last time you or any other policeman will get the red carpet treatment from me again.' Bates immediately reported the incident to Morrow, who 'attached some significance' to a statement of this kind from a Superior Court judge. He asked for a written report, which was 'turned over to Mr. Justice Rand for his information.'[13] Landreville's judgment clearly left a lot to be desired; however, so too did Ivan Rand's.

Rand's *ex parte* approach to the Law Society was a case in point. The society had been largely responsible for the Rand Commission being struck. It had reported to the minister of justice that Landreville was not fit to continue as a judge, and it asked that he be removed. When Rand was appointed, he was provided with a copy of the Law Society report. While it is quite ordinary for commission counsel, in preparing a case, to interview prospective witnesses to determine if they have anything useful to contribute to the proceedings, commissioners themselves usually stay above the fray in order to maintain at least a semblance of impartiality in studying the matter under review. For some reason, Rand did not apply this normal rule.

In February 1966 Rand asked for a private meeting with the treasurer of the Law Society. He wanted to know why the Law Society report was considered confidential. Over lunch at the University Club, John Arnup set him straight. The report was sent to the minister of justice, but the Law Society at no time took the position that it was confidential. Once received by the minister, it was 'his communication' and he 'was free to do what he liked with it.'[14] Rand invited the Law Society to appear before his commission to present its views. Arnup took the matter under advisement.

Arthur Pattillo, the chairman of the kangaroo court that 'convicted' Landreville, insisted that the Law Society appear. 'Having been the responsible party for initiating this enquiry,' Pattillo wrote, 'we owe a duty to make representations to the Commission.'[15] This view did not prevail, and Rand's invitation was declined. 'Having in mind the material that you ... are obtaining for consideration by the Commission,' Arnup wrote Morrow, 'and in view of the fact that it is Mr. Rand who is Commissioner, the Law Society does not desire to make any representations during the hearings.'[16] The society had every confidence in Rand's grasp of the 'ethics which ought to govern a judge.'[17] After Arnup's account of his luncheon discussion, the society could be satisfied that there was no need for it to air its views publicly, and be cross-examined about its activities.

For his part, Attorney General Wishart told Rand that the government of Ontario had no interest in becoming involved. 'Having ordered and seen to the carrying out of the prosecution of Mr. Justice Landreville, I feel that my duty as Attorney General in the matter has been completed.' Wishart went on to say that 'all of the facts which were available to us were, I believe, presented in a hearing lasting some six days. Anything which I might now add would be merely an expression of opinion, and it would be presumptuous of me to trespass on the area where you have been commissioned to render judgment.'[18]

Landreville began to give evidence on 25 April 1966 in a practically empty courtroom located in the Supreme Court of Canada building in Ottawa. Rand's mind was already made up, but Landreville was still given the opportunity to present his version of events, which he did over the course of two long days. Insofar as the facts were concerned, Landreville, like so many of the other witnesses, offered nothing new. At times, Landreville was confident; at other times, his voice would become thick with emotion, his eyes filled with tears. 'If I had stayed in Sudbury,' he told Rand, 'I would have peace of mind and my health.'[19] If Landreville was searching for sympathy, however, he was looking in the wrong place. Without any evidence, Rand suggested, mid-way through Landreville's first day of testimony, that he had a 'good imagination.' Landreville, apparently, could see 'what was underway,' and the real reason he ran for mayor in 1954 was in order to 'play a part ... in the carrying out of this rather astonishing enterprise.'[20] Incredibly, Rand was suggesting that Landreville ran for mayor in December 1954 having determined that gas was on its way and that he would cash in on the development.

When Landreville suggested otherwise, and pointed out that he had campaigned on a platform of municipal amalgamation, Rand, clearly annoyed, directed him to change the topic.

Virtually all the events under review had taken place a decade earlier. Yet Rand had difficulty in accepting Landreville's assertion that his memory was not perfect and that, as he heard the evidence of different witnesses in different proceedings, his own memory was refreshed. While this explanation might account for relatively minor variations in his overall account, it *was* disturbing that Landreville gave several different accounts, over the course of his evidence in these different proceedings, on when exactly it was that he first approached Farris about acquiring shares in NONG. This conversation was critical.

The first time Landreville testified before the Ontario Securities Commission in 1958, he said that he approached Farris some time between 1 June and 15 July 1956, after first and second readings on the Sudbury franchise had taken place. By the time Landreville appeared before Rand, he had changed his account. He recalled that the approach was made late on the evening of 17 July, after the bylaw received final reading. Well, which one was it, Rand wanted to know. All Landreville could do was repeat his explanation that his memory had been refreshed, and assert that he now believed that the discussion took place later than he thought originally. It was better, from Landreville's point of view, to situate it after the franchise bylaw had passed, rather than before it received third and final reading. If it took place before the franchise was granted, there would be more reason to believe that it had been offered as an inducement to ensure speedy passage. Rand was clearly troubled by Landreville's shifting accounts: 'Well, all I have to say to you, Mr. Landreville,' the commissioner said, 'is that you impress me as a person of a bright mind with a good memory.'[21] Rand had formed the view that Landreville was modifying his evidence to suit the circumstances. Also noteworthy was the fact that Landreville and Farris had now testified to somewhat different versions of events.

Legal proceedings eventually come to an end, and on 27 April 1966 commission counsel Morrow began his final argument by referring to the order in council. 'You are charged,' he told Rand, 'with deciding whether anything done by Mr. Justice Landreville in the course of his dealings with NONG constituted misbehaviour in his official capacity as a judge or whether Landreville had by such dealings proved himself unfit for the proper exercise of his judicial duties.'[22] In Morrow's view, it was appropriate, in answering these questions, to consider Landreville's conduct both before and after he was appointed a judge.

Turning to Landreville's conduct as mayor, Morrow suggested that in discharging his mandate, Rand had to answer a number of questions. First, was Landreville's 'energy and drive' directed at facilitating the passage of the franchise bylaw 'prompted by the hope or expectation of a later benefit?' Second, did the share option, granted in the immediate aftermath of passage of the bylaw, if not before, 'reflect the possibility of an arrangement or reward for the passing of the franchise?' Third, was the exercise of the option arranged in such a way as 'to keep secret the transaction and to keep Landreville's name off the share registry?' It was up to Rand, in answering these questions, Morrow argued, to determine whether there was evidence 'of a degree of moral turpitude, or lack of ethics that may affect this man's usefulness as a Judge.'[23]

In Morrow's opinion, there were a number of problems with Landreville's conduct after he was appointed to the bench which Rand had to confront. Had Landreville lied when he told Officer Bates in September 1962 that he had bought the NONG shares through a Sudbury broker? If Rand found that he had, rejecting Landreville's explanation that he had merely expressed the view that it was likely that he had purchased the shares in this way, then the commissioner would have to draw some conclusions about the propriety of a judge telling falsehoods to the RCMP. Rand also had to determine whether Landreville had used his position to avoid or impede a police investigation.

It was also incumbent on Rand, according to the commission counsel, to decide whether Landreville had had an obligation to present himself to the Ontario Securities Commission in 1958 when he learned of its investigation into the distribution of NONG shares. If Landreville had a duty to do so, did his disregard of it indicate some lack of the moral fibre necessary in a judge? Rand must also, Morrow argued, review all of Landreville's sworn testimony, before the 1962 OSC investigation, the Farris preliminary inquiry, the Farris trial, and his own preliminary inquiry, in order to decide whether Landreville had told the truth. In doing so, it was important to recognize that some discrepancies could be the result of the passage of time. However, Morrow added, there was always the possibility that the confusion 'may show a callousness or carelessness in giving serious testimony, and a disregard for the consequences which may arise ... it may be ... an abrogation of one's normal duty as a judicial officer.' Characterized in this way, the callousness or carelessness was arguably 'contempt of court.'[24]

Robinette saw things differently, and when he made his final submissions he explained why. Referring to the order in council, he pointed out that there was no evidence suggesting any misconduct or misbehaviour by Landreville in relation to his official capacity as a judge. There was nothing to suggest neglect of duties, bad manners, corruption, or any action that would indicate 'bad behaviour'; he pointed out that the Act of Settlement, together with section 99 of the British North America Act, guaranteed security of tenure for judges 'during good behaviour.' That being the case, Robinette suggested to Rand, the sole issue before him was whether Landreville had in his dealings with NONG proved himself unfit for the proper exercise of his judicial duties. Here, too, Robinette argued that all the evidence indicated he had not.

'Fitness,' like 'beauty,' is in the eye of the beholder, and to assist Rand in focusing on the issue before him, Robinette suggested a test: 'Has he so conducted himself that reasonable litigants, knowing the true facts, would not desire or permit their cases to be tried before him? Put slightly differently, has he so conducted himself that reasonable litigants, knowing the true facts, would justifiably lack confidence in his keenness of perception, his sense of fairness, his objectivity, his ability to distinguish between right and wrong?' Given the constitutional guarantee of security of tenure for superior court judges, Robinette took the position that unfitness must be proven according to the strictest of standards, and with the clearest of evidence, before a 'Superior Court judge could properly be destroyed, and not only destroyed as a Judge, but destroyed as a man.'[25]

There was, on the contrary, considerable proof of Landreville's good character, and Robinette referred to Judge Cooper's testimony in support of that point. 'It must also be remembered,' Robinette continued, 'that Landreville was prepared to sacrifice the monetary advantages of continuing in a busy practice for the position on the bench. It seems to me reasonably clear from what occurred that he deemed it to be his duty to his profession and also to his racial origin as a representative of the French-Canadian group, and as I know, one of the few leading French-Canadian lawyers then practising in Ontario, he felt it his duty to accede to Mr. St. Laurent's perfectly legitimate and proper persuasion that he should accept the post in the Supreme Court of Ontario in succession to the late Mr. Justice Chevrier.'[26]

Robinette pointed out that no Sudbury City Council member felt cajoled by Landreville to support NONG. All the testimony was to the opposite effect and established that he had done nothing wrong in his capacity as mayor. To be sure, there was, by the spring of 1956, a sense of urgency in approving the franchise arrangements, but that haste was communicated by C.D. Howe, A.R. Crozier, and others, not by Leo Landreville. Not only was NONG the sole contender, but Landreville did not even participate in the vote. The selection of NONG was a *fait accompli*. That decision had been effectively made the previous year. When Sudbury finally approved the deal, it was bowing to the inevitable, but was doing so having achieved the best overall franchise deal. These facts, Robinette argued, hardly suggested that Landreville, years later, was somehow unfit to serve as a judge. There was no evidence that Landreville 'improperly exercised his powers as Mayor or put any undue or improper pressure on anyone, or that he, in any respect, betrayed his municipality or disregarded his duties to the municipality and to his ratepayers, in his capacity as Mayor.'[27]

Even if Landreville had made an error of judgment in accepting the NONG stock option, the Rand Inquiry had established that Landreville 'did not permit his duty to the municipality to conflict with any interest which he may have had resulting from the opportunity given to him to acquire shares in NONG.'[28] This option was given after the NONG franchise had, for all intents and purposes, been awarded. There was no possibility for conflict, Robinette concluded, and no conflict had taken place.

Robinette then reviewed the history of the piece, beginning with Landreville's fall 1954 meeting with Attorney General Dana Porter. He argued that Landreville had acted as a prudent and careful mayor, one who zealously safeguarded the interests of Sudbury. In Robinette's submission, Landreville had not, at any time, done anything wrong, and he therefore took offence at Morrow's suggestion that Landreville had demonstrated some disregard for the truth by failing initially to recall when exactly the first approach to Farris was made.

Now, it is difficult for a person to be certain, and Mr. Landreville at no time has said that he is certain as to the date. He said to you that his impression is now, that having heard the other evidence, that it was July the 17th, but he quite frankly admitted that it could have been earlier in July.

It would have been utterly foolhardy for Mr. Landreville to disregard his prior evidence, which he has read carefully, and in my submission, having read that evidence, and having heard the evidence of witnesses here, it was rather a conscientious effort to be as accurate as he could be with respect to the fixing of that date, and there would be no motive, nor no reason why there should be any transposition, and I think the net result of this testimony is, as he has said, he can't be certain, but he is under the impression that it was late at night.

In my submission you ought not to draw the inference, or the conclusion that there was any callousness, to use my friend's expression, but in my submission it was rather a deliberate attempt by a conscientious witness to try to get at the true date.[29]

Similarly, there were no inferences to be drawn from the fact that Officer Bates and Justice Landreville had differing accounts of exactly what was said when the police came calling. Interjecting, Rand made it clear which version of events he believed. In February 1957 Landreville had sent a telegram to McGraw reporting that he had sold all his NONG shares, when he had not. Rand now suggested to Robinette that this telegram provided sufficient proof to conclude that Landreville had lied. Robinette rejoined that Landreville may not have told the truth on this occasion, but this transgression was only a 'white lie,' and was hardly the basis upon which a finding of credibility could be made.

Frustrated by Rand's constant interruptions, Robinette continued in his attempt to justify Landreville to the commissioner. Landreville should not, Robinette argued, be attributed with responsibility for Farris's 'cloak and dagger activities in connection with Convesto.'[30] Landreville knew nothing about the operation of the Convesto account, and had nothing to do with the gifts of shares to the other mayors. Landreville could hardly be found guilty by association. Rand, however, would have none of it, and continued to break in with caustic remarks. 'I couldn't get over it,' Robinette later recalled. 'Rand just hated the guy.'[31]

As Robinette was concluding his remarks, there was one final interruption. What did he have to say, Rand asked, about the Law Society report? Until that point the report and the resolution that followed had not once been raised in evidence. Robinette was clearly taken aback. What possible relevance did that report have on these proceedings and the discharge of Rand's mandate? The answer, at this stage, was none. If the report was relevant, it should have been properly introduced. Witnesses should have been called and subjected to cross-examination. How was the report prepared? What facts were considered? What was the nature of convocation's debate? Only if the report was properly tested could it be relevant. It had never been proved. It was simply a document filled with hearsay. The report was useless, and Robinette attempted to explain why. 'Well sir, I would say this. First of all, now one thing I want to make plain is that I am a bencher of the Law Society and a former treasurer and I took no part in the deliberations with respect to that report, for obvious reasons, because I was counsel and had been counsel for Mr. Landreville.' Robinette obviously knew a conflict of interest when he saw one. He went on, however, to outline the deficiencies in the report:

The fact of the matter is that the Committee didn't give Mr. Landreville any opportunity to be heard. It purported to make a decision. It refers in the body of the document to speculation and then, from this speculation, the Committee draws certain inferences. Now, I don't like to be critical of my brethren on the bench, but it is sufficient to say that this is something that ought to be investigated. Now if it had gone just that far, there would be no objection to it ... but when a Committee purports to make a decision affecting an individual, the first rule of natural justice, the elementary rule of natural justice, is to permit that person to be heard.[32]

That was all very interesting, but what Rand wanted to know was whether Robinette had any objection to his making public a copy of the report and the resolution convocation had passed calling for Landreville to be removed. 'I have it on vested authority,' Rand advised Robinette, that 'so far as the Law Society is concerned, it is a matter of indifference whether the Minister or whether this Commission should make it available, as you might say, as an attachment to its proceedings.' Personally, Rand did not think it made any difference. What did Robinette think? 'No, I wouldn't think it made any difference at all.'[33] Rand now had what he wanted, and Robinette, distracted by the discussion, continued with his summation.

It was important to remember, he told Rand, that when a judge went on the bench, he abandoned a great deal. He gave up his practice. He lost his earning capacity. Accordingly, it was proper, and consistent with legal principles that had survived the test of time, that only in the clearest cases should a judge be impeached. He asked Rand, as he went about considering the evidence and writing his report, to keep these principles in mind. The inquiry was not, however, formally over. It was only adjourned, Rand announced, *sine die*.

Over the course of the proceedings, Landreville became concerned that Rand was moving away from an inquiry into the facts and towards an inquisition into his morals. Morrow's concluding remarks convinced him that Rand was clearly heading in that direction. Landreville therefore urged Robinette to be 'bold' and to write to Rand, reiterating that the inquiry was not about ethics and that it would be wrong for Rand to impose his own moral code on Landreville. After all, as Landreville observed, Rand was not 'born in my century.'[34] Robinette suggested that it might offend Rand to make an intervention of this kind, and so the matter was dropped. As it turned out, Landreville's fears were justified.

Rand's report started out normally enough. It sketched the history of the discovery of natural gas and the efforts to bring that gas east. Various developments were discussed and, by and large, Rand got the chronology right. By the spring of 1956, Sudbury alone among the major northern municipalities had not yet signed with NONG. On 26 April 1956, however, Rand found that something extraordinary had occurred. Farris travelled to Sudbury and had dinner at Landreville's home. According to Rand, Farris was 'a business executive with a receptive mind ... a man of sensitive imagination which seems to have been set aflame with the prospect of a unified gas distribution from Manitoba east.'[35] It was from this point forward, after the festivities on Elm Street, that Rand characterized every event, insofar as they related to Landreville, in the most negative light.

Rand concluded that Farris and Landreville, when they met, cooked up a deal, not dinner. Landreville then rammed a resolution through the Board of Control recommending that City Council give the franchise bylaw first and second reading. The only explanation for this outcome was that an agreement had been reached between Farris and Landreville: support at City Council in exchange for NONG shares. Standing in the way of that conclusion, however, was the judgment of Magistrate Marck, His judgment must, Rand found, 'be accorded a respectful recognition.' However, even if the facts establishing municipal corruption and conspiracy did not satisfy the requirements of the criminal law by constituting the elements necessary to establish an offence, that did not mean that Landreville was necessarily fit to serve as a judge.

According to Rand, Landreville's personal history suggested concern. He was a man of 'roving mind.' He had a 'sharp eye for business and is now of considerable wealth.' He invested in real estate. Once, Rand observed, Landreville bought a property with his law partner, the future judge, and they sold it a few years later for a profit. Landreville was 'plausible in statement and his resourcefulness, superficially, is considerable. His emotions are active and he can be highly expansive; he is fascinated by the glitter of success and material well-being. His outlook is indicated by a residence in Mexico, as well as a lodge some miles from Sudbury.' He was also 'capable of being disingenuous' and had been caught making more than one 'utterly false statement.' In short, Rand concluded, 'he presents the somewhat versatile character of a modern hedonist of vitality whose philosophy is expressed in terms of pragmatic opportunism for public prominence, financial and social success, tinctured with arrogance towards subordinates and confidence in his ability to move around.'[36] Rand continued his amateur psychology exposition by saying that a man like Landreville was likely to settle in the north.

That section of Canada, for the past sixty years, has been nurtured in speculation; beneath ironized masses of rock lay the substance of colossal wealth; fortunes shot up over night; and the response to the proposed gas developments exhibited the inherited trait of its people. Everybody, as it was said, wanted to 'get in on the ground floor.' Such a land with such a spirit was as a magnet to the young lawyer fresh from law school and itching for action. It is not surprising that he should have been caught up even in 1955 by the vision of the bold project and it may be that from the first he viewed it as presenting a rare opportunity for public and personal profit. In Farris he met a kindred spirit, between whom there would be mutual loyalty serving personal interest, the determinant of the shortsighted and disastrous course of action which has been somewhat detailed.

Farris, a man in his early 50's born and brought up in Vancouver, with a mind sharpened by the keenness of the struggle for fortune, of a driving energy, who viewed the petty morality of the middle class as no more than a hindrance to the public and private interest of large scale enterprise, found a congenial associate in Justice Landreville. In both, the titilating speculative prospects were irresistible and in the northland of Ontario an unsurpassable locus presented itself. For the past sixty years it had furnished foundation wealth to many sections of Canada and the United States: gold, silver, cobalt and other metals and minerals drew adventurers to what was otherwise a wilderness; and in the course of those years there has been built up a spirit for speculative fortune that in 1956, in a somewhat minor degree, broke out anew.[37]

After only four months of mutual acquaintance, Farris and Landreville developed a 'mutuality of understanding ... an instinctive recognition apparently by each of an identity of outlook, attitude and interests, an "affinity,"' so much so, according to Rand, that Landreville felt comfortable in approaching Farris for shares.[38]

If any more evidence of impropriety was required, Rand declared it could be found in the correspondence between the two men. The night after Farris dined at Landreville's home, he sent Mrs Landreville some flowers. Landreville then wrote Farris a letter: 'Do come back soon as I note any delay in your return – I shall purposely sabotage this contract to compel a return visit. Further, you and I have a few important things to discuss – re co.' Landreville testified that the important business to be discussed was the passage of the bylaw. Rand concluded that no legitimate business would be mentioned in such 'occult language.' The letter was of interest to Rand for another reason as well: the use of 'what is called the "first name" relation.' Rand was convinced, notwithstanding the lack of evidence proving this to be the case, that the whole transaction involved the sale of influence, and that it was artfully designed to keep Landreville's identity off of NONG's books. Farris, Rand added, was a 'denizen of the market place,' and his actions were hardly appropriate for the nephew of the former chief justice of British Columbia.[39]

Rand subjected not only Landreville's character to analysis, but the correspondence between Landreville and Farris as well. There was no doubt that Landreville chose his words poorly. There was also no doubt that the timing of the letters offering and accepting the stock option raised cause for concern. But the letters did not prove anything. The evidence against Landreville was all circumstantial, and, as circumstantial evidence goes, it left much more than a reasonable doubt. Rand saw things differently. 'It must be apparent,' he wrote, 'that those circumstances though short of a sufficiency for the purpose of a criminal proceeding, do raise a deep suspicion of a secret understanding. Suspicion is not sufficient in itself to establish criminality nor is this Commission a Court. But for the purpose here the question arises why has there been so much obvious concealment about the share acquisition?' No one corroborated Landreville's evidence that he made his purchase option known, and his failure to come forward at the first opportunity to reveal the truth was, 'considering his public office, extraordinary behaviour, and its implication serious.'[40]

Also extraordinary, according to Rand, and equally if not more serious, was Landreville's behaviour on the witness stand. His evidence in all the proceedings in which he testified was 'vague, indefinite, qualified, noncommittal, replete with half-truths, overstressed accounts of indifferent or non-significant facts, irrelevant digressions, emphasis on the obvious, indignant assertion in the nature of shadow-boxing, protestations of anxiety to vindicate himself, and airy looseness with truth in small matters: all bringing about an essentially misleading picture of governing facts.' Landreville's memory left a lot to be desired: 'His remark on that faculty that for some matters it was good and for others bad, can, without reserve, be accepted; but the classification becomes extremely simple: on the vital items where the probing touches the nerve there is failure; on the unimportant, a quick and clear recollection.'[41]

Landreville was not a man to be believed. He was not fit to be a judge.

No question is raised of misbehaviour in the discharge of judicial duty; this inquiry goes to conduct outside that function. What is to be examined consists, first of matters surrounding the negotiation for and the acceptance of 7,500 shares of stock following the granting of the gas franchise by Sudbury; secondly, of conduct thereafter in relation to the investigation of that acquisition by the Mounted Police, the Securities Commission of Ontario, indirectly by the Courts of the Province, and finally directly by this Commission.

The acquisition was the conclusion of relations which bear in their train a deep suspicion of impropriety. It is originally related to Justice Landreville as Mayor, as a reward for influence in bringing about the grant of the franchise or in hastening the grant, and possibly looking also to future relations with the community of Sudbury as they might be made more harmonious by the support of a man prominent and capable of influencing public opinion. It is clear that once an all-Canadian route for the pipe line had been settled, the introduction of gas to Sudbury, though it faced a heavy cost for the lateral from North Bay, was inevitable. The scheme promised a boon to the whole northland; delay was the most that could ultimately be brought against it; but that would not have been tolerated for long. But the urgency in the spring of 1956 was real and the considerations focussed were weighty. They might be looked upon as in any event overriding any adverse influence of the Mayor, but that would not affect the character of an agreement if any, to advance NONG's interest. Notwithstanding these possibilities, the acquisition can reasonably be associated with his action from the latter part of April to the conclusion on July 17, 1956, and beyond doubt public opinion tends to attribute, not unreasonably, the one to the other.

When the donee of such a gift with such a background is a member of the highest court of a province, is that an act or dealing beyond coercive control? What it tends to do is to shackle the independence of the recipient; and where the office calls for the exercise of judgment or discretion, in the adjudication of conflicts of interests between third persons, the possibility of improper even unconscious influence is too obvious to be given easy toleration.

Some observations of Justice Landreville in the letter of September 19 are here relevant; his description of judges: 'An all-inspriing [sic] unapproachable, staid class of people'; his concern for the future: 'I want to assure you that my interest in your company, *outwardly aloof*, will, nevertheless, remain active'; his keenness for the promise of shares, 'I am keeping your letter of July 20 carefully in my file.' This letter was addressed to 'Ralph' and signed 'Leo.' Making all allowances for a tendency to display cleverness and for the speech and thought of one familiar with the market place, these are strange remarks from a person just about to enter into membership of a Supreme Court; it demonstrates an astonishing insensitiveness to the plenary importance of that public office. The one absolute condition required of a Judge is a free mind, untrammelled in judicial action by foreign or irrelevant interests, relations or matters which might colour or distort judgment.

Rand had concluded that Landreville lacked the qualities necessary to serve as a judge. As he elaborated:

[I]t can be affirmed that in the overwhelming majority of the judicial officers of this country, issues presented are dealt with as if the parties before them were anonymous. That the dangers of close acquaintance and intimate personal relations are to be guarded against by abstention from any participation in matters which may involve them, is a rule ethically obligatory in our courts ... 'Outwardly aloof, my interest in your company will remain': 'your company' might easily become engaged in disputes; already there have been two gas explosions in Sudbury, one causing serious injury to a person and damage to a home; there may be contention over rates and other features of service which might reach the courts; possibilities of this sort abound. If the language is to be taken literally and seriously, words could not be more repulsive to any person holding the courts in high respect. For one whose relations towards others are easily charged with emotion and are influenced inordinately by acts of financial liberality, as seems to be the case here, the expressions can be taken only as demonstrating disqualification for the function: if its influence could be present in one case it could equally be so in others.

Such an attitude, such an act of assurance, followed by the acceptance of such a gift, issuing from circumstances clouded by deep suspicion, make up conduct incompatible with the standards of probity, detachment, independence of mind and fidelity to duty which appertain to judges. Followed by the message of February 16, 1957, 'Should I be of any assistance to your firm for the promotion or betterment of this company in Ontario, please do not hesitate to contact me,' it is sufficient and calculated to destroy, certainly, to impair materially, public confidence essential to the administration of justice under the rule of law ... against the danger of impairment of independence and impartiality we must remain alert and uncompromising.

His conduct as a witness and in extra judicial action is of an equal if not of a greater infringement of the standard of conduct demanded of a judge: the facts show an astonishing departure from what is dictated by an elementary conception of a judge's personal behaviour. By a course of presenting a confused picture of facts before judicial and administrative tribunals, the purpose of discovering the truth of certain matters sought by both an important agency of government and by the courts of the province, has been or has attempted to be frustrated. That conduct was to prevent disclosure of facts touching the administration of regulations relating to shares and securities of a company incorporated in Ontario; and to protect directly an official of that company in a prosecution arising out of such matters. The desire of the Justice in each case was to shield both himself and the other and is quite understandable. But the moral standard for a judge in his private capacity cannot admit such an interference with the course of government or of the proceedings of courts of justice. That is the duty of every citizen but it is supremely so for a judge: he cannot make his conduct an example of tolerated obstruction.

That such conduct is a breach of the duty which our conception of the judicial office sets for a judge cannot, in the opinion of the undersigned, admit of any doubt. He is sworn to the administration of Justice as our evolving ethical intelligence has fashioned it; but that obligation is not limited to the adjudicative role. He comes under another but equally sensitive duty. To respect the Law which he administers and to promote its processes to their proper ends. For a judge in his private capacity so to impede and defeat those processes is a grave dereliction, a gross infraction of the canons of conduct governing him.[42]

Rand then turned to the matter of the independence of the judiciary.

Mr. Robinette properly stressed the independence of judges and, rightly conceived, that principle admits of no limitations. It enables the guarantee of security to the weak against the strong and to the individual against the community; it presents a shield against the tyranny of power and arrogance and against the irresponsibility and irrationality of popular action, whether of opinion or of violence; it enables the voice of sanity to rise above the turbulence of passion; and it is to be preserved inviolate. But what does the independence of judges imply? That can be nothing short of this: that the minister to whom such an authority is committed shall himself be the first to respect what has been entrusted to him, the administration of the rule of Justice under Law, including loyalty to its institutions. The public acceptability of character for such a function is of that which exhibits itself in action as beyond influences that tend to taint its discharge with alien factors.[43]

Rand concluded his report with three findings:

I – The stock transaction between Justice Landreville and Ralph K. Farris, effecting the acquisition of 7,500 shares in Northern Ontario Natural Gas Company, Limited, for which no valid consideration was given, notwithstanding the result of the preliminary inquiry into charges laid against Justice Landreville, justifiably gives rise to grave suspicion of impropriety. In that situation it is the opinion of the undersigned that it was obligatory on Justice Landreville to remove that suspicion and satisfactorily to establish his innocence, which he has not done.

II – That in the subsequent investigation into the stock transaction before the

Securities Commission of Ontario in 1962, and the direct and incidental dealing with it in the proceedings brought against Ralph K. Farris for perjury in 1963 and 1964 in which Justice Landreville was a Crown witness, the conduct of Justice Landreville in giving evidence constituted a gross contempt of those tribunals and a serious violation of his personal duty as a Justice of the Supreme Court of Ontario, which has permanently impaired his usefulness as a Judge.

III – That a fortiori the conduct of Justice Landreville, from the effective dealing, in the spring of 1956, with the proposal of a franchise for supplying natural gas to the City of Sudbury to the completion of the share transaction in February 1957, including the proceedings in 1962, 1963 and 1964, mentioned, treated as a single body of action, the concluding portion of which, trailing odours of scandal arising from its initiation and consummated while he was a Judge of the Supreme Court of Ontario, drawing upon himself the onus of establishing satisfactorily his innocence, which he has failed to do, was a dereliction of both his duty as a public official and his personal duty as a Judge, a breach of that standard of conduct obligatory upon him, which has permanently impaired his usefulness as a Judge.[44]

'In all three respects,' Rand found, 'Justice Landreville has proven himself unfit for the proper exercise of his judicial function.' Landreville's conduct gave rise to suspicions, and it was up to Landreville to prove his innocence. He had failed to do so. This conclusion led to one of only two possible results: if Landreville failed to resign, he must be removed.[45]

Rand submitted his report on 11 August 1966, and the cabinet considered the report at a meeting twelve days later. 'Mr. Rand's conclusions were highly critical of Mr. Justice Landreville's behaviour in the matter,' the minutes recorded, 'to the extent that it would be impossible for Judge Landreville to remain on the bench.'[46] Cabinet decided to forward the report immediately to the governor general, but also to give Landreville an opportunity to meet privately with the minister before the report was released in order to discuss its 'implications.' On 25 August cabinet again discussed the matter, deciding to release the report quickly, in part to avoid the impression that the government was unduly favouring Judge Landreville. Before doing so, however, Landreville had to be advised formally of the contents, and he was summoned to Ottawa for an urgent meeting with the justice minister.

While Landreville was provided with a copy of the report before his interview with Cardin, its contents were no real surprise. A summary of the report had leaked and had been published in the *Globe and Mail*. Once again, Landreville was headline news: 'Report called devastating to Landreville,' the *Globe* announced, adding that it had been learned that Landreville was treated 'roughly' by Rand.[47] The *Telegram* had better sources, and some of the contents of the report were published on its front page.[48] The next day, the *Globe* reported that the Rand report had enough in it to warrant impeachment proceedings in parliament.[49]

When Landreville met with Cardin on 25 August 1966, he was prepared for the worst.[50] Cardin told him that the government had no choice but to table the report and move for his dismissal. Landreville was told to resign, and the government's wish in this matter was again indirectly communicated to Landreville with the assistance of some sympathetic friends.[51]

Once the report was leaked, and after Landreville was given a copy, the government tabled it in the House of Commons, before formally releasing copies to the press. That was done on 29 August 1966, and it was a deliberate decision. Government ministers, concerned that Landreville might sue Rand for libel, decided to insure against that result by tabling the report in the House where it would be, because of parliamentary privilege, immune from attack.[52] At the same time as he tabled the report, Cardin told the House that he was giving 'notice that it is my intention to make a motion ... at the first opportunity for an address to His Excellency praying that the judge be removed from office on the grounds set forth in the report.' It was also the government's intention to refer that motion to a joint committee of the House and Senate, 'so that the fullest inquiry can be made by Parliament itself and so that the judge can be given an opportunity to appear and speak on his own behalf.'[53] Landreville announced that he would fight any impeachment attempt.[54]

Landreville's complaint was simple: he was convicted of a crime of which he had not been charged. As he noted in a letter to the minister of justice, Rand's findings were not based on his dealings with NONG in 1955 and 1956, but on the commissioner's review of events after that date, a review coloured by his negative assessment of Landreville's character. 'Mr. Rand's report,' Landreville added in a statement given to the *Sudbury Star*, 'is based entirely on my manner of giving the evidence on several occasions on which I appeared in court and before a commission. It draws a malicious portrait of me in contrast and contradiction to what all witnesses have said about my character.' Landreville insisted that he had engaged in no wrongdoing, legally, morally, or ethically, and he made it clear that he had no intention whatsoever of stepping down because of a 'malicious, iniquitous, unjust and prejudiced' report.[55]

Reaction to the report was mixed. One commentator wrote that it was 'highly significant' because, 'for the first time in Canada the qualities required of a judge have been set forth by a high authority in an official publication.' Rand's enumeration of these qualities was 'masterly.'[56] 'The Rand Report on the former Mr. Justice Landreville,' the *Law Society Gazette* editorialized, 'may well be proven to be one of the most important constitutional documents on the judiciary.'[57] Many newspapers demanded immediate action. 'Boot Judge Off Bench' was the way one put it.[58] More careful readers, however, took issue with the presentation of the facts, if not the conclusions that were reached. The report was rambling and, in places, incoherent. Particularly noteworthy, and questionable, was Rand's repeated use of hearsay to support the conclusions he reached.

Relying on newspaper clippings, a notoriously unreliable source, for example, Rand had reported that Landreville and his former law partner had made a nice profit on the sale of some real estate: 'In 1955–56, while the gas development was taking place he was a party in equal interest with a former partner, now a County Court Judge, in the sale of land in Sudbury, acquired by them in 1949 for $173,000 and sold in 1956 for $325,000. That he is not to be taken as an innocent in such dealings is demonstrated by language addressed to the Tax Appeal Board in the course of an appeal from a gift tax arising out of that sale.' Rand either did not know, or did not care, that Landreville and Cooper had bought a vacant shell, gutted by fire, rebuilt it, and, some time later, sold it. That information would put the sale – and the profit – into perspective, but it was exactly that kind of information which Rand either did not seek or ignored. Moreover, there was nothing wrong with buying a building, fixing it up, and selling it for a profit. That transaction, like the fact that Landreville owned a home in Mexico and a hunting lodge up north, was completely unrelated to the issue of whether he had committed an improper or illegal act and was, as the result, unfit to serve as a judge. Very simply, there was nothing inconsistent about owning a second home, or having been a successful businessman, and later becoming a judge.

Another strange conclusion was Rand's finding that Landreville was a 'snob.'[59] When asked about his lobbying efforts on NONG's behalf, and, in particular, about a party he was reported to have held to introduce Farris to members of City Council, Landreville testified that he 'was not on a social basis with many of the Aldermen and Controllers; I would not invite them to my home.' And then, 'I am looking over the list of Aldermen, and I can say there would not be more than two with their wives, if at any time I had made an invitation.'[60] In his report, Rand made an extraordinary finding based on this testimony: 'He stated that there could be no social gathering in his home of the City Council of Sudbury for the purpose of promoting NONG's application for a franchise because there were too many members of the Council who were not of his social rank and would not be invited.'[61]

Landreville was anything but a snob. Snobs are not apt to get elected to progressively senior positions in municipal government over a period of twenty years in a multi-ethnic community like Sudbury. Rand read Landreville wrongly, from start to finish. The report's findings about Landreville's personality and wealth, his home in Mexico, and his hunting lodge in the north had nothing to do with evidence Rand heard, but everything to do with what he had read in the newspapers, particularly the *Toronto Star*.

Rand also appended to his report a copy of the Law Society's report, thereby giving it authority and respectability, neither of which it deserved. As Donald S. Macdonald, a future justice minister, pointed out in the House of Commons, the Law Society, in investigating Landreville and issuing a report, had exceeded its jurisdiction and had acted contrary to established principles of natural justice. The Law Society's report, Macdonald stated, was nothing more than an 'attack ... on a judge.'[62] If he was interested in balance, Rand might have also appended a copy of Magistrate Marck's decision, or his letter to the Law Society. Significantly, he did not.

There were other problems with the report. Rand found Landreville guilty by association. Farris may have had reasons for hiding the NONG transaction, for example, but Landreville could hardly be faulted for that. He never hid his dealings in NONG shares; he even wrote Convesto on his Osgoode Hall stationery acknowledging receipt of the shares. There was absolutely no evidence that Landreville had ever shown contempt for the law, 'gross' or otherwise. Maybe he should have presented himself to the Ontario Securities Commission in 1958, but he had no legal obligation to do so, and there was absolutely no evidence that he knew, at that time, that Farris might have attempted to conceal the beneficiaries of the sale of the 14,000 shares. Moreover, in finding Landreville guilty of 'gross contempt,' Rand exceeded his mandate by a considerable extent, for even the most liberal interpretation of his terms of reference did not require him to determine whether Landreville had engaged in this misbehaviour. Had the government wanted a general investigation into Landreville, the terms of reference would have indicated as much. Instead, Rand was directed to inquire into Landreville's dealings with NONG and whether anything done 'in the course of such dealings constituted misbehaviour ... or whether Landreville has by such dealings proved himself unfit for the proper exercise of his judicial duties.' The investigation was limited to Landreville's dealings with NONG, and Rand had strayed far off course.

Most importantly of all, Rand ignored section 13 of the Inquiries Act, the statute under which his commission had been constituted. Section 13 provided that before any findings of misconduct were made against someone, that person should be given an opportunity to respond to them. Landreville had no reason to believe that he was being charged with 'gross contempt,' and he had had no opportunity to refute that allegation. Rand had adjourned the inquiry *sine die* and, before concluding the proceeding, he had a legal obligation to advise Landreville of this finding and to provide him with an opportunity to refute it. These legal concerns aside, and they were important ones, the language Rand used in describing Landreville was intemperate and unnecessary. Ultimately, it was not only unfair but it coloured and discredited the basic conclusions he had reached.

There were more than enough facts on which to find that Landreville had, by his conduct, 'proved himself unfit for the proper exercise of this judicial office.' The share option was highly questionable. Why would a public company give a judge more than $100,000, if Farris's evidence in this inquiry was to be believed? The share option was not against the law – Marck's judgment established that – but it was a clear conflict of interest. It said something very important about Landreville and about his fitness to serve as a judge, no matter when the option was requested or when it was obtained. Rand could have reached some significant conclusions based on this single fact.

In addition, Landreville's letters and public statements in the aftermath of the disclosure of his ownership of NONG shares did not reflect well on his character, or on the temperament and disposition the public rightly expected in a Supreme Court of Ontario judge. Many people would consider the option, and the circumstances in which it was obtained and exercised, inconsistent with the type of behaviour required of a judge. At least Rand got that part of the report right, and in that respect he set out a useful and appropriate test: 'Would the conduct, fairly determined in the light of all circumstances, lead such persons to attribute such a defect of moral character that the discharge of the duties of the office thereafter would be suspect? [H]as it destroyed unquestioning confidence of uprightness, of moral integrity, of honesty in decision, the elements of public honour? If so, then unfitness has been demonstrated.' The public did have expectations of the judiciary, and judges should be held to the highest standards. Unfortunately, instead of dispassionately stating the facts, and then applying the larger principles to Landreville and reaching a reasoned decision, Rand had attacked the man in an offensive and demeaning way. Like the Law Society before him, Rand had failed to give Landreville his due by providing him with an opportunity, which he was entitled to by law, to refute negative findings that Rand was making against him. As Robinette justly complained, Rand never, not once, gave Landreville a break.[63] The result might have been right, but the process was wrong.

After the report was released, a citizens' committee in Sudbury was established on Landreville's behalf by two 'housewives,' some labourers, and an engineer. 'The Citizens Committee for Factual Information on the Landreville Case' occupied itself with passing resolutions in defence of the judge and communicating these views to members of parliament and the press. They also kept Landreville informed. He made it absolutely clear that he had no intention of resigning, and every expectation, if parliament intended to proceed further, of appearing before a parliamentary committee to state his case. Instead of reserving further comment to an appropriate time and place, Landreville told curious reporters immediately after the report was released that if 'making money was a crime,' he was 'guilty,' adding for good measure that if he was given another chance to obtain stock in the same way he had obtained his shares in NONG, he 'would do so.'[64]

Unwisely, Landreville also told reporters that the source of his troubles was one reporter at the *Toronto Star* who had lost his job at the *Sudbury Star* as a result of Landreville's complaints about the fairness of his coverage of Sudbury City Hall. Blaik Kirby was, Landreville told the newspapermen camped outside his Hull, Quebec, motel room, the person responsible for the whole mess, and he suggested that his motives for doing so could be traced to this earlier event. While Kirby had made one major mistake in his coverage of the story – an article written about Landreville during the Farris trial was wrong and the *Star* later apologized for the mistake – all that the newsman had done was pursue the story. For good measure, Landreville accused Ontario NDP leader Donald MacDonald of being the other villain in the piece. MacDonald had, Landreville claimed, taken up Kirby's cause and commenced partisan attacks.[65]

Landreville told the press he would not step down. 'To resign,' he said, 'would be to admit guilt.'[66] This point was reinforced by Landreville's new lawyer, the colourful and controversial David Humphrey of Toronto, who also had a judicial appointment in his future. Robinette was acting as counsel in the Leitch Gold Mines case and could not take on another brief. As it happened, Humphrey, retained to represent Landreville before parliament – for that is where Landreville's case was now heading – would not be defending him for some months, as various procedural questions had still to be addressed. This was, after all, the first time in Canadian history that the government had moved to impeach a judge.

Humphrey advised Cardin that Landreville would vigorously oppose any impeachment attempt, and predicted that the proceedings would be protracted. He strongly objected to Rand's report, which was the product of a gratuitous investigation into matters completely extraneous and foreign to Rand's terms of reference and to Cardin's 28 December 1965 promise to limit the investigation to the determination of the facts. 'It is obvious,' Humphrey wrote, 'from Mr. Rand's statement of facts, undisclosed by the transcript of evidence, that he has proceeded on an inquiry of his own.'[67] That was true, but it was also true that Robinette had been shown a draft copy of Rand's terms of reference, and those terms clearly entitled Rand to consider and report whether Landreville was a fit person to continue sitting as a judge.

There was no way that Landreville could stop parliament from proceeding. He did, however, want to know what case he had to meet, and on 21 September 1966 he wrote to the minister of justice asking for 'particulars of the allegations which will form the basis of the proceedings.' Only if he knew the 'exact complaint upon which impeachment was sought' could he 'intelligently refute the allegations' made against him.[68] Cardin never replied. Instead, he introduced a motion in the House of Commons on 21 November 1966 establishing a joint committee of parliament to inquire into and report on the expediency of presenting an address that called for Landreville's removal as a judge in view of the facts set out in the Rand report and the conclusions that Rand had reached.[69]

Humphrey took issue with this approach. First, he questioned the propriety of the tabling of Rand's report. In his view, the government should have examined its contents before presenting it to parliament. If that step had been taken, it would have been clear that the report did not do what it was supposed to do. What it did do was offend natural justice. In addition, Humphrey took issue with the government's suggested approach. A joint committee of the House and Senate was not the correct way in which to proceed. 'There should,' he stated, 'be a committee of the House of Commons which reports to the House following which, if its resolution and recommendation is accepted, *thereafter* is studied by the Senate or its committee.'[70] Humphrey's comments were noted, but they did not change the government's decision about how best to proceed.

Given the conclusions that Rand had reached, Cardin might have been expected to set the committee to work with only minimal delay. However, after tabling his resolution in November, and inviting Humphrey in December to make any suggestions he wished about the manner in which the committee might proceed, the minister of justice gave Humphrey and Landreville no further information about the timing or form of the proceedings. Landreville remained on the payroll, although he had again stopped sitting as a judge. In early January 1967 Humphrey wrote to Cardin and asked for a status report. He wanted to know when the committee was going to meet and what evidence it intended to review. He also repeated his request to be apprised of 'the particulars of the ... accusation which Mr. Justice Landreville must meet.'[71] Humphrey again received no reply. Landreville, however, was invited to appear before the joint committee when it met on 20 February 1967.

8

'Pleading for My Honour'

On Monday, 20 February 1967, an event took place in Ottawa that had never previously occurred, and has not happened since. One of Her Majesty's judges arrived at the Parliament Buildings to defend himself before a joint committee of parliament charged with investigating and then recommending whether he should be removed.[1] Looking elegant in a charcoal grey suit with a light grey waistcoat, Landreville was accompanied by three lawyers, David Humphrey, Terrence Donnelly, and Gilles Guenette, but he was, he immediately announced, representing himself. The four men proceeded to the committee room, where six senators and twelve members of the House of Commons were waiting to decide the fate of the diminutive judge. Seventeen of the eighteen members were lawyers, and one was a clergyman.

The joint committee, co-chaired by Senator Daniel Lang and Ovide Laflamme, MP, had been established the previous November, but other than deciding to introduce into evidence copies of the Rand and Law Society reports, the committee had not accomplished any work of consequence. Preliminary discussions about procedure had taken place, but nothing of significance would be decided until Landreville and his counsel had appeared. The hearings were pivotal. If Landreville conducted himself well, if he established to the satisfaction of a majority of the committee members that he had done nothing wrong as a judge, and if he could prove that the independence of the judiciary was truly at stake, then, even at this late stage, he had a fighting chance of retaining his job – and restoring his reputation.

The Rand and Law Society reports were notoriously unfair, and it would not take much to show that he had, on both counts, been a victim of a legal system gone awry. But that would not be enough. Landreville also had to demonstrate that he was judicial in attitude and temperament. Unfortunately, the hearing got off to a bad start, and the negative impression he conveyed in his first appearance was only exacerbated with the passage of time.

In a prepared statement, Landreville objected to the Rand report and described it as an 'illegality.' He declared that a judge of a superior court did not fall under the Inquiries Act, though he and Robinette had privately agreed to the inquiry being conducted under that legislation and had also undertaken not to attack its constitutionality. Landreville did, however, have a relevant legal objection to the Rand Inquiry. The Inquiries Act provided 'that no report shall be made against any person until reasonable notice has been given to him on the charge of misconduct alleged against him and until he has been allowed full opportunity to be heard in person or by counsel.' Landreville had never been given that notice. He also observed, poignantly, that he had agreed to an investigation to ascertain the facts, not to a psychiatric analysis.

Landreville further charged that the joint committee was without jurisdiction to hear his case. He was appalled that the Rand and Law Society reports had been introduced into evidence, although, as the committee's terms of reference had specifically mentioned the Rand report, it was only natural that it would be introduced. The Law Society report was another matter. Rand's decision to append it to his report was questionable: it was not real evidence, and no one had come before Rand to testify to the circumstances in which it was prepared. J.J. Robinette had, after a fashion, agreed to its coming before the Rand Inquiry, although for a very limited purpose. Landreville was understandably concerned about its prejudicing his case. It was improper and unfair, in Landreville's view, for the parliamentary committee to rely on unsworn, untested evidence, particularly where the truth of that evidence was put into question. If the committee had decided to accept evidence of this kind, then it also ought to have accepted into evidence a copy of Magistrate Marck's reasons for decision.

Most significant of all, Landreville had repeatedly asked for, but had never received, notice of the specific charges that were now being made against him. What allegations had to be answered? What was, in brief, the exact complaint before the parliamentary committee which Landreville had to meet? 'I came to meet my accusers,' Landreville stated; 'where are they?' 'I came to face accusations; what are they?'[2] The joint committee had already held two meetings in his absence. This, he claimed, offended the tenets of natural justice.

Landreville then spoke in French, addressing the francophone members of the committee. 'Out of the 32 judges of the Supreme Court of Ontario, these events have befallen the only judge of your language. I feel this very deeply.' He was being attacked because of language and ethnicity. Completing his statement, Landreville uttered an old French saying: 'Honi soit qui mal y pense' [evil to him who thinks evil]. Then, with his coterie of lawyers and supporters following behind, Landreville got up and left, leaving the senators and members of the House of Commons gasping in stunned silence. There was embarrassed laughter, followed by general confusion. Gordon Fairweather said it was more 'fun than Sunday.' More seriously, he urged the committee not to be taken in by Landreville's theatrics. What was important, Fairweather reminded his committee colleagues, was whether they agreed with the findings of the Rand report, written by another former attorney general of New Brunswick. Landreville was free, he pointed out, to call evidence on his own behalf.[3]

Meanwhile, Landreville was holding a press conference outside the hearing room, no doubt contrary to his lawyers' advice. He reiterated his complaints, particularly his charge that the real reason for the controversy surrounding him was that he was Ontario's only French-speaking superior court judge.[4] The *Toronto Star* would have none of it. In an editorial published several days later, it urged the committee to ignore Landreville's 'insolent antics.' 'This man's behaviour is a disgrace to the Ontario bench. The parliamentary committee should go ahead and consider his case,' the editorial concluded, 'and recommend appropriate action, whether he cooperates or not.'[5]

Notwithstanding Landreville's performance, many of the members of the joint committee were sufficiently disturbed about his legitimate concerns, not to mention the intemperate language and unsupportable conclusions found in the Rand report, to ask the committee counsel, Yves Fortier, for a report. Fortier was a rising young Montreal lawyer with good Liberal connections. He advised the committee that its procedures were lawful and that the hearings could proceed.

On 23 February 1967 the committee began the process of considering the conclusions reached in the Rand report. They were assisted in this task by a lengthy submission from Fortier, who outlined in great detail the evidence Rand had heard and elaborated the basis on which Rand had reached his conclusions. The only aspect missing from this overview was any consideration of Rand's persistent *ad hominem* attacks. Those were, Fortier claimed, 'flagrant examples of *obiter* which do not ... bear repeating.' In his view, it was unfortunate that 'some of these remarks have been the most publicized remarks of the report.'[6] While they might not have been worth repeating, surely the fact that Rand made these remarks was relevant. After all, they said something about the manner in which he had judged Landreville. As Senator John Hnatyshyn pointed out, it may be *obiter dicta*, but if 'I was convinced that he is overdoing it, I would not pay much attention to his other recommendations.'[7] Exactly.

This point was made repeatedly in the question period following Fortier's submissions. Fortier had read all the evidence adduced before Rand, and that given by Landreville in other proceedings considered by Rand. A thorough review of the documents followed, and while Fortier did not find any documentary evidence that was favourable to Landreville, the 'interpretation given by Commissioner Rand to some of the documentary evidence on occasion was not as favourable as it could have been.'[8] The commissioner had not, in another example, paid much attention to the extremely favourable character evidence given by former members of the Sudbury City Council. By participating, Landreville could bring this and other evidence forward, and in the process establish that he was not the man Rand had portrayed. It was an opportunity for Landreville to establish that his treatment by Rand was unfair, that he was fit to serve as a judge, and that important principles dating back hundreds of years to the Act of Settlement were at stake.

Eventually, Landreville realized as much, and when the committee reconvened on 28 February 1967 he said he was ready to testify. Sitting between his lawyer, Terrence Donnelly, and Senator Lang, Landreville began his remarks. The outlines of Landreville's defence, for that is what it was, were clear and, by now, familiar. Everyone in Sudbury wanted natural gas; even the three city councillors who voted against the franchise deal on final reading did so only in the hope of obtaining an even better deal from NONG. Sudbury did sign with NONG, but so had virtually every other northern municipality. Just the way Farris wanted it, NONG had the field virtually to itself; there were no competitors to speak of, and no northern municipality ever seriously considered establishing a public utility for the distribution of natural gas. Attorney General Dana Porter had made it clear from the outset that the province would not support any publicly owned gas distribution scheme.

Sudbury City Council had taken its time to reach a franchise decision, in part because INCO took so long to make up its mind. Once that decision was made, and because of the urgency for action occasioned by the closure debate, the telephone call and telegram from C.D. Howe, and the persistent representations of A.R. Crozier, the chair of the Ontario Fuel Board, City Council acted with dispatch. Landreville insisted, however, that when the bylaw granting a franchise to NONG finally came to a vote, he did not influence anyone's decision. Nor did he take any part in the debate, or work behind the scenes. Every city councillor who had testified before Rand had stated – and Landreville now cited the transcripts, chapter and verse – that 'Mayor Landreville' acted properly and honourably throughout. The evidence established that the city of Sudbury ended up getting the best overall deal, and that its former mayor was a leader and man of integrity. He had not used his position to influence City Council, or to secure some special advantage for himself.

Landreville did not deny asking for NONG stock, but when he did make the request, the franchise application was, for all intents and purposes, settled. The stock option was asked for and received solely in the context of an agreement providing that Landreville, when he stepped down as mayor, would join NONG management. He also asserted that, when the option was received, it was hardly a sure thing. In the summer of 1956 no one anticipated an explosion in the price of NONG shares. At the time, $2.50 a share was a fair price. Besides, as Marck's decision proved, neither asking for nor receiving that option was against the law.

Nor was there evidence that he had ever done anything, since being appointed a judge, that would render him unfit for judicial office. To be sure, he had not volunteered to give evidence before the 1958 OSC investigation, but he was under no obligation to do so. He had, when he testified in 1962, and on several occasions since, told the truth, and he had never sought to camouflage his purchase of NONG shares. His name appeared in Convesto's books, and he had signed a receipt for the share certificates he received. Writing letters about his NONG shares on his official stationery was not consistent with an effort on his part to conceal his participation in NONG. These were not, very simply, the actions of a man with something to hide (although they may have been the actions of someone who thought he would never be held to account).

As the proceedings dragged on – the parliamentary calendar being what it is, hearings are rarely held on consecutive days – Landreville was breaking under the strain. 'His hands and arms seldom stopped moving. He stabbed a finger in the air and swept his hands in a horizontal motion in front of him to emphasize points.'[9] Overcome with tears, Landreville was forced on more than one occasion to call a temporary halt to his testimony, which, in any event, was regularly interrupted by division bells summoning MPs in a minority parliament to a vote.

Fortier asked most of the questions, although from time to time other committee members interrupted Landreville's presentation to question him more carefully on some of his remarks. There were many aspects of his involvement in the affair that Landreville could satisfactorily explain, and others he could not. He succeeded in explaining to the committee members how he could be granted a stock option in exchange for his promise to work for NONG. What he could not explain, however, was how the option survived when he was appointed to the bench. By the time Landreville went to exercise his option, there was no prospect of his being employed by NONG. Giving stock options to future executives was one thing; honouring options given on a broken promise of future service after a significant increase in the value of the shares was quite another. What possible benefit to the shareholders could there have been in honouring the stock option in Landreville's case? And why did neither the option letter nor the company's minute books ever report the fact that the option was being given in consideration for and anticipation of Landreville's promise to join the executive ranks?

The timing of the transaction also bothered committee members. Sudbury had dragged its feet for months. Then, all of a sudden, the application was quickly considered and approved. Rand might be right that Landreville had pushed it through in return for the future promise of illicit and cheap NONG stock. Landreville denied the contention and pointed out that there was no evidence establishing it to be so. The correspondence between him and Farris, not to mention his discharge at his preliminary trial, was to the opposite effect. However, even accepting Landreville's evidence about when the request was made, and granted, raised more questions than answers. How could acceding to the request be seen as anything but as a reward for delivering Sudbury City Council to NONG, with the explanation of future employment merely an alibi constructed after the fact?

If the deal was completely above board, why had Landreville kept it a secret? Landreville had long claimed that he had, in fact, mentioned his future arrangements with NONG to several council members. Unfortunately for him, no one else had the same recollection. This inconsistency aside, and it was not an insignificant one, Landreville asserted that his arrangements with NONG were a 'private matter.' He did not have to tell anyone, he explained, since the transaction with NONG was completed and City Council had no further business with the company for the remainder of his term. This was absurd. The signing of an agreement with NONG marked the beginning of a relationship with City Council, not the end. All Landreville could say was that *his* term as mayor was coming to an end, and City Council had nothing further of consequence for the remainder of that term to negotiate with NONG. Had he actually owned the shares at the time – which, he hastened to add, the Municipal Act permitted – he would have disclosed his ownership if some matter relating to NONG had come before council for a vote. The stock option, he explained, raised no such requirements. It also did not impose any disclosure obligations to the Ontario Fuel Board when he appeared before it some ten days after the option was received.

It was disturbing to the committee that Landreville had no satisfactory explanation for failing to come forward in 1958 when he knew the Ontario Securities Commission was investigating allegations that some municipal and provincial politicians were corrupt. Was this appropriate conduct for a judge? Everyone knew that the OSC investigation was taking place. Did not Landreville, as an officer of the court, feel some obligation to come forward, identify himself, and tell what he knew? All he could say in his own defence was that, as a judge, he was reluctant to meddle in politics. This was nonsense.

Landreville was not reluctant, as a judge, to write Convesto on his Osgoode Hall stationery, on 16 February 1957, thanking the firm for the delivery of 7500 free NONG shares and concluding: 'Should I be of any assistance to your firm for the promotion and betterment of this company in Ontario, please do not hesitate to contact me.' There was nothing 'sinister' about this statement, Landreville insisted. He had no intention, he told Fortier, of actually acting on behalf of NONG. Fortier was not, however, prepared to accept this explanation. In what way, he asked, could a judge of the Supreme Court of Ontario promote or better a company? All that Landreville could suggest was that, as a director of the Canadian Tourist Association and a frequent after-dinner speaker, he would have been in a position to place a 'good word' for a company such as NONG. Nor did he find anything extraordinary about his letter of 19 September 1956 to Farris where he said that his 'interest' in NONG, while 'outwardly aloof,' would remain 'active' nevertheless.[10] Evidence of this kind seriously damaged Landreville's credibility.

In a great many respects, Landreville was his own worst enemy. On 9 March, for example, he testified about a 28 February 1957 telegram he had sent to a Vancouver stockbroker, claiming that he had sold all his NONG shares. In fact, he had sold some and was in the process of selling the others. Faced with these facts, Landreville admitted the truth: 'Well, gentlemen, I did send that telegram and that was a lie.' He added, unnecessarily, 'I only can say to you that ... I lie often. I might say to a woman – she has a beautiful hat or advise my secretary to tell the other party I am not in, even advise others to lie, but let anyone attack me on a matter of seriousness – a serious matter, that is a different thing.'[11]

The procedure the committee followed may have had something to do with Landreville's response. As in a medieval Star Chamber, the onus was on Landreville to prove his innocence, not on some other party to prove his guilt. In discharging this evidentiary burden, Landreville was hampered in many important respects. He had no control over the presentation of his case. He had, for example, wanted to subpoena Rand. 'I want to question him as to where he obtained some of the factual information contained in parts of his report, information which never came out in the inquiry ... as a character analysis it is contradicted by the testimony of every witness heard by the inquiry.'[12] Committee members, however, had no intention of agreeing to this request, and it was pointed out that it was Landreville, not Rand, who was effectively on trial.

Personal attacks on Rand were not shrewd tactics. Landreville should have focused on the inadequacies of the Rand report. It would not have taken much to discredit the report, and a number of committee members had already publicly signalled their concern that the commissioner's bias had unduly influenced the conclusions reached. The refusal to allow Landreville to call Rand was both understandable and predictable. The committee's refusal to allow Landreville to call character evidence was another matter. Time after time, Landreville was told that his character was not in issue, and that the committee would not be considering Rand's observations when they went to write their report. After all, Fortier pointed out, when Jonah Barrington wanted to call evidence about his general conduct and character in the 1800s, he too was denied the opportunity to do so.[13] But this precedent did not make it right. It was largely because of Landreville's character that Rand had concluded he was unfit to serve as a judge. Landreville should have been given the opportunity to rebut this finding.

In all, Landreville testified for six days on eleven separate occasions. He pointed the committee members to evidence supporting his version of events, and to evidence that he suggested Rand had ignored. He succeeded in introducing a copy of Marck's judgment, but failed in his effort to get the committee to agree to allow the Hamilton magistrate to attend and speak personally on Landreville's behalf. It would have been most unusual, and certainly unprecedented, if Marck had been allowed to testify. Judges speak through their decisions, not through the press or on the witness stand. The committee had Marck's decision; it had been entered into evidence. There was nothing more that the magistrate could say.

Landreville was similarly unsuccessful in his efforts to call former justice ministers Favreau and Cardin to testify about his numerous requests for the appointment of a commission. Robinette was also waiting in the wings. He was prepared to testify how he and his client went before Commissioner Rand 'prepared to play tennis and were called upon to play rugger.'[14] In the end, Landreville was not allowed to call a single witness on his own behalf. Parliamentary procedure dictated that all witnesses be called by the committee, and it had no interest in calling any of the witnesses Landreville had named. Questions of procedure and propriety aside, it was probably true that none of Landreville's proposed witnesses offered the promise of adding anything substantial. In one forum or another, every relevant fact was now on the record, including the evidence of Landreville's 'good character.' The attendance record of some committee members was irregular, however, and only Fortier had read all the evidence. There was thus no reason to believe that every fact – especially the evidence of Landreville's good character – was known to every member of the committee. Moreover, reading transcripts of evidence in other proceedings is hardly the same as actually seeing the key witnesses and hearing their testimony.

Ultimately, Landreville appealed to fairness. On 14 March 1967, his speech quickening and his face flushed, he asked the committee members to allow him to remain as a judge. 'Had I known every event in the future that was to take place, do you believe for a moment, gentlemen, that I would have accepted the Northern Ontario stock even at $117,000? Do you believe for a moment that I would exchange my life's career for any sum of money? One does not do it that way if he is an honourable man. I am here before you,' he stated, 'pleading for my honour, basically; that is why I am here.'[15]

There was more to it than that, and Landreville continued with some remarks about the standards properly required of judges. 'I do contend, gentlemen, that the standard Mr. Rand imposes on a judge is too high a standard. I believe that a judge is entitled to a private life.' It was not right to examine a judge's past, and find that the judge is unfit because of 'suspicions of impropriety.' Judges were appointed, not anointed. He insisted he had done nothing wrong, and that if similarly placed he would request and accept the stock option again. After being pilloried in the press and in parliament for years, Landreville still did not understand that many citizens considered his conduct questionable, to say the least. If only he had, years earlier, apologized and expressed regret, the whole matter might have gone away. Instead of appearing remorseful and judicial, he seemed a man who had learned nothing, and who believed, notwithstanding all the evidence to the contrary, that he had nothing to learn. Continuing in this vein, he declared that soliciting and accepting the stock option was not misconduct of the sort that rendered him unfit, after eleven years of service, to continue to sit as a judge. After thirty years of public service, he did not deserve being attacked, his reputation destroyed, and his family left on the brink of financial ruin. 'I have no lessons to give on integrity to anyone,' Landreville concluded, 'but I will not take any lessons either.'[16] With that remark, the public hearings of the special joint committee investigating Leo Landreville came to an end.

That night the committee met in camera. The discussions continued for two days, and committee members were well aware that they were engaged in a historic task.[17] Party discipline was not imposed, and the discussions were intense. 'Among the most pervasive of my recollections of the Parliamentary Committee,' Gordon Fairweather later recalled, 'was the sick feeling many of us felt about the responsibility for the future of Leo Landreville.'[18] On 17 March 1967 the committee issued its report, brief but to the point. It stated that Rand's 'reflections' on Landreville's character were not considered pertinent and played no part in the committee's deliberations. Despite Rand's flights of judgmental rectitude, the committee concluded on the basis of the Rand report (which had in turn stated that there was no evidence of judicial misconduct), and on the basis of Landreville's own testimony before the committee, that he had 'proven himself unfit for the proper exercise of his judicial functions.' Accordingly, the committee, 'with great regret' recommended removal.[19]

The committee's report suggested unanimity. In fact, it was approved by a vote of 12 to 4. A clear majority, to be sure, but disquieting nonetheless, as only four members regularly attended and were in a position properly to weigh Landreville's evidence and demeanour. On more than one occasion, mid-way through the proceedings, the committee came close to losing its quorum of seven, and on several occasions Landreville had to repeat evidence given earlier to accommodate committee members who had missed some of the proceedings. A majority of the members of the joint committee, through inadvertence, disinterest, or the press of other commitments, did not take their responsibility seriously, at least insofar as attendance was concerned. Presumably, they studied the complete transcript of the committee's proceedings, and any questions they had were answered by Fortier. But it will never be known how the majority came to its decision, because the report is bereft of rationale and analysis. It simply stated that the Rand report was reviewed, that Landreville was heard, and that he should be removed.

When Landreville received notice of the committee's recommendation, he immediately contacted the Speaker of the House of Commons and asked for an opportunity to appear at the bar of the House to address the honourable members if a removal address was introduced. There were no Canadian precedents, but there was the oft-cited case of Sir Jonah Barrington, who had been allowed to address the British House of Commons. Landreville now claimed this as his right.[20] He also wrote to the prime minister and argued that the parliamentary proceedings were unfair. He had not been permitted to call witnesses, and 'most of the committee members had been absent more often than not.' He publicly appealed to the prime minister to set matters right. 'There being no accusation, no trial, there being no question as to the performance of my duties as a judge for over ten years, I must conclude, therefore, that I am in jeopardy of being liquidated out of office on mere suspicion of an act done prior to my appointment.'[21] Nothing less than the independence of the judiciary was at stake, and Landreville urged Pearson not to forget that fundamental fact.

Privately, Landreville told Pearson that if he were allowed to retire with his pension, he would consider doing so because it was questionable whether he had any further usefulness as a judge. Rumours soon spread that Landreville was willing to go quietly if he had a guarantee on his pension. When the *Globe and Mail* heard the story, an editorial quickly followed. Landreville 'has clearly no conception of the essential ingredients of the judicial mind.' The protracted affair demonstrated the need for a cleaner and more effective method of dealing with judges whose fitness to serve was called into question. A permanent judicial council was one possible solution.[22]

In the highly charged political climate of the day, the government was unlikely to be receptive to any arrangement that involved pensioning Landreville off. As Cardin wrote to Pearson, giving Landreville a pension was not a good idea for reasons that were 'self-evident.'[23] Landreville therefore insisted to Pearson that he had the right to appear before the

House of Commons and fully state his case.[24] This request preoccupied some senior civil servants throughout the spring. After considering the issue in some detail, a consensus was reached: Landreville would, if the matter proceeded, be given an opportunity to appear,[25] although, as Cardin observed to Pearson, such an appearance was sure to be 'a rather unpalatable spectacle.'[26]

Justice Minister Pierre Elliott Trudeau announced outside the House of Commons that Landreville would be allowed to appear before the bar of the House and to call relevant witnesses if he wished. Landreville would, Trudeau stated, be given every protection of the law.[27] However, given Landreville's performance before the special joint committee, the government was understandably nervous about the prospect. Opposition leader John Diefenbaker, sensing the government's discomfort, repeatedly insisted that Landreville be accorded his due.[28] Diefenbaker was one of Landreville's earliest and most caustic critics and he regularly railed against giving him a pension, but he could not resist any opportunity that might make the governing Liberals look bad.

Landreville aside, the government had a lot to do. Five by-elections were pending, including one in Sudbury in late May 1967. On 8 May the governor general read a new speech from the throne, and it was expected that the ensuing debate would last at least eight days. Pearson was rumoured to be considering his retirement, and candidates were already jockeying for position in the leadership contest that would follow. In this context, the Landreville affair needed to be resolved. Instead, it was on the verge of getting out of hand.[29]

On 31 May Trudeau advised the House that when the Senate reconvened on 6 June, a resolution would be presented 'for the adoption of a joint address to His Excellency the Governor General requesting the removal of Mr. Justice Landreville from the office of judge of the Supreme Court of Ontario.' Trudeau went on to say that, if the resolution was adopted in the Senate, it will 'then be brought before this house for its consideration.'[30]

Away from Parliament Hill, the issue was becoming something of a *cause célèbre*, particularly in Sudbury.'[31] The government lost the by-election there, and it was widely understood that Sudbury did not appreciate the treatment of its adopted son. Still, every time a question about Landreville's pension was raised in the House, Pearson and Trudeau received scores of letters urging the government not to give in. Insofar as these letters accurately portrayed the public mood, Landreville, accused of everything from incompetence to corruption, had little support. Many members of parliament took the initiative to write to the prime minister to express their negative views.[32]

Landreville did have some supporters. When the cabinet met at the beginning of May, George McIlraith, the leader of the government in the House of Commons, 'expressed deep concern at the manner in which the Committee had conducted its sittings and at the nature of its report.' He noted that only three of the twelve government members on the committee had attended all the sittings, and that several of the points made by Justice Landreville in his 22 March 1967 letter to the prime minister had not been considered by the committee. McIlraith suggested that the matter be considered carefully and at length by the cabinet as a whole 'if a dangerous and damaging issue were to be avoided.' Other ministers echoed this view, and it was reported that there was 'a growing feeling in the legal profession that Judge Landreville was being impeached for actions which took place before he became a member of the Judiciary.'[33] Pearson's parliamentary secretary, John Matheson, urged the prime minister to proceed cautiously. There was a basic principle of British justice at stake. For all his faults, Landreville had done nothing as a judge to warrant impeachment.[34] That might have been true, but it was too late.

Early on 6 June 1967, just hours before the impeachment resolution was set to be introduced in the Senate, Landreville met with Ovide Laflamme, the member of parliament for Quebec-Montmorency who had been co-chair of the special joint committee. Earlier, Laflamme had been approached by the leader of the government in the Senate, J.J. Connolly, who, on behalf of the cabinet, was seeking a deal. Laflamme now told Landreville to resign because of his ill health. Following his resignation, Laflamme advised, Landreville should apply for a pension proportionate to his years of service. According to Landreville's account, Laflamme told him that this arrangement had the approval of Prime Minister Pearson. Laflamme apparently urged Landreville to put his trust and faith in him and the government, and assured him that he would personally attend to the matter.[35] Landreville did not have a lot of time to consider his situation; the impeachment resolution was introduced in the Senate later that day. A vote was scheduled for the following day.

Landreville was not prepared to resign on the basis of Laflamme's promises. He wanted better assurances than that and, on 7 June, he met with Senator Salter Hayden (like Robinette, a member of the law firm McCarthy & McCarthy). Connolly was also there. Landreville was advised that the Senate would probably adopt the special joint committee's report and pass the resolution, although there was some reason to believe that his Senate support was growing. The four members of the special joint committee who voted against the report were senators. Liberal Senator Sarto Fournier, a former mayor of Montreal, had, moreover, been quietly lobbying on Landreville's behalf.

While few senators had any personal sympathy for Landreville, there was a fairly widespread appreciation that his conduct as a judge had been satisfactory, and that an attack on this judge was an attack on the entire judiciary. In the House of Commons, Pearson had a minority government, and a number of MPs in his own party, including John Matheson, had told him they would actively oppose the government if it moved to impeach this judge.[36] Matheson, a war hero who had been badly wounded in the Battle of Ortona, understood, as a lawyer (and future judge), some of the important principles at stake and attempted to explain them to Pearson. Matheson may have been bluffing. Opposing one's party in the abstract was easy; voting against one's own party and the government, particularly in a minority parliament, was difficult. Still, there was also no way of predicting what would happen if the government's resolution was put to a vote.

Landreville, however, had no way of accurately gauging his support and little reason to believe that he could survive a government motion calling for his removal. He had no way of knowing that the cabinet believed that the resolution might fail in the Senate, and was undecided about what it would do in that result.[37] He had every reason to believe that he was about to be impeached, and, in the circumstances, resignation was his only option.[38]

Connolly had obtained some figures from the Department of Justice indicating what Landreville's prorated pension would be. Landreville was told exactly how much he would get, and how much his wife would get in the event of his death. After receiving this information, and based on the assurances that had earlier been given, Landreville dictated a resignation letter. The first draft stated that he was resigning conditionally upon receipt of a pension. Senator Connolly reviewed the letter and bluntly advised that it was politically unacceptable. The document was revised with Senator Hayden's assistance, and then given back to Connolly.

Having lurched from scandal to scandal in the past few years, the government was determined that there should be no hint of any kind of deal. Accordingly, Landreville was advised that his pension application would have to be handled separately and that he should place his faith in the prime minister and the minister of justice, both of whom, Connolly said, were sympathetic and determined that justice be done.[39] After receiving these assurances, Landreville signed the letter. The Senate had been scheduled to vote on the resolution calling for Landreville's removal later that night.

'After five difficult years and appearing in seven hearings,' Landreville wrote, 'my health and wealth are impaired. I cannot continue. In any event my usefulness as a judge has been destroyed by the publicity and harassment arising out of such proceedings.' There was no way, Landreville wrote, that he could remove the 'unfounded suspicions.' There was never any question that he had fully and faithfully discharged his duties as a judge: even Justice Rand acknowledged as much. However, Landreville could not continue as a judge and he asked the minister of justice to accept his resignation, to be effective at the end of the month.[40] The letter did not specifically request a pension on the grounds of permanent infirmity, but had referred to an impairment in 'health.' Cabinet considered the letter the next day and, after accepting Landreville's resignation, it tabled the letter in the House of Commons.

Cabinet, when reviewing Landreville's resignation letter, recognized that a decision to give him a pension would be made at some political cost. Nevertheless, Senator Connolly reminded his colleagues that 'in discussions which he had had with Judge Landreville's advisers, it had been made clear that the letter of resignation had been written in the expectation that ... favourable consideration would be given' to Landreville's pension application. Connolly pointed out that no formal 'commitments' had been made, but that the matter should be considered 'in the context of difficulties which might have arisen had the Senate rejected the Joint Address for Judge Landreville's removal from the Bench, as appeared likely in the circumstances.'[41] There was really no doubt but that a deal had been made, and it was now up to the government to honour its part of the arrangement. Cabinet, however, decided otherwise. Since no formal request had been made, and since there was no point in responding until it became necessary to do so, cabinet decided, if the question of a pension arose, that the minister of justice should indicate to the House of Commons that the matter would be considered by the government.[42]

Politics intervened, and it did not take long for questions about a pension to be asked. Diefenbaker, Landreville's stalwart supporter when the judge wished to appear before the House, had changed direction. The day after Justice Minister Trudeau announced that Landreville's resignation letter had been received, Diefenbaker was demanding to know whether the former judge had been pensioned off. The answer, for the time being, was no. 'I can only say,' Trudeau told the House on 8 June, 'that as far as I know there is no question of bounty.' Meanwhile, the NDP wanted to know if there was anything in the correspondence leading up to the resignation, and the acceptance of the resignation, which mentioned or dealt with the question of Landreville's entitlement to a pension. The answer to that question too was a truthful 'no.'[43]

Notwithstanding these denials, the question was raised almost every day in question period. The replies were more or less the same. There was no 'deal.' Trudeau claimed that there were no arrangements to provide Landreville with a pension, and that he was not 'induced' to resign on the promise of receiving one. That was not quite true, as Senator Connolly had reminded his cabinet colleagues when they first met to discuss Landreville's resignation letter on 8 June. As another of Trudeau's cabinet colleagues put it more bluntly, it was understood and agreed that Landreville would receive a pension if he stepped down without a fuss.[44] Prime Minister Pearson, Justice Minister Trudeau, and the rest of the cabinet were well aware of the exact nature of this understanding. It was fair to Landreville, and his resignation had prevented an embarrassing spectacle in the House and Senate. However, instead of simply awarding the pension, taking the inevitable criticism, and then moving on, the government allowed the issue to drag.

In response to question after question in the immediate aftermath of Landreville's resignation, the justice minister refused to state categorically that Landreville would not receive a pension.[45] The tactic did not dampen debate, because it left the issue unresolved. The door was a little ajar, and Diefenbaker, who had well-honed political instincts, knew what was coming next. 'Can the Minister of Justice now inform the House,' he asked in parliament on 20 June, 'as to whether Mr. Landreville, formerly a justice of the Supreme Court of Ontario, has filed with his department a certificate of ill health so as to qualify for an $18,666 pension?' Diefenbaker wanted Trudeau to give an assurance to the House that 'in all the circumstances this bountiful harvest will not be reaped.'[46] Trudeau replied that he was not aware of any pension application.

Needless to say, a request was on its way. On 23 June Landreville wrote to Trudeau to apply for a pension on the grounds of permanent infirmity. The Judges Act provided that the Governor in Council might grant a pension to 'a judge who has become afflicted with some permanent infirmity disabling him from the due exercise of his office, if he resigns his office.'[47] Landreville's resignation became effective at the end of the month.

In his application, Landreville provided evidence of his disabilities. Letters were enclosed from two doctors. One, from a specialist in internal medicine, diagnosed Landreville as suffering from disc disease and osteoarthritis. The second was from Dr Arthur M. Doyle, an associate professor in psychiatry and medicine at the University of Toronto. Dr Doyle, who examined Landreville on 21 June, concluded that Landreville was in a poor state:

He has become increasingly depressed for many reasons. He finds his reputation demoralized. He is unable to make fit judgements, even for family affairs. He feels quite inadequate to resume the practice of law ... His family has suffered much. His wife is in a state of anxiety, and his son who is at University decided to give up his intentions of proceeding in law because his name would make it difficult for him to pursue this profession.

Mr. Landreville himself is in a state of deep emotional distress and depression. He has no idea about his future activity. He feels that he could not go near a court-room. He feels that neither he nor his wife can appear in public without a feeling of degradation by the public opinion that has resulted from his many legal hearings, and press comments that have been derogatory to his character. His depression has been quite severe, and he has contemplated self destruction on many occasions. Recently he has been arrested for driving ninety miles an hour on highway #7 near Peterboro. At this time he was ... clutching the wheel, and even then contemplating self destruction. I understand he has never had any previous violations for his driving, but it must be remembered that this happened when he was driving to Ottawa to give his resignation.

This man is suffering from severe depressive reaction with considerable anxiety, obviously precipitated by the events of the past five years, particularly his complete frustration resulting in his decision to resign his judgeship.

Until today I have never known Judge Landreville personally, except in 1946 when I examined an accused person whom he was defending, and subsequently a few years ago ... when he was the presiding judge at a Supreme Court hearing. My examination today represents a striking difference from the lawyer and judge composed with interest, understanding and continued judgement, compared to the depressed, emotionally disturbed patient that I see today. He is indeed not fit to continue on the bench.[48]

Landreville pointed out to Trudeau that Law Society regulations prohibited former judges from practising in the courts, and that, in any event, he did not have the capacity to do so. What he did have was financial need, and he reiterated that at no time were there ever any findings made against him even hinting that he had misbehaved as a judge. Landreville therefore asked Trudeau to take whatever steps were necessary to grant him a pension.[49]

Cabinet again discussed the matter on 29 June. Virtually every minister had something to say. Senator Connolly pressed the cabinet to live up to its bargain, and pointed out that if the government turned down Landreville's pension application it would be the 'first time' that it had gone 'beyond the medical certificates brought forward by a judge who offered to resign.' Connolly also observed that there were precedents of judges being granted a full pension after serving eight years in one case, and two years in another. He urged his colleagues to honour their undertaking. Other ministers concurred. Should a pension be refused, the minister of forestry pointed out, 'Ministers would be going back on their word to Senator Connolly.'[50]

Trudeau was annoyed. He noted that Landreville had turned down an earlier opportunity to resign with pension in hand, 'when the matter had not been placed before Parliament.' Instead, he 'had preferred to bluff as long as possible, until his bluff had been called.' Trudeau also pointed out that it could easily be said that Landreville had himself brought about his psychological malaise. 'As for the allegation of need,' Trudeau suggested that 'the Government would be laughed at if it paid too much attention to it, given the extravagant ways of Mr. Landreville.'[51] Ultimately, the cabinet decided not to make a decision on Landreville's pension request. However, in the aftermath of this meeting, Trudeau's public posture changed. In response to yet another question about the government's intentions, he advised the House that he had not yet made up his mind 'whether the punishment which has been meted out to this man for something which was not done in the discharge of his duties should extend indefinitely.'[52]

Nevertheless, the government failed to act, and when he had heard nothing for several months, Landreville again wrote to the justice minister. This time, he decided to be more blunt. He told Trudeau that just prior to tendering his resignation, 'indications' were given to him that a pension would follow. Trudeau knew this to be true. Landreville also informed the justice minister that he needed the money. His wife had nothing, and all he owned was the modest bungalow in Mexico and an even more modest property – 'a shack really' – in northern Ontario. His expenses had been enormous; more than $30,000 had been spent on legal fees. All he wanted was eleven-fifteenths of his pension, reflecting the number of years he had served on the bench.[53] Trudeau advised Landreville that the matter was being studied by the government.

There the issue stood until Montreal mayor Jean Drapeau, one of Landreville's oldest friends, intervened. He arranged for Landreville and Trudeau to meet on 21 November, in the minister's West Block office. Landreville asked for justice, and he told Trudeau about the accommodation he and Laflamme had reached, not to mention the 'understandings' he had received from 'others.' Trudeau questioned some of Landreville's actions, particularly the timing of his decision to resign, given that he had some prospect of success in the Senate. Trudeau also told the ex-judge that he had been repeatedly questioned about the case in the House, and that if Landreville were to receive a pension, he, Trudeau, would be a target. He nevertheless agreed to give the matter further thought.[54]

Trudeau, independently wealthy himself, had difficulty in understanding that others could be in straitened circumstances. More important, however, he had other things on his mind. On 14 December 1967 the seventy-year-old Pearson announced his resignation as leader of the Liberal Party of Canada. No one had expected Pearson to stay on to fight an election against the new Conservative leader, Robert Stanfield, although it was not immediately obvious who his successor would be. There was no shortage of volunteers. Within ten days in January, seven Liberals announced plans to compete for the prize at a convention set for Ottawa in April. Cabinet ministers Paul Martin, Paul Hellyer, and Mitchell Sharp were viewed as the front-runners, but none of them seemed likely to capture the attention of delegates. In the meantime, media attention began to focus, increasingly, on the justice minister. Trudeau entered the race on 16 February 1968.[55]

Landreville was understandably concerned, given these events, that his case would not receive the attention he thought it deserved. His pension application could easily be overlooked by this government, and he had no reason to believe, should the Conservatives come to power, that they would honour the understanding that had been reached.

Landreville again approached the prime minister, but Pearson refused to see him.[56] On 4 March Landreville wrote to Trudeau, and sent a copy to every cabinet minister. Setting out his version of the events that led him to resign, Landreville 'begged' Trudeau to place his request before cabinet. He was, he added, fifty-eight years old, without a profession, in ill health, and in financial need. He pointed out that 'there were representations clearly made to me, corroborated by facts, which guide the

Cabinet in the exercise of its discretion.'[57] Landreville reiterated the circumstances that led him to resign, including the nature and source of the representations he had received. Behind the scenes, Senator Connolly was pressing both Trudeau and the prime minister to live up to their word. The effort was wasted.[58]

On 5 March Trudeau finally replied. He had been about to write to Landreville when the latest letter arrived, he said. 'My Cabinet colleagues and I have given very anxious consideration to the merits of your request, and it is with regret that I must inform you that the Government has decided, at this time, against taking the steps necessary to grant you a pension or annuity.'[59] In fact, the cabinet had not yet formally considered the request, although it had discussed it the previous year. When it met on 7 March, it denied the application.[60] How then could Trudeau claim, on 5 March, that cabinet had, in effect, considered the matter, when it did not do so for another two days? The question was an important one, and it would return to haunt Trudeau.

Grasping at straws, Landreville interpreted Trudeau's letter as indicating that the government had decided to grant him a pension, but had chosen not to do so 'at this time.' On 13 March he wrote to Trudeau and asked when the government intended to complete the negotiation.[61] Trudeau responded the following week that the government had decided against providing Landreville with a pension.[62] In the meantime, however, in response to a question from John Diefenbaker – no longer opposition leader, but still a commanding presence in the House – Trudeau advised the House that the government had 'decided at this time against taking the steps necessary to grant Mr. Landreville a pension or annuity.'[63] Landreville continued to believe that, as no 'final decision' had been made, there was still a possibility of convincing the government to change its mind.

In the meantime, the Liberal leadership race was in full swing. Although he had been in parliament less than three years, and in the cabinet less than twelve months, the justice minister was different enough from the Liberal veterans to gain enormous attention. Trudeau was irreverent, brilliant, and French, and he projected a youthful image, although he was almost fifty years old. He also appeared as a reluctant leader, a valuable trait in an era of public restlessness and disenchantment brought about by the scandals, disappointments, and turmoil of the 1960s. Paul Martin's early lead in the polls quickly evaporated. Quiet, behind-the-scenes support by Lester Pearson undoubtedly helped Trudeau, but the battle was still close. On 6 April Trudeau captured the prize.[64]

Fourteen days later, on 20 April, Trudeau was sworn in as prime minister, and on 23 April the new leader dissolved the House and called a general election. 'Trudeaumania' arrived in full force. Trudeau said little of substance in the campaign; his musings on a 'just society,' however, drew remarkable crowds – 40,000 in Toronto and 35,000 in Montreal as voting day approached.[65] Stanfield ran what was widely viewed as a solid campaign for the Progressive Conservatives, but in contrast to Trudeau he appeared as a stodgy relic from an earlier day. The results, on 25 June, surprised no one. Trudeau and his Liberals won 45.3 per cent of the vote and a clear majority of 155 seats. John Turner, himself a leadership contender and future prime minister, was appointed minister of justice in the new government. It did not take long before Landreville began a renewed campaign of appeals directed at him.

The new justice minister met with Landreville, and then advised him by letter that he was not prepared 'to propose or sponsor legislation that would in my judgment be necessary to authorize the payment of a pension to you.'[66] Landreville continued to write to Lester Pearson, and the two finally met at Pearson's home in August 1968. Pearson promised to do what he could as a 'civilian.' He made some inquiries, but told Landreville that there was really nothing he could do. Pearson was out and Trudeau was in. The former prime minister did, however, 'regret the whole business.'[67]

Landreville moved around a lot: to San Diego first, where he wandered the waterfront and played chess with other retired men; then to Mexico, to his second home, 'Landra Villa,' after his wife was badly injured in an automobile accident; and finally back to Ottawa, where he had been born. His letter campaign did not flag. He continued to write to the prime minister, the justice minister, to sympathetic reporters, to his friends in government and outside. He asked everyone and anyone for their help. Meanwhile, his case attracted political and public attention. His name was brought up on numerous occasions in the House of Commons. Members of the public wrote letters urging the government not to give him a pension, reinforcing the unsympathetic opinion found among most House members.

Eventually Landreville returned to the practice of law with an Ottawa firm, Binks, Chilcott, Lynch & Simpson. Binks was a Tory and a close friend of the leader of the opposition, Robert Stanfield. He raised the Landreville case with Stanfield, who agreed not to make a fuss if a pension was granted. J.J. Robinette intervened and contacted Donald Macdonald, a colleague from the McCarthy & McCarthy law firm, and now a member of the Liberal government, to urge him to do what he could.[68] These efforts failed, but an important message was communicated: if the Rand report was set aside, the government would almost certainly grant a pension. The government had a majority in the House, and it was early in its term. Whatever political considerations might have influenced its decision not to grant a pension in 1967 or early 1968 were gone.

Moreover, Rand had died in January 1969. Writing to a friend after he heard the news, Landreville said: 'It was eight years too late,' adding, 'May God bless his soul, he needs that blessing.'[69] Landreville was, however, more concerned with temporal matters, and began to work on securing justice from the courts, if it was not to be forthcoming from the executive.

He consulted various lawyers about the matter, but nothing was accomplished until he retained Gordon Fripp Henderson for the case in September 1971. It was an inspired choice. Henderson, a bencher and a future president of the Canadian Bar Association, had a bit of the renegade in him, and from time to time he took on unpopular causes, because that was his responsibility and because it was right. Landreville presented exactly such a case.

After Henderson agreed to take Landreville on, he sometimes came to regret his decision.[70] Landreville was a difficult client, one who did not hesitate to bring Henderson's real and imagined deficiencies to his attention. Landreville documented every conversation and instruction in writing. He took, as lawyers say, a real interest in his case. At the same time, he continued to possess a certain charm, and he was as effusive in his praise when things went well as he was scathing in his criticism when they did not. Henderson took it all in stride. He and his firm were essentially acting without fee, since only disbursements were paid. As it turned out, the brief would extend over the course of the next ten years.

9

Vindication?

The case began, as most cases do, with a meeting with the client. Preparation of legal research came next, and the opinion of J.R. Cartwright, the former chief justice of Canada, was sought. Cartwright, who had joined Gordon Henderson's firm, Gowling & Henderson, as counsel on his retirement from the bench, believed that there was an arguable case that Landreville was entitled to a pension under the Judges Act. There was little chance of suppressing the Rand report, Cartwright opined, because too much time had elapsed.[1] Landreville nevertheless urged Henderson and his team to attack the report and obtain his pension.

Time was short. Rand had presented his report on 11 August 1966. There were both federal and provincial limitation periods, and they required, with certain exceptions, that legal actions be initiated within six years. Henderson, Cartwright, and another senior Gowling & Henderson lawyer, E. Peter Newcombe, worked on the case throughout the summer of 1972. They were later joined by Y.A. George Hynna, Robert M. Nelson, and George Addy. Various jurisdictional questions were addressed. Should proceedings be initiated before Ontario courts, or before the Federal Court? Were Landreville's claims for a pension and for the suppression of the Rand report somehow inconsistent, because in the former claim he said he was disabled, and in the latter he said that Rand had slurred his reputation? And what would the courts say about the delay? Almost six years had elapsed before Landreville took action against the

Rand report, and a long period had passed since he was denied his pension. What had he been waiting for?

By the end of August 1972 the legal papers were ready and filed in court. Two separate legal actions were placed before the Federal Court. The first sought to set aside the Rand report. It was invalid, Henderson and the other lawyers claimed. The relief sought was straightforward: a declaration suppressing Rand's report. The action for the pension claim was even simpler in scope. It stated that Landreville was entitled to support by reason of infirmity as provided for in the Judges Act, and that the Governor in Council had not, as it was required to do, considered his application and reached a decision with respect to it.

It was decided to proceed first with the action aimed at quashing Rand's report. What Landreville wanted was a declaration that Rand had been invalidly appointed and that his report was, therefore, *ultra vires*. Moreover, Landreville also sought through judicial review a writ of *certiorari* to have the records of the commission removed to the court and to have the report set aside. The Crown responded with an interlocutory motion seeking to strike Landreville's statement of claim. The matter of the jurisdiction of the Federal Court to grant the relief Landreville sought proceeded to a hearing in the fall of 1973 before Mr Justice Pratte.

The Department of Justice, representing Her Majesty under whose authority Rand had served as royal commissioner, took the position that Landreville's claim should not proceed because the Federal Court was without jurisdiction to grant any of the relief he wanted. As is common in cases of this kind, it was decided to determine the jurisdictional issue first, and three specific questions were asked: Did the Federal Court have the jurisdiction to issue an order of *certiorari* against the Queen? Did the Federal Court have the jurisdiction to quash Rand's report? Could the Federal Court grant a general declaration of the kind sought by Landreville?

In brief, Landreville made three main legal claims. First, he argued that the conduct of a judge of a superior court could not be the subject of an inquiry under the Inquiries Act, and that for this and other reasons the order in council establishing the Rand Inquiry, and everything that took place as a result, was unconstitutional, unlawful, and void. The second claim asserted that in making his report, Rand had failed to act judicially, that he acted outside of and exceeded his jurisdiction, and that he ignored the principles of natural justice. In support of this claim, the pleadings pointed out that Rand's report went beyond his mandate, that he made findings about irrelevant matters, and that he introduced into his report statements of fact for which there was no evidence. Rand also came to conclusions about Landreville's character and personality, and appended to his report a copy of the Law Society report, which had not been properly proved and had been issued without giving Landreville an opportunity to be heard. Finally, Landreville sought a declaration that Rand violated section 13 of the Inquiries Act, because at the conclusion of the evidence in his hearing he stated that the proceedings were adjourned *sine die*. Yet he wrote his report without giving Landreville any notice that he intended to find him guilty of misconduct.

On 11 December 1973 Mr Justice Pratte issued his reasons for decision. He held that there was no need to determine whether *certiorari* lay against the Crown, as there was no basis to proceed with such a claim in this particular case. The *certiorari* remedy, Pratte pointed out, lies only to quash something that is a determination or a decision. Rand's report was neither. Pratte readily disposed of the second question as well. He held that the Federal Court had no jurisdiction to suppress Rand's report. He noted that the report itself had no legal effect. Pratte then turned to the heart of the matter: whether the Court had the jurisdiction to issue a general declaration of the kind sought by Landreville – namely, that Rand had violated section 13 of the Inquiries Act.

It was commonly agreed, Pratte wrote, that the court had jurisdiction in a proper case to grant declaratory relief against the Crown or the attorney general. 'The plaintiff,' Pratte wrote, 'seeks two declarations: first, that the appointment of the Commissioner was *ultra vires* and, second, that the Commissioner did not conduct the inquiry as he should.'[2] The Department of Justice argued that the Court should decline to grant this relief because it was purely academic. Government lawyers had argued that the inquiry was conducted and the report released years earlier; no benefit could possibly be reached in issuing one or more declarations of the kind Landreville sought.

The matter was not moot, according to Henderson. He argued that a declaration that the commissioner had conducted his inquiry in disregard of principles of natural justice would contribute to a restoration of Landreville's reputation. It might convince the government that it was right and just to compensate Landreville for the damage suffered by him as a consequence of the inquiry. Henderson also took the position that it was in the public interest to know that the conduct of a superior court judge cannot be the subject of an inquiry under the Inquiries Act.

Faced with these two opposing positions, Pratte had to make a decision: 'The question to be answered is therefore whether this Court has jurisdiction to make a declaration on a legal issue in a case where the declaration would be devoid of legal effects but would likely have some practical effects.'[3] Pratte undertook a lengthy review of the law, and concluded that the Court did have the jurisdiction to issue such a declaration. This finding constituted an important development in Canadian law.[4] Landreville's 'reputation' may not have had legal significance to the government lawyers, but it was important to Landreville. Pratte's decision, establishing that declarations could be given even if no legal consequence would necessarily follow, was critical. It provided Landreville with a legal basis for continuing his claim. Pratte's decision did not determine any of the questions at issue, but it did allow the case to proceed. Landreville had won an important first victory.

If Landreville was hoping for speedy justice, however, he was quickly disappointed. By August 1974 his action against the Rand report was in abeyance. Trial dates came and went. The Department of Justice demanded particulars. What irrelevant matters, the department wanted to know, had Rand considered in his report? How had Rand failed to act judicially? Lengthy pleadings and pages and pages of particulars were exchanged. More legal wrangling ensued. In the meantime, his pension suit had not yet even reached the discovery stage. That did not occur until the fall of 1974, and even then that process barely began. Eventually, it was determined that the pension action would proceed to trial in March 1975; the one attacking the Rand report in April or May. Those dates too were postponed. Landreville was becoming increasingly concerned. Many of his key witnesses, such as Lester Pearson, Guy Favreau, and Senators Connolly and Hayden, had either passed away or were becoming very advanced in age. Landreville himself was not getting any younger, although his health had greatly improved.

Eventually, the application attacking the Rand report proceeded to trial before Mr Justice Frank U. Collier, an independent westerner, who heard evidence and arguments on 2, 3, and 4 February 1977. Henderson made three principal submissions. First, that the Rand Commission was not validly constituted, and that the only procedure to be followed was set out in section 99 of the British North America Act. Second, that if the Rand Commission was validly constituted, the commissioner lost jurisdiction by exceeding his terms of reference. And third, again assuming the legality of the commission, that the commissioner failed to comply with the requirements of section 13 of the Inquiries Act. On 7 April 1977 Collier issued his reasons for decision. After a thorough review of the background facts, he turned his attention to the issues. Collier found that the conduct of judges was a matter connected with good government, and so the Governor in Council was authorized to order an inquiry under the Inquiries Act. For the sake of completeness, or because he was aware of the possibility of appeal, Collier also observed, for whatever it was worth, that Landreville's request for the inquiry was 'not a real or free one';[5] and, if there was no constitutional power to initiate this inquiry, 'then the plaintiff's consent or request for it, and the agreement not to object to it, cannot cure the defect.'[6]

With this issue out of the way, Collier confronted the conclusions Rand had reached about Landreville's acquisition of NONG stock, testimony before various tribunals, and role in the Sudbury franchise negotiations. It was not for him, Collier wrote, 'to decide whether the evidence or materials referred to by the Commissioner ... were relevant, cogent or trustworthy.' Nor was it his job 'to decide whether the comments of the Commissioner, on what amounted to the personality and credibility of the plaintiff, were justified or valid.' In Collier's view, the royal commission's terms of reference were wide enough to embrace those portions of the report and its conclusions. 'The quarrel,' he wrote, 'is really with how the Commissioner dealt with the issue, and the facts or matters he chose to rely on. I do not think his method of dealing with the question, though others might have done differently, amounted to going beyond the terms of reference, and so losing jurisdiction.'[7]

That left section 13. It provided that 'No report shall be made against any person until reasonable notice has been given to him of the charge of misconduct alleged against him and he has been allowed full opportunity to be heard in person or by counsel.' Henderson had argued that Rand's findings, in his second and third conclusions, constituted a finding of misconduct which nullified the report, because Landreville was never notified that these findings would be made, nor was he ever given the opportunity to make representations with respect to them. The transcript of the Rand proceedings clearly indicate that the commission adjourned *sine die*. In Henderson's submission, after this adjournment, but before issuing his report, Rand should have given Landreville the opportunity to respond to the misconduct charge. Obviously, section 13 rights arise only after a commissioner has reached a tentative conclusion that a person has committed some misconduct, and, having reached that conclusion, the commissioner is statutorily required to notify that individual, specify the allegations of misconduct, and afford the person concerned with a fair and proper opportunity to prepare and present a defence.

Henderson asserted, for example, that if Landreville had known that the giving of evidence before the Ontario Securities Commission and as a prosecution witness in the Farris trial would be found to constitute 'gross contempt,' he might have led some evidence of his own in rebuttal. At the same time that Rand was investigating Landreville, Mr Justice Wishart Spence was conducting his royal commission into the Gerda Munsinger affair, Canada's first major parliamentary sex scandal. Allegations of misconduct were made in that inquiry against a number of people, and Mr Justice Spence notified all of them of their section 13 rights.[8] Given the potentially wide scope of royal commissions, combined with the power of the commissioner to set his or her own procedure, section 13 provided extremely modest protection to individuals subject to inquiry. Rand either forgot about the existence of the provision or chose to ignore it, determined as he was to secure Landreville's removal from the bench. Collier now set that wrong right. The assertion, he wrote, 'of gross contempt was a very serious one.'[9] Rand had written in his report that 'there was conscious contempt before all three tribunals; it may or may not have passed the borders of criminality; but to confuse, to raise doubts by the juxtaposition of contrived and emphatic assertion and nullifying qualification and reservations, is not to be distinguished in effect from deliberate falsity.'[10] In Collier's view, this statement was nothing less than a finding by Rand that Landreville had committed 'perjury.'[11]

Counsel for the Crown asserted that Landreville was notified, by Rand's terms of reference, that he was charged with misconduct and that findings would be made with respect to that. After all, what did Landreville think the Rand Commission was about, if not an investigation into allegations of his misconduct? Was it realistic for Rand to reconvene his commission to advise Landreville that the allegations were proven? Investigations lead to findings and reports. However, Collier, having reviewed the requirements of section 13 and the commissioner's mandate, held that Rand had strayed beyond his terms of reference and violated the Inquiries Act in the process:

I do not agree that the matter of gross contempt of the other tribunals can be said to be included, by implication or necessary intendment, in the terms of reference.

This was a somewhat unusual Royal Commission. The majority of Royal Commissions seem to be constituted to investigate a particular subject, thing or state of affairs. Rarely do they relate to one person. This Commission was, however, directed to the investigation of one particular person and his dealings with a certain company, its officers, or its shares. The Commissioner was requested to inquire into those dealings and to express an opinion whether, in the course of them, there had been misbehaviour by the plaintiff as a judge, or whether the plaintiff, by the dealings, had proven himself unfit. I am unable to see how those general terms indicated to the plaintiff there would, or might be, an allegation of gross contempt of certain tribunals, amounting to misconduct.[12]

Rand should have given Landreville notice of the allegations of misconduct set out in his second and third conclusions. He had not done so, and that left Collier with no choice but to find 'with diffidence' that Rand 'failed to comply with the mandatory requirements of Section 13 of the Inquiries Act.' Collier added that he had 'come slowly to that conclusion.'

The Commissioner was an eminent and renowned judge of the Supreme Court of Canada ... As a mere trial bench judge, I feel some reluctance in concluding that this distinguished Commissioner omitted to comply with one of the terms of the statute governing his inquiry; that this was error in law. But my function cannot be affected by diffidence or reluctance. I am required to apply the law, as I conceive it to be, to the issues between the parties to this suit.[13]

There were only two matters left for Collier. The Crown argued that the case should be dismissed because of 'the doctrine of laches' – a legal principle that prevents parties from seeking redress if they wait too long to assert their rights. This doctrine requires the passage of a substantial length of time, which was certainly present in this case, but also necessitates the presence of some prejudice to the other side caused by the delay. There was no prejudice to the Crown in this case, and so its application was dismissed.

So too was an application by the Crown that the case be dismissed because any declaration issued would be without legal effect. That issue had been earlier determined by Mr Justice Pratte. Having heard the evidence, Collier was satisfied that a declaration of his findings would serve a useful purpose. It will be, he wrote, 'a matter of public record that the plaintiff did not, at the commission hearing, have full opportunity to refute the allegation or finding he had committed, as a judge, gross contempt in his testimony before certain tribunals.' Collier also noted that Landreville had launched a parallel proceeding seeking a declaration that he was entitled to a pension as of the date of his resignation as a judge. 'It may be,' Collier concluded with some understatement, 'that the declaration I find he is here entitled to will serve some useful purpose in the prosecution of that other suit.'[14]

The effect of the judgment was to declare that Landreville had been entitled to, but did not receive, notice of Rand's second and third conclusions. There was still the first conclusion, that Landreville's acquisition of NONG stock 'justifiably gives rise to grave suspicion of impropriety.' Since Landreville had failed to remove that suspicion and to prove his innocence, he was understandably concerned that that conclusion, which had not been effectively set aside, would give the government a justification for maintaining the status quo on his pension request. As such, it provided a basis for tabling Rand's report, establishing the special joint committee, and introducing the impeachment resolution in parliament leading to his resignation.[15]

In the meantime, the discoveries, pre-trial legal manoeuvres, and delays in Landreville's pension suit finally came to an end. The Department of Justice had been dragging its feet, but there is only so much an unwilling litigant can do to delay a civil proceeding. However, just before that case was to begin in the spring of 1978, the minister of justice and attorney general of Canada, Ron Basford, contacted Henderson. 'In light of the Reasons for Judgment of Mr. Justice Collier in the other action brought by your client in respect of the Rand Report,' Basford was 'prepared to see that Mr. Landreville's application for a pension is once more brought to the attention of Cabinet so that any decision taken by the Cabinet can then be considered by the Governor in Council.' He did not wish unduly to raise expectations. 'My desire in writing you,' he concluded, 'is to tell you that in light of the comments of Mr. Justice Collier, I, as the Attorney General, will review the matter, hear whatever representations you want to make, and have the matter considered by Cabinet.'[16]

Basford met with Henderson and Hynna in early May 1978. The minister told Landreville's lawyers that the pension application had been dealt with once in cabinet, and so their claim that Trudeau's letter denying the request was premature was simply without foundation. In preparing his case, Henderson sought access to the cabinet minutes and other related documents concerning Landreville's pension application. Not surprisingly, the Department of Justice asserted that all the cabinet minutes were secret. A provision of the Federal Court Act, section 41(2), allowed ministers to submit affidavits stating that the 'production or discovery of a document or its contents would be injurious to international relations, national defence or security, or to federal-provincial relations, or that it would disclose a confidence of the Queen's Privy Council for Canada.' The mere filing of such an affidavit served as a complete defence to any disclosure request.[17] The judge was not even entitled to examine the document in order to assess whether the exemption was being properly claimed. Section 41(2) was a Draconian provision, and one subjected to

considerable and indiscriminate abuse. In the early 1980s, when comprehensive freedom of information legislation was passed, the provision was
finally repealed, although cabinet documents could still be subject to
exemption under the Access to Information Act.

When Landreville's case was proceeding to trial, section 41(2) was in
full force and effect. On 27 May 1976 C.M. Drury, the minister of state for
science and technology and minister of public works, who had had no
direct involvement in the affair, submitted an affidavit declaring that disclosure of any documents relating to Landreville's pension application
would violate this provision.[18] An appendix to the affidavit listed all the
cabinet meetings at which Landreville was discussed. The oddest thing
about the affidavit was that the last date given, 7 March 1967, was just
three days after Landreville had again asked Trudeau for a decision and
two days after Trudeau wrote to state that the cabinet had rejected Landreville's request. Moreover, Landreville had received encouraging letters from Trudeau's cabinet colleagues, and these letters were dated after
Trudeau claimed that the cabinet had already considered the question.
The Drury affidavit claimed that the production or discovery of any of
these documents would constitute a confidence of the Queen's Privy
Council for Canada.[19] This action deprived Landreville of a vital source of
information.

Accordingly, Henderson rejected Basford's assertion that the cabinet
had actually considered the matter. Landreville was entitled, his lawyer
said, to know that his pension application had been properly considered
by the Governor in Council as was required under the Judges Act. It simply was not proper for the government to hide behind cabinet secrecy
when circumstantial evidence led to the conclusion that, when Trudeau
advised Landreville that his application was denied, cabinet had not yet
met to consider his request. While cabinet may have discussed the
request when it met on 29 June 1967, it did not make any decision with
respect to it. Moreover, cabinet did not notify Landreville that it had
made a decision. In none of the correspondence is there any suggestion
that the request was determined on that date. In fact, cabinet deliberately
decided not to decide when it was called upon to do so in the immediate
aftermath of Landreville's resignation.

The issue now before the courts was whether the Governor in Council
had ever, as was statutorily required, turned its attention to Landreville's
pension request. Now, almost twenty years after the fact, with the cabinet
minutes released under the Access to Information Act, what really happened can be told. When Trudeau wrote Landreville advising him that

the cabinet had considered and rejected his pension request, he was not telling the truth. When cabinet met in the immediate aftermath of Landreville's renewed pension request, and following Trudeau's rejection of that request, the justice minister advised his colleagues that he had already written Landreville turning him down, and that his letter doing so had been approved by the prime minister and the leader of the government in the Senate.[20] Following discussion, at which time Trudeau was again reminded that Landreville had been 'encouraged' to 'expect a pension if he resigned,' cabinet again decided not to take 'any further action at this time on a pension for former Justice Landreville.'

Based on the circumstantial evidence that he had available, Henderson had correctly figured out that the Governor in Council had never actually considered Landreville's pension request. This explained to Henderson why the government took so many measures to ensure that its records were not released. After all, if the Governor in Council had considered Landreville's request, it could simply prove that it had done so, and having proved that point it was unlikely that any judge would interfere with what was clearly an executive act. The fact was that Landreville was entitled under law to have his request for a pension determined, yet the Governor in Council, while it had several times considered the request, had never reached a decision with respect to it.

Once that legal position, and the consequences flowing from it, were made clear, Henderson proceeded to outline the merits of Landreville's case to Basford. The justice minister was apparently interested in Landreville's financial situation, and was advised that he was receiving a salary of $12,000 per year from his legal practice, such as it was, and had no other income to speak of. The discussion then turned to settlement. Henderson advised the justice minister that Landreville would accept $100,000 tax free plus his legal costs. The discussion concluded with Basford requesting further particulars on Landreville's financial situation.[21]

This information was provided, and both Landreville and Henderson were hopeful that the matter would finally be resolved without going to trial. When Basford departed the justice ministry on 2 August 1978 and was succeeded by Otto Lang, it seemed it might be necessary to start all over again. Landreville urged Henderson to set the matter down quickly for trial, and a trial date of 27 September 1978 was set. Seven years had now passed since Landreville first approached Henderson about taking his case. One week before the trial was about to begin, Henderson consented to an adjournment. Landreville was furious, but Henderson explained that he had been in touch with Lang's office and the minister was committed to resolving the matter once and for all.[22]

Landreville still wanted a lump sum representing pension arrears, future entitlement, and legal costs. This the government could not accept. Lang did not want to bring the matter before cabinet. That would simply provoke all sorts of debate and might fail to achieve the desired result. Since Landreville was now working full time as a lawyer, he could hardly claim that he was incapacitated by reasons of health. Lang had a simpler solution in mind – payment of some sum in settlement of Landreville's suit. This would not require Lang to bring the matter before cabinet, and the settlement terms could be worded in some way so that the government was not assigned responsibility for Rand's failure to provide Landreville with due process in the preparation of his report.

Like any good lawyer and judge, Landreville knew that there was no possibility of guaranteeing legal results – predicting them was hard enough. Moreover, with Collier's judgment on the record, Landreville believed he had restored his good name. He therefore told Henderson to settle the suit. An election was expected any day, and there was no reason to believe that a new government – and one was expected after more than a decade of Trudeau rule – would be at all sympathetic to Landreville's case. On 3 October 1978 Henderson wrote to the Department of Justice. Explaining that Landreville and his wife each had a future life expectancy of about thirteen years, a future pension of $30,000 annually required a lump-sum settlement of $264,000. Henderson further calculated Landreville's arrears as amounting to $175,000, and he asked for $15,000 in legal costs.[23]

Settlement discussions continued through the fall of 1978. As each day passed, Landreville became more and more concerned that parliament would be dissolved and an election held before the settlement discussions were successfully completed. He was very anxious to proceed. He claimed that he had no money, and his case was not even set down for trial. Finally, on 12 December 1978 Henderson wrote to the department and insisted that the matter be resolved before the end of the year.[24] The Department of Justice considered an annual pension of $30,000 too rich, and proposed a settlement providing for a pension of $20,000. Landreville refused. He would settle for $22,000 a year and not a penny less.[25] The discussions continued, and Lang was succeeded as minister of justice by Marc Lalonde. Then, as Landreville feared, in March 1979 an election was called for May. Landreville contacted Henderson and insisted that the matter be immediately set down for trial.

Henderson had other ideas. He had been advised that it was not the time to 'rile' Trudeau. Rather, he advised, it would be better to wait until after the election was over. The government would then deal with the matter early in its term.[26] To press the issue now would embarrass Trudeau, and this would not be appreciated as his government sought a new mandate. Landreville had heard it all before, but was willing to accept Henderson's advice.

On 22 May 1979 Canadians went to the polls and defeated Trudeau's Liberals. The Conservatives, under leader Joe Clark, were the new minority government. Landreville pressed for a summer trial, but the chief justice of the Federal Court refused. A new trial date was set, 29 October 1979. In the meantime, Landreville's law partner Ken Binks, who was well connected with the incoming Tories, was raising the matter privately with the minister of justice, Senator Jacques Flynn.

Binks and Flynn met on 10 July 1979. Binks reviewed the case, presenting the minister with a copy of Basford's letter of the previous April and briefing him on the settlement discussions that took place after that date. According to Binks, the Landreville matter was 'unfinished business' and should be dealt with without further delay. Flynn promised to investigate. He told Binks to advise Henderson to see him in August.[27] That meeting took place on 7 August, and it went well. At Flynn's request, Henderson wrote to the deputy minister, Roger Tassé, the following day, bringing him up to date on the dispute which was now just two months away from trial. Henderson pointed to two facts that had never been questioned: that Landreville served with distinction as a judge, and that when he resigned from office he was incapable, by reasons of mental and physical infirmity, of continuing to serve. Henderson also noted that Collier had effectively quashed the Rand report, and that this report had been the basis for the action taken by the Special Joint Committee of the Senate and House. Landreville was, Henderson told Tassé, in financial need and remained willing to provide complete disclosure to this effect. The whole sad affair ought to be resolved on 'its merits and on compassionate grounds.'[28]

After the Department of Justice considered the matter, Henderson was advised that the trial should proceed. The Clark government would not take responsibility for the unfinished business of its predecessor. Henderson began in earnest to prepare his case, and it proceeded to trial at the end of October 1979 before Mr Justice Collier, who, of course, was well acquainted with the underlying facts.

At the commencement of the proceedings, Collier expressed the view that it would be difficult, in the absence of the cabinet minutes, to do justice between the parties. He asked Department of Justice lawyers J.A. Scollin and Leslie Holland to inquire whether the materials requested could be released. However, even if the government was willing to release them, political convention dictated that it could not do so. It is established practice in Canada that a succeeding government does not have access to the cabinet minutes and documents of the preceding government. Collier was advised of this fact. It did not, however, satisfy him. The failure to provide Landreville with these documents, Collier stated, affected his ability 'to do true and real justice between these parties.' The Federal Court judge was aware that he must decide the case on the basis of the evidence before him.

I cannot come to a decision not to decide. My decision when I reach it, will be, as I see it, to dismiss the action or to give some kind of declaratory relief. In reaching my decision and recording my reasons, I may well refer to the state of the evidence and the position taken by the previous administration and by the present administration in respect of these Cabinet Minutes and Memorandum. My remarks may well not be flattering to either group, particularly if I think true justice is not being done.

I am therefore making certain assumptions ... The decision to invoke section 41 of the Federal Court Act was, I assume, authorized by the then Attorney General. Since then the Government has changed. Nevertheless it is my view the conduct of the defence of this action and the instructions in respect of it are with the present administration and the present, presumably, Attorney General. In my opinion, one cannot because of some political convention or understanding, avoid giving the necessary instructions to the Deputy Attorney General and to Council as to the position taken at this Trial ...

To sum up and put it as briefly as I can, these matters I raise cannot, to my mind, be brushed aside because of some understanding in respect of changes in Government. Nor can the conduct and instructions in respect of this law suit in October and November of 1979 be somehow said to be that of the previous advisors to the Defendant and not that of the Canadian people present. Nor can it be said that the instructions really come just from the Deputy Attorney General in my view.

Lastly and purely as a footnote, I understand that there is tentative legislation in hand at present which will, if enacted, largely do away with section 41 of the Federal Court Act.[29]

Collier was, in effect, telling the government that while it was legally entitled, pursuant to the Federal Court Act, not to provide the documents in question, its failure to do so would be held against it. A settlement by the Crown would have been the prudent course, but the trial continued. Henderson argued that Landreville ought to have been given a pension when he resigned because he was 'afflicted with some permanent infirmity disabling him from the due execution of his office.' Collier was asked to issue a declaration to that effect. As an alternative, Henderson asked the judge to direct the Governor in Council to consider Landreville's pension application.

It was Henderson's submission that the Governor in Council, when acting under the Judges Act, fulfils a judicial or quasi-judicial function. In his view, the Judges Act required the Governor in Council to consider pension requests, but in Landreville's case there was no evidence indicating that his pension application was ever put before it. Moreover, it was Henderson's position that, although the Judges Act stated that the Governor in Council 'may' give a pension to a judge who has become infirm, the independence of the judiciary required that the word 'may' be interpreted, for the purposes of this provision, as 'shall.'

Landreville gave evidence on his own behalf. He testified about his meetings with Laflamme, Lang, and Connolly, not to mention his encounters with Justice Minister Trudeau and his deputy, D.S. Maxwell. Landreville told the Court about the assurances he had received that a pension would be forthcoming. The Crown objected to all this evidence on the basis that it was hearsay. Hearsay, evidence of what one has heard rather than what one knows from first-hand knowledge to be true, is generally inadmissible in civil proceedings on the basis that its probative value is limited. There are a number of exceptions to the hearsay rule, and one of these exceptions permits the introduction of such evidence, not for the purpose of establishing the truth of that evidence but for establishing the hearer's state of mind. On the basis of this exception, Collier allowed the evidence in to show why Landreville 'took the courses of action he testified to.'[30] At the conclusion of the proceedings, the decision was reserved.

On 29 April 1980 Collier delivered his decision. Given his remarks to the Crown, presented in open court, his decision was not a great surprise. He found, just as Henderson had argued, that section 23 of the Judges Act indicated in effect that the Governor in Council must give consideration to a pension for an infirm judge; otherwise, 'the accepted theory of the independence of the judiciary is transgressed; the intention and effect of the applicable provisions of the *B. N. A. Act* is eroded, if not contradicted.'

Collier noted that 'the temptation by the executive to intervene, even with no improper motive, in the carrying out of judicial functions, is not unknown.' Accordingly, 'more than mere lip service must be paid to those constitutional safeguards.'[31]

The result of this finding was that the Governor in Council must, when a judge seeks a pension for reason of infirmity, consider the application. The pension decision, Collier wrote, 'cannot, to my mind, be postponed indefinitely. Nor, in my opinion, can the Governor in Council refuse to decide.'[32] But this is exactly what had occurred in Landreville's case. In the examinations for discovery it was established, when justice department officials testified, that all section 23 applications were considered by either a special committee of council, the committee of cabinet that handles regulations and other proposed orders in council on a regular basis, or by the full cabinet. The decision of the ministers was always recorded in the form of an order that was brought forward to the governor general for signature and thereafter issued as an order in council. There was no evidence that this long-established procedure was followed in Landreville's case.

The Crown argued that Drury's affidavit, listing in an appendix various cabinet meetings when Landreville was discussed, was proof that the cabinet had discharged its statutory responsibility under section 23 and had considered Landreville's pension request. In Collier's view, the Drury affidavit proved nothing of the kind. The Crown had refused to disclose those documents, claiming cabinet secrecy, and it did not call any evidence at trial. It was open to the government to lead evidence that Landreville's application was considered in accordance with section 23 of the Judges Act; it did not do so, and Collier was left with little choice but to conclude that the cabinet had decided not to take the steps either to grant or to refuse Landreville's pension application. Trudeau's letter of 5 March 1968 established this fact. Collier went on to find that cabinet was legally obliged to render a decision, one way or the other, and that it had failed to meet its obligations.

On the evidence before me, I conclude the Governor in Council did not carry out the duty, that is, in law, required by paragraph 23(1)(c) of the *Judges Act*. There was a duty to act on the plaintiff's application. The Privy Councillors were required to give advice. That advice was as to whether or not the plaintiff had a permanent disabling infirmity. If the decision or advice was 'no,' the Governor in Council should have acted, probably by order-in-council, refusing the application. If the decision or answer was 'yes,' then a pension was mandatory.

But the Governor in Council did not go through those steps. The then Minister of Justice merely said he and his cabinet colleagues had considered the plaintiff's request, and 'the Government' had decided, at that particular time, not to take the 'necessary steps.' There is nothing to indicate the question of 'permanent infirmity' was considered or decided on, and appropriate advice given to the Governor General. There is nothing to indicate the matter ever got to the Governor General for action one way or the other.[33]

Accordingly, Collier held that Landreville was entitled to 'a declaration that the Governor in Council must consider and decide' whether he had, as of 30 June 1967, 'become afflicted with some permanent infirmity disabling him from the due execution of his office.'[34]

Collier made it clear that Landreville had a very good case. Section 23(1)(c) of the Judges Act had to be given a reasonably wide interpretation. Affliction was definitely not confined to physical infirmities. 'It can,' Collier wrote, 'embrace emotional and mental infirmity as well.' In his view, a wide approach made considerable sense:

It seems to me, in this modern day, a judge because of adverse publicity, criticism and comment, whether deserved or undeserved, proved or unproved, might, combined with other non-disabling physical and emotional problems, be afflicted with a permanent infirmity preventing him from reasonably functioning. A judge, could, on that view, in the eyes of the public, lawyers and litigants, be effectively disabled from performing a plausible judicial role.

Nor do I think the expression 'permanent infirmity' must be interpreted to mean an infirmity probably lasting forever. There is always the possibility, in cases of affliction, of dramatic remission, or new cures.[35]

In an alternative claim, Henderson had asked Collier to direct the Governor in Council to grant Landreville a pension. The Federal Court judge was not prepared to accede to this request. After all, parliament had, in section 23 of the Judges Act, directed the Governor in Council to determine this issue. It had not given Collier this responsibility. It had, however, given him the authority to direct the Governor in Council to do its job, and that is exactly what he did.

Nevertheless, the experienced judge issued the declaration with some reservations. He felt, he wrote in the concluding portion of his judgment, that the 'whole story' had not been told:

The difficulty was caused by the invoking, by the government in power in 1975 and 1976, of the absolute non-disclosure provisions of s. 41 of the *Federal Court Act*. From a technical evidentiary point of view there was almost nothing, other than the letter of March 5, 1967, to indicate Cabinet had considered, and decided on advice to be given. From a layman's practical point of view, it seems Cabinet considered the question. But s. 41 was invoked. That, for legal purposes in this Court, imposed an initial curtain of silence. The ringing down of that curtain of silence did two things. It affected the plaintiff's normal rights as a citizen and a litigant: The right to know what happened. Was his application treated according to law? It affected equally the rights of the citizens of this country. Had the Governor in Council, in fact, carried out the duty I say was imposed? Was there consideration given, and a decision made, on the plaintiff's letters and medical reports, that he had not, indeed, become afflicted with a permanent disabling infirmity?

I am unable to see, on the materials before me, why, in respect of those questions and those rights, it was thought necessary, in this case, to resort to the statutory non-disclosure provision. Because of the effect of the course chosen by the defendant's advisers, in respect of s. 41 of the *Federal Court Act*, I may be doing, in effect, an injustice to the citizens of this country. I may be giving the plaintiff relief to which, if all the facts were known, he is not entitled.

Equally, if I had decided to dismiss this action, I may have done him an injustice.[36]

When this case first came on for trial, the government that had invoked section 41 had been replaced. The new government, relying on political convention, refused to release the documents in question. Between the date of the hearing and the issue of his judgment, the new government was itself replaced by the old one. Joe Clark and his Tories faced and lost a motion on a money bill in the House in December 1979. An election was held and the Liberals, still under the leadership of Pierre Trudeau, returned to power. Collier was aware of these events, even if he was not, as a judge, entitled to vote. And so he had contacted Department of Justice counsel, after the trial had been completed, but before he had issued his judgment, to inquire whether the Crown wished to avail itself of one last opportunity to disclose the documents. He was advised, once and for all, that the cabinet minutes would remain secret. In those circumstances, he had little choice but to conclude that his assumptions were correct. In addition to issuing a declaration to that effect, he ordered the government to pay Landreville's legal costs.[37]

Collier's decision was an important one, and it had implications beyond Landreville's case. The government would no longer have a choice, if it ever did, when a pension application from a judge was received, but to consider that application and to make a decision with respect to it. Landreville may not have presented an attractive case, but there was a principle at stake, and that principle, dating from the 1701 Act of Settlement, was that judges were guaranteed security of tenure, and part of that guarantee necessarily required the Governor in Council to grant pensions to persons who, by reason of infirmity or disability, were unfit to continue to sit as judges. Moreover, the government had now been told that if it wished to rely on outmoded and unjustified claims of cabinet secrecy in civil suits where it was the defendant, it would do so at its peril.

The decision was received with general approval. *Globe and Mail* columnist Geoffrey Stevens embraced the principle behind the result. If the cabinet, Stevens commented, 'is to continue to act as the final arbiter in regulatory and administrative matters which affect the rights of individuals, it is going to have to clean up its act. It is going to have to abandon its stupid, self-serving secrecy. It is going to have to adopt sensible, orderly procedures which are not only fair, but seen to be fair.'[38]

On 6 June 1980 the Crown filed notice that it intended to appeal Collier's decision. Government lawyer Leslie Holland advised Henderson, however, that the government would settle for a lump-sum amount, and a new round of negotiations ensued. The department had in mind a settlement of between $175,000 and $200,000. Just a few years earlier, the government could have jettisoned the case for half that amount. Landreville now estimated his true loss as being in excess of $600,000. Had he been granted a pension in June 1967, Henderson explained, he would have already received more than $300,000, and that sum would be required as a capital amount to provide a future annuity for Landreville and his wife. In these circumstances, Henderson wrote to the justice department in June 1980 and stated that the government's offer was far too low. Landreville would, however, accept $500,000 in full settlement of his claim.[39] The request was summarily rejected. Henderson was told that the appeal was on.[40]

Henderson did not, however, give up. He had no wish to see the case appealed, but wanted a settlement on reasonably equitable terms. Further negotiations continued throughout the summer and fall of 1980. Would the government agree to a tax-free payment of $250,000, Henderson asked? That suggestion was received with some interest. A tax ruling was required, and Henderson was told that if it was favourable, the basis of a settlement might exist. More time elapsed. The ruling was obtained, the result was satisfactory, and the settlement reached. In February 1981 the

Governor in Council authorized payment to Landreville of $250,000, on an ex-gratia basis, 'in order to settle the claims of Mr. Landreville in respect of a pension pursuant to the Judges Act.' This payment was subject to Landreville and his wife 'forever discharging Her Majesty from all manner of claims, actions or demands he or she ever had, now have or may in the future have ... in respect of his judicial service.'[41] On 20 February 1981 Landreville received a cheque for a quarter of a million dollars.

Conclusion

Some facts in this saga are unassailable. The provincial government was opposed to public ownership of the natural gas distribution system, and encouraged the northern municipalities to sign with one carrier. When most of the northern municipalities chose NONG in early 1955, the choice for the remaining communities was effectively made. In any event, there was, as Ralph Farris preferred it, no real competition for NONG – the only barrier was that imposed by the individual municipalities in negotiating individual franchise arrangements. Sudbury, under Landreville's leadership, adopted a cautious approach and accelerated consideration of the NONG application only as a result of intense pressure, from the federal government, Trans-Canada Pipe Lines, the Ontario Fuel Board, and NONG itself. These events were a small part of a much larger drama playing out on Parliament Hill. When Sudbury City Council went on to consider the deal, the pros and cons had been thoroughly aired and there was no alternative. It was NONG or nothing. The people of Sudbury, and the owners of INCO, were fully behind the plan to bring in natural gas.

Numerous proceedings – the 1958 and 1962 Ontario Securities Commission investigations, the Farris preliminary inquiry, the Farris trial, the Landreville preliminary inquiry, and the Rand Inquiry – all looked into the circumstances of Sudbury City Council's 17 July 1956 decision to grant a franchise to NONG. None of these investigations ever found that Landreville had done anything to influence his council to vote in favour of the deal. How Sudbury City Council would have voted had Landreville disclosed his future plans is anyone's guess.

The evidence is not conclusive, but what there is suggests that it is more likely than not that Farris and Landreville made a deal. Landreville claimed that he agreed, or arranged, when his term as mayor expired, to join NONG and, like other executives, was given the opportunity to purchase company shares at then prevailing prices. Timing is everything, however. And, at the very least, the evidence demonstrates that Landreville expressed his interest in NONG shares some time before third reading – he testified to that effect before the OSC – and broached Farris about employment with NONG immediately after Sudbury City Council gave the franchise bylaw third and final reading. The letter of 8 May 1956 stating that 'we have important things to discuss – re co.' supports this conclusion,[1] as do the letters Farris and Landreville exchanged after the NONG franchise had finally been approved. None of these documents, and none of this evidence, however, is sufficient to support the allegation that the share option was granted in return for Landreville's assistance in obtaining council approval. That is why Landreville was discharged following his preliminary inquiry.

No matter when the stock option was requested and granted, Landreville was not legally required to disclose this arrangement. Moreover, his conduct in failing to do so pales somewhat in comparison with that of Phil Kelly, Colonel William Griesinger, and Clare Mapledoram. These 'stalwart citizens' had direct conflicts of interest. They had been ordered to dispose of their pipeline shares. Not only were these instructions ignored but the shares were retained. About the only thing that can be said for John Wintermeyer is that he was not a cabinet minister when he dealt in NONG shares. He was, however, the finance critic for his party when he bought the shares, and he had been the leader of his party for some time when he finally disposed of them. The claim that he alone of all the early NONG insiders failed to profit from his transaction is preposterous. Landreville, in marked contrast, did not vote when the franchise deal was before Sudbury City Council. And, as it turned out, Sudbury got the best overall franchise agreement.

Landreville's conduct in soliciting shares and keeping that fact quiet must also be put in perspective. Innumerable northern mayors, members of council, and city clerks also enjoyed NONG's largesse. Their names were forwarded to NONG headquarters in Toronto, and they were given the chance to participate in the hugely successful and highly oversubscribed public offering. Those who sold early made quick and easy profits; they also escaped any public censure for their actions. Some, like Sudbury mayor Joseph Fabbro, who drafted a list of Sudbury residents he believed should be favoured by this special arrangement, were indemnified by the company when the price of their NONG shares declined. Who, in this whole affair, could throw the first stone?

For his part, Ralph Farris ran NONG as if he owned it, which he did not. NONG was a public company, owned by the shareholders. Farris gave shares to his friends and, on his evidence, assuming it is to be believed, he arranged for Landreville to reap a huge windfall, even though there was no longer any prospect of his rendering any service to the corporation. It was NONG's shareholders who should have earned the profits.

Ultimately, the Landreville affair is all about public trust: how to separate righteousness from rascality and rapacity, plunder and blunder, and the peddling and buying of influence; how to distinguish between the public interest and private greed. Landreville, Kelly, Griesinger, Mapledoram, and Wintermeyer, like so many politicians before and since, did not recognize the difference between public and private. They did not understand that political power, high and low, involves trust, and that public office is bestowed for the good of country, province, and community, not for the benefit of the individual. Leo Landreville also had the misfortune of coming along at a time when corruption in government was declining, but moral sensitivity about what remained was increasing.[2]

None of the key players in this story, with the exception of CCF–NDP leader Donald C. MacDonald, really understood what the scandal was all about. MacDonald is the real and only hero of this piece. As leader of the CCF and then the NDP at a time when that party stood for something, MacDonald believed in right and wrong and, more important, knew the difference between the two. Alone at first, but later joined by others, particularly the *Toronto Star*, he made it his business, and the public's business, to get to the bottom of the scandal – and he succeeded.

In marked contrast, Leslie Frost, who made a virtue out of necessity, belatedly called the OSC investigation in 1958, and was just as happy when it was quickly wound up having established that no one had done any wrong. The fact that the one lead arising out of that investigation was not pursued is proof positive that what Frost and his attorney general, Kelso Roberts, really wanted was for the scandal to go away. Nevertheless, the 'Gas Scandal,' as he referred to it, caused Frost 'more anxiety and distress than any other incident in my long public life.' The premier realized, when Griesinger and Mapledoram went down to defeat in the provincial election that followed their resignations (despite his having campaigned on their behalf), that it was the perception of conflict, and not the amounts involved, that led to the election results. In public life, Frost later observed, 'it is not only what one does but what people think one does that counts. The mere fact that they had a very small number of shares in the Company was completely unacceptable to the people and the press and no explanation would then suffice.'[3] Unfortunately, Frost, who had very high personal standards of honesty and integrity, applied quite different standards on behalf of his party, as his attempted cover-up of the Gas Scandal makes clear.

Landreville, of course, was given a great many shares and reaped a substantial gain. If the circumstances surrounding the request and receipt of the stock option were not questionable enough, his behaviour as the facts of his involvement became known confirmed the conclusion that he had to go. Neither his private nor his public statements about his role in the affair inspired confidence. His claim, when interviewed by the RCMP in September 1962, that he had bought the NONG shares through a Sudbury broker was simply untrue. Although Landreville remembered the conversation differently – he informed the Rand Commission that he told the RCMP officers he *might* have bought the shares through his Sudbury broker – the fact of the matter was that the officers prepared virtually contemporaneous reports, and they presented a more credible account of the conversation that occurred. Landreville's assertion, reported in the *Toronto Star*, that he had purchased NONG shares for 'cold hard cash' was a lie.

In many respects, Landreville was his own worst enemy, and when the public finally had the opportunity to see him, he was not at his best. He had lost what little was left of his composure, and he appeared before the joint committee as a man thrashing about in distress. As MP John Matheson observed to the prime minister, 'Had his bearing and deportment been more genteel from the moment of the NONG disclosures, I suspect he would now be in a safe position.'[4] One can only marvel at Landreville's persistent self-destructiveness and his continuing bad judgment.

But Landreville was also a victim of the scandals of the Pearson years: Pierre Sévigny and the Gerda Munsinger affair, Hal Banks and the Seafarers' International Union, Yvon Dupuis and his $10,000 bribe, Guy Favreau and the Dorion Inquiry, Maurice Lamontagne and René Tremblay, and Mr Justice Meunier. Most important of all, he was a victim of the times: 'It [was] a time of political confusion and instability and pettiness; of the revitalization of French Canada resulting in Family Compact backlash.'

The absurdity of the time was shown, wrote one of Landreville's old Dalhousie Law School classmates and lifelong friends, Murdoch MacPherson Jr, 'by the fact that the government reached back to find someone to conduct your inquiry; and so you were tried against the mores of a former period.'[5] Had Landreville been named Fleming or even, perhaps, Cohen, had Pearson enjoyed a clear majority, had the various scandals not taken place, had Farris not lied, had Landreville acted with dignity, had he admitted to making a mistake and expressed contrition instead of saying he would do it all again, had he come forward and given a statement to the Ontario Securities Commission in 1958, had he lived a little more modestly and with better taste, had he been less emotional, had Rand been more human and forgiving – well, it might have ended differently.

The Landreville case is important for some of the questions it asked. What standards of conduct did the public expect, and did the law require, of municipal politicians? Considered more broadly, what ethical standards were required of all politicians? Were political leaders required to declare conflicts of interest, and, if not, should they have been? Eventually, some changes were made to the law. In 1961 the Municipal Act was amended to require municipal politicians to disclose any financial interest they might have in matters under civic consideration. A disclosure obligation was a good first step, but it was no more than that. Unless the provisions extended to family members as well, and unless it was accompanied by sanctions for breach, the law was, as the Toronto *Telegram* commented at the time, 'a pretty toothless affair.'[6]

Nevertheless, it was the government's preferred approach. As Frost told the legislature when the bill came up for debate, conflicts of interests had 'all sorts of ramifications and possibilities.' It was therefore difficult to attach any statutory penalty for breach. That job was, in Frost's view, better performed by the voters. 'In the end the penalty is really this: That the public has the opportunity of assessing the conflict of interests and attaching the penalty to it.'[7] The deficiencies of Frost's approach were obvious. Only a comprehensive scheme requiring disclosure of conflicts, direct and indirect, contractual and non-contractual, and of interests, both personal and corporate, and imposing real penalties for breach, had any likelihood of ensuring appropriate behaviour by municipal officials and providing an effective mechanism for dealing with those persons who placed their interests before their duties. As Frost knew, recent history established that there were many bad apples in the barrel.[8] It took the legislature until 1972 to pass comprehensive conflict of interest legislation respecting municipal councils.[9]

The Landreville case is also important because it revealed the deficiencies in our system for the disciplining and removal of judges. The Law Society, in investigating Landreville, convened a kangaroo court and then relied on its findings. The process was deplorable. Yet there was perhaps one justification for what the Law Society did. After all, there was no established mechanism for bringing concerns about sitting judges to the attention of the authorities in some manner consistent with established notions of judicial independence. Individual lawyers could not complain about a sitting judge – the bench was sufficiently small and inbred to raise a real fear of judicial reprisals. Provincial chief justices did not have any authority to deal with errant judges, nor did the chief justice of Canada or any of the provincial attorneys general. There was, in short, nowhere to go. Believing as they did that Landreville had, by his own actions, demonstrated that he was not fit for the bench, the treasurer and benchers of the Law Society felt duty-bound to take appropriate action on behalf of the bar and bench. Still, that was no justification for the Law Society to destroy Landreville as a judge, and as a man, by taking the action they did. 'Anxious to appear righteous before the people,' John Matheson observed to Lester Pearson, 'they retired to their carpeted dining hall and without granting Landreville so much as one word in his own defence, unctuously came to conclusions which were calculated to ruin him forever in the eyes of his brother judges, the legal profession and the public generally.'[10]

Parliament was entrusted with guaranteeing the independence of the judiciary, and instead of initially discharging that trust, the government did nothing. It was only after the Law Society forced its hand that it referred the Landreville case to a royal commission. The Rand inquiry and its report illustrated some of the problems with the use of royal commissions to investigate allegations of individual misconduct, and raised, not for the first or last time, some of the problems in appointing judges and retired judges as royal commissioners. Was it really consistent with judicial independence to embroil judges in political and partisan matters? There were other problems as well.

Not only were the legal rules governing these commissions unclear, but the process itself, with the commission counsel calling the evidence, made the exercise nothing more than a glorified trial of an individual, without the safeguards that usually accompany such proceedings. Royal commissioners were entitled to establish their own procedures; the courts had made it clear they had a wide discretion in doing so. However, Canadians had a right to a trial if they were criminally accused. A royal commission charged with investigating the acts of an individual, any royal commission, threatened that right by effectively putting the individual on trial in a forum more closely resembling a Star Chamber than one of Canada's courts.

Rand had been given clear terms of reference, but that did not stop him from wandering far off topic. With no restrictions on his right to compel attendance of witnesses, and no fetters on the procedure he decided to pursue, the commission became nothing more than a fishing expedition desperately searching for something to justify the recommendation that was reached. When the evidence failed to disclose that Landreville had broken the law, Rand was forced to broaden his scope.

The press, unhampered by any restrictions on what it could report, made the most of the travelling spectacle. The inquiry inevitably became an inquisition, and character assassination on a national scale became a national sport. It was unfair, and it served no useful purpose. The government did not obtain any new information about Landreville and his activities. All it received was a questionable rubber stamp for its decision to have Landreville removed.

Even if Rand had done a good job, even if he had been fair, there were still principled reasons for concern about this particular approach. If the party in power could strike an inquiry any time it claimed the 'good government of Canada' was involved, that would potentially allow it to inquire into the activities of any judge with whom it took issue over the interpretation of law, or any other issue for that matter. That prospect was remote, but worrisome nevertheless, and avoiding it was a strong argument in favour of establishing some mechanism to deal with complaints against judges consistent with their constitutionally recognized independence.

Section 99 of the British North America Act provided that 'Judges of the Supreme Courts shall hold office during good behaviour, but shall be removable by the Governor-General on Address by the Senate and the House of Commons.' As these events made more than clear, a mechanism was needed to receive and review complaints made against judges. Something had to be done, the *Toronto Star* pointed out, so as to 'give Parliament the authority to take removal proceedings against any judge who by his behaviour, whether on or off the bench, and whether before or after his appointment, has clearly established that he is not a fit person to sit in judgement of others.'[11] The allegations against Landreville had been allowed to drag on for too long, and even when the government responded, its method of doing so was *ad hoc* and, as a result, both inadequate and unfair. By any interpretation, the Rand Commission and the report were a travesty of justice. In many respects, Rand was a throwback to another day. Ironically, Rand, like Landreville, rose from humble beginnings. But unlike Landreville, he was a man with little experience of the real world. His musings on the role and conduct of judges were idealized, unreal, and unrealistic; no one could meet his standard of conduct. His diatribes against Landreville showed that he himself had lost the ability to judge impartially and stripped his report of any usefulness it might otherwise have enjoyed. The Rand Commission was an unfitting end to the brilliant career of a great Canadian judge, and out of step with much of Rand's life and work.

There are important lessons to be drawn from the Landreville case. Parliament is equipped for many things, but not for conducting the trial of a judge. The proceedings of the special joint committee more than prove this point. The members of that committee did not always take their task seriously, and their attendance record provides persuasive evidence of that. There was also something unseemly about the fate of a judge being thrust into political hands. In the midst of all these events, Justice Minister Cardin, in a letter to Landreville's lawyer, J.J. Robinette, took the position that it was 'open to Parliament to make an address for the removal of a judge on any ground it sees fit, whether it constitutes misbehaviour or not.'[12] Obviously, parliament was not bound by common law definitions of terms such as 'good behaviour.' However, judicial independence would be quickly undermined if parliament used its removal power except in the clearest case.

The Act of Settlement of 1701 established an independent judiciary, and since that time the separation between the executive, the legislature, and the judiciary has been a hallmark of democratic life. In order to promote and guarantee this independence, judges are granted security of tenure and remuneration. Without either, they could easily become pawns of the state, and in totalitarian societies they invariably do.

It is true that parliament is supreme, and that is how it should be. However, this episode demonstrates that political considerations and partisan affiliations could have something to do with the exercise of the removal power, and this was and is not consistent with an independent judiciary. If parliament could remove a judge for good reasons, it might also, as Cardin's letter suggests, do so for questionable ones. In 1964 the chief justices of all the provinces met in Toronto. Landreville's difficulties had barely begun, but the assembled jurists agreed that judicial conduct should be supervised, and that they should be in charge of the supervision. Judges, not politicians, should judge other judges.

John Matheson wrote to Prime Minister Pearson in October 1967 with one suggestion: that the Judges Act be amended, along the lines proposed by Dean William Lederman of Queen's University Law School, so that 'hereafter allegations of misconduct against any Superior Court Judge will be first fully investigated by a Commission of other Superior Court Judges who will conduct a fair hearing. Such Commission should ascertain the facts and report them and also make a finding whether in their opinion the misconduct has been proven to their satisfaction. They could then recommend removal if they did find the necessary misconduct. Upon such recommendation the Cabinet would accept the recommendation, introduce the motion for removal and stand behind it in Parliament as a Government measure.'[13] It was a good idea, and four years later, in the summer of 1971, at the same time that the Judges Act was amended to raise the annual stipend and to increase survivor benefits, Lederman's proposal was given effect. Legislation was passed, with all-party support, establishing the Canadian Judicial Council.[14]

Without a doubt, the Landreville case figured prominently in the decision to establish the council. At second reading, Albert Béchard, parliamentary secretary to Justice Minister Turner, explained that while the government had the power, under the Inquiries Act, to investigate complaints against a judge, that was not the most appropriate way of doing so. 'Because the independence of the judiciary is an integral part of the Canadian democratic process, it is important that the judiciary become, to some extent, a self-disciplining body. The executive or legislative branches,' Béchard continued, 'should not ordinarily intervene in the management or control of the judiciary. To do so might result in an abuse of the executive power of government and would diminish the respect and independence now held by the bench, and destroy the delicate balance of powers that Canadian democracy has enjoyed since Confederation.'[15] Other politicians, clearly referring to Landreville, rose in the House to give this government measure their full support. Establishment of the Canadian Judicial Council would ensure, on the one hand, that judges were accountable for their behaviour, and, on the other, that their independence was preserved.

The council, whose membership is composed of the chief justices, senior associate, and associate chief justices of the federal, provincial, and territorial superior courts, with the chief justice of Canada as chair, was

empowered to conduct investigations of complaints about the compe-
tence of judges, as well as to look into allegations of judicial misconduct.
Investigations can begin in one of two ways: at the request of the federal
minister of justice or a provincial attorney general, or if the council
decides to conduct an investigation as a result of a complaint it receives.
In most cases, an independent counsel is retained initially to undertake a
fact-finding investigation and prepare a report, which is considered by a
panel of the judicial conduct committee. Usually that ends the matter,
and most complaints are dismissed at an early stage. Sometimes, as a
result of this investigation and report, where the conduct complained of
is insufficient to support removal, the council issues an 'expression of disapproval.' The panel may also recommend further investigation by the
council, and an inquiry committee may then be struck.

Only rarely are complaints against a judge referred to a formal investigation by an inquiry committee. One recent case involved, oddly enough,
one of Leo Landreville's former law partners, but the judge resigned
before the inquiry committee actually got to work.[16] These committees,
comprising judges and persons designated by the minister of justice,
enjoy the powers of a superior court. At the conclusion of an inquiry, the
committee reports to council, which, in turn, is required to report to the
minister of justice. Council may recommend that the judge be removed.
In most cases where complaints alleging grounds serious enough to warrant removal are received, the judge resigns prior to the initiation of any
of these proceedings. For the most part, the council relies on admonitions
and informal conciliation. In dealing with conduct that is serious enough
to merit investigation and review, sanctions short of removal are applied.
Generally, they are both conciliatory and educational in nature.[17]

The act sets out the grounds necessary to support a removal recommendation. A formal investigation must have taken place, and the council, as a result of that investigation, must have formed the opinion that the
judge has become incapacitated or disabled from the due execution of
office by reason of age or infirmity, having been guilty of misconduct,
having failed in the due execution of his office, or having been placed, by
his or her conduct or otherwise, in a position incompatible with the due
execution of office. Obviously, this definition goes some way in providing scope or definition to the term 'during good behaviour.'

Having received a report from the council recommending removal, the
minister may then proceed in one of two ways. He or she may ask parliament to establish a special committee to consider the council's report as
well as to conduct its own inquiry, or, somewhat more likely, if a full

hearing had already been held by the council, the minister may simply and immediately introduce a motion for a joint address of parliament requesting the governor general to remove the judge.

This process is not problem free (and it is worth noting, has not been tested to any significant degree). The council has no formal disciplinary powers, and the issue, from time to time, of 'expressions of disapproval,' while undoubtedly salutary, is not provided for in the legislation. Perhaps this is the way it should be. This book demonstrates that a judge cannot be wounded: the judge is either destroyed or left alone. Once a judge has been discredited, there is no turning back. Still, the process of the Canadian Judicial Council could be improved. The absence of any public participation in the investigation and complaints process has understandably attracted criticism. Is it really appropriate that only judges should judge other judges? Might the public interest be served by public participation?

The amendments to the Judges Act and the creation of the Canadian Judicial Council also fail to answer one of the real problems raised in Landreville's case. What should be done about conduct that occurred before the judge was appointed, but which comes to light only after the appointment has taken effect? As Mr Justice Edson Haines of the Supreme Court of Ontario observed in a letter of 16 April 1967 to John Matheson, which he asked Matheson to forward to the prime minister, this was the real issue that had to be addressed. As soon as a lawyer accepted appointment as a judge, Haines suggested, he or she accepted immediate responsibility for his or her conduct from that day forward. 'Once appointed, however, it seems to me that the curtain should be drawn on all prior conduct unless that conduct constitutes a most serious crime of a very grievous character. Were it not so, then every judge's confidence would be placed in jeopardy by anyone possessed of secret information which he could hold over the head of the judge.' Haines also pointed out that most, if not all, of the allegations against Landreville dated from before his appointment to the bench. He noted that few people have unblemished careers; there is always something that could be made the 'subject of adverse comment or accusation.' There was, therefore, a need for some guidelines for future cases, since this was an issue that affects 'all of us.'[18]

Ultimately, Rand's question will have to be answered when the conduct of a judge, either before or after appointment, is brought into question: 'Would the conduct, fairly determined in the light of all circumstances, lead such persons to attribute such a defect of moral character that the discharge of the duties of the office thereafter would be suspect?

[H]as it destroyed unquestioning confidence of uprightness, of moral integrity, of honesty in decision, the elements of public honour? If so, then unfitness has been demonstrated.' These questions, alone among all the findings in the Rand Report, will probably stand the test of time.

No administrative process is perfect, especially one that must review the conduct of judges in a way that respects the integrity and independence of their office. Creation of the Canadian Judicial Council, and institution of a mechanism for the receipt and investigation of complaints, whatever its faults, is, by any measure, an improvement over what had previously existed.

How Landreville would have fared had the council been in existence in 1958, 1962, or even 1966 is anyone's guess. He had done nothing wrong as a judge, but did his conduct in responding to the complaints against him place him in a position incompatible with the due execution of his office? Ultimately, there was nothing questionable about the government moving against Landreville. His usefulness as a judge was at an end. It was the process employed that left so much to be desired.

Landreville, however, deserves a fair share of the responsibility for that process. Well into the piece he was given the opportunity to resign, and he was informed that appropriate pension arrangements would be made. A resignation following his preliminary inquiry would have made considerable sense. Landreville was in a battle he could not win, and the longer he fought, the worse his situation became. But Landreville was not a quitter, and he did not believe that he had done anything wrong. By the law of the land, he was right. He had committed no crime. His discharge from the preliminary inquiry permanently answered most allegations to that effect, Rand and his report notwithstanding.

While Landreville had not broken the law, his bad judgment caused him to forfeit a career and a position in society he would have otherwise long enjoyed. Taking the NONG stock option was not illegal, but it was wrong nevertheless. Landreville's constant protestations of innocence led people to believe that he had done something wrong and did have something to hide. While Leo Landreville made no efforts to keep his stock sales secret, Ralph Farris obviously thought their arrangement was best kept quiet. The manner in which he concealed the exercise of Landreville's stock option is suggestive of nothing else. In the end, Landreville got some money, but he never restored his good name. All that he established was that he had been treated unfairly.

NONG, however, was quite successful. In 1958 gas arrived in the north, the industrial climate immediately improved, and a number of industries expanded operations. The availability of natural gas influenced one of the Lakehead's larger industries, Canada Malting Company Limited, to launch an expansion program there instead of Winnipeg. Gas contributed to the decision of Jones & Laughlin Steel Corporation to locate a $30 million iron-ore pelletizing plant near Kirkland Lake. In Cochrane, NONG's industrial promotion department helped coax a new plywood plant to town, bringing with it a hundred new jobs.

By 1962 NONG itself employed three hundred people and had spent more than $40 million building its distribution system. That year, it earned almost one dollar per share. These were positive results, but NONG was, by any measure, a modest venture: its $2 million net profit for 1964 on sales of $24 million illustrated that. Nevertheless, in possession of a captive market, and selling in a regulated environment, it was all but guaranteed some profit. The utility was sure to endure as a steady, if unspectacular, earner.[19] Just as Farris had planned, NONG threw off fabulous profits for its promoters, and year after year, under a variety of owners, it paid steady dividends to its shareholders. Monopolies are like that.

After Farris was convicted of perjury, his public role in the company had to come to an end. He resigned as president in 1965, returned to Vancouver, and lived in relative seclusion. He died at the age of sixty, on 21 January 1970. Landreville, however, was a survivor. He had travelled a long way from the Ottawa walkup in which he was born to Benvenuto Place. It was a long climb up, and it was a long fall down. He made the most of his situation, which was not an attractive one. He had his family. He had his friends. He travelled. He practised law after a fashion. And he continues to believe that he did not do anything wrong.

Notes

1 NORTHERN ONTARIO NATURAL GAS

1 Matt Bray and Ernie Epp, eds., *A Vast and Magnificent Land: An Illustrated History of Ontario* (Thunder Bay, Ontario: Lakehead University 1984), 7
2 Much of the following section is derived from ibid., 7–16; Ken Coates and William Morrison, *The Forgotten North: A History of Canada's Provincial Norths* (Toronto: Lorimer 1992), 48–9; and Lise Kimpton, *The Historical Development and the Present Situation of the French Canadian Community of Ontario* (Ottawa: Carleton University, Department of Sociology and Anthropology 1984), 1–10
3 Marc Cousineau, 'Belonging: An Essential Element of Citizenship – A Franco-Ontarian Perspective,' in William Kaplan, ed., *Belonging: The Meaning and Future of Canadian Citizenship* (Montreal: McGill-Queen's University Press 1993), 137
4 Quoted from Bruce Hodgins et al., *The Canadian North: Source of Wealth or Vanishing Heritage?* (Scarborough, Ontario: Prentice Hall 1977), 161–2
5 Bray and Epp, *A Vast and Magnificent Land*, 14
6 This section is drawn from William Kilbourn, *PipeLine: TransCanada and the Great Debate, A History of Business and Politics* (Toronto: Clarke, Irwin 1970), 3ff.
7 Ibid.
8 Canada, House of Commons, *Debates*, 13 March 1953, 2927–31
9 This account is substantially derived from Robert Bothwell and William Kilbourn, *C.D. Howe: A Biography* (Toronto: McClelland and Stewart 1979), chapter 17.

10 *Re Trans-Canada Pipe Lines Ltd. and Western Pipe Lines, Alberta-Montreal Line* (1954), 73 CRTC 37 (Canadian Railway and Transport Commission)

11 Alexander Ross, 'The Life and Times of a Wheeler-Dealer,' *Maclean's*, September 1963, 18–9

12 Ibid., 64

13 However, see the evidence of C. Spencer Clark before the 1958 OSC investigation in which he claimed, somewhat improbably, that it was a matter of relative indifference to NONG whether the northern or southern routes were chosen. While the former would involve, Clark claimed, a somewhat smaller capital expenditure, the scheme was feasible in either case, provided that monopolies were obtained throughout the north. *In the Matter of NONG Ltd.*, evidence of C. Spencer Clark, 29 May 1958, 21ff, Ontario Archives (OA), OSC Papers, RG 4-02, file 249.6

14 *In the Matter of NONG, etc.*, evidence of Ralph K. Farris, 23 October 1962, Landreville Papers, 308

15 Ross, 'The Life and Times of a Wheeler-Dealer,' 64

16 *R. v. Farris*, evidence of Gordon Kelly McLean, 10 April 1964, Landreville Papers, 442

17 Ottawa *Citizen*, 25 January 1966. See also Donald C. MacDonald, *The Happy Warrior: Political Memoirs* (Markham, Ontario: Fitzhenry and Whiteside 1988), 76. Gordon Kelly McLean, however, insisted, at least for a time, that the idea was his, and that his uncle did not get involved until well into the piece. See *In the Matter of NONG Ltd.*, evidence of Gordon Kelly McLean, 2 June 1958, 62, OSC Papers, RG 4-02, file 249.9

18 Northern Ontario Natural Gas Company, *Annual Report*, 28 April 1958, 16

19 'Had anyone,' Farris testified before the Ontario Securities Commission in 1962, 'realized, or could have read into the future, how successful it was going to be, there would have been little difficulty in putting up that sum but it was a speculative company right up to the day it was financed.' *In the Matter of NONG, etc.*, evidence of Ralph K. Farris, 23 October 1962, 311

20 Northern Ontario Natural Gas Company, *Annual Report*, 28 April 1958, 8

21 Ibid.

22 R.W. Herring to R.K. Farris, 15 June 1966, L.A. Landreville Papers, private collection, Ottawa

23 Northern Ontario Natural Gas Company, *Annual Report*, 28 April 1958, 8

24 See report of Controller Monaghan cited in *In the Matter of NONG, etc.*, examination of Leo Albert Landreville, 3 and 4 October 1962, 102–3. See also Royal Commission, *Report: Inquiry Re: the Honourable Mr. Justice Leo A. Landreville* (Ottawa: Queen's Printer 1966) (Commissioner: the Hon. Ivan C. Rand), 5.

25 Minutes of a Joint Meeting of Northern Ontario Municipalities Held at Township Hall, Kirkland Lake, Ontario, 9 February 1955, Landreville Papers

26 Ibid.

27 Ibid.

28 North Bay *Daily Nugget*, 11 September 1956

29 A 50 per cent interest was purchased in June 1956. Full control was obtained through a June 1958 share exchange. Ontario Securities Commission, *Final Report*, 22 July 1963 (Counsel: H.S. Bray), 10, 235ff, Landreville Papers

30 See D.M. LeBourdais, *Sudbury Basin: The Story of Nickel* (Toronto: Ryerson Press 1953), 1; C.M. Wallace, 'The 1880s,' in C.M. Wallace and Ashley Thomson, eds., *Sudbury: Rail Town to Regional Capital* (Toronto: Dundurn Press 1993), 11.

31 See LeBourdais, *Sudbury Basin*, 12 .

32 Economic Council of Canada, *Performance and Potential: Mid-1950s to Mid-1970s* (Ottawa: Information Canada 1970), 9

33 O.W. Saarinen, 'The 1950s,' in Wallace and Thomson, *Sudbury*, 200; Charles Dorian, *The First 75 Years: A Headline History of Sudbury, Canada* (Devon: Arthur H. Stockwell 1959), 44–5; Economic Council of Canada, *Performance and Potential*, 196

34 Dorian, *The First 75 Years*, 196; Saarinen, 'The 1950s,' 192

35 Dorian, *The First 75 Years*, 88–92; Saarinen, 'The 1950s,' 207–8

36 LeBourdais, *Sudbury Basin*, 206

37 Report on the Economic Feasibility of Natural Gas Service to Designated Communities in Ontario, Canada, Phase 11, Fish Service & Management Corporation, Houston, 15 June 1956, 8–10, Landreville Papers

2 THE HONOURABLE LEO LANDREVILLE

1 Leo A. Landreville File, Law Society Archives, Toronto

2 Innis Christie, former dean of law, Dalhousie University, to author, 9 August 1994

3 Landreville Autobiography, chapter 1, 2 (unpublished manuscript of Leo Landreville)

4 Peter Sypnowich, 'The Case of Mr. Justice Landreville,' *Canadian Weekly*, 13 December 1965, 2–7

5 Ottawa *Journal*, 1 November 1958

6 L.B. Pearson to L.A. Landreville, 2 October 1953, L.A. Landreville Papers, private collection, Ottawa

7 Landreville Mayoralty Speech, December 1954, ibid.

8 J.J. Kelly, city solicitor, to the mayor and members of council, 10 September 1954, ibid.

9 Ibid.

10 *In the Matter of NONG, etc.*, evidence of Ralph K. Farris, 17 October 1962, 29–31, ibid.

11 J.J. Kelly to the mayor and members of council, 10 September 1954, ibid.

12 Memo for Board of Control, 14 April 1955, ibid.; Minutes of Meeting of the Board of Control, 20 April 1955, ibid.

13 J.C. Grey to L.A. Landreville, 7 April 1955, ibid.

14 See *Proceedings of Inquiry into the Dealings of the Honourable Mr Justice Leo A. Landreville with NONG Ltd. before the Honourable Ivan Cleveland Rand*, evidence of John W. Tomlinson, Toronto, 5 April 1966, 768ff, evidence of A. Crozier, Toronto, 5 April 1966, 804ff, National Archives of Canada.

15 Ibid., evidence of C. Spencer Clark, Vancouver, 14 March 1966, 91–2

16 *In the Matter of NONG, etc.*, evidence of Ralph K. Farris, 17 October 1962, 30ff

17 Report Re: Delegation, Trans-Canada Pipe Line, Office of the Prime Minister, 22 July 1955, Landreville Papers

18 L.A. Landreville to J.C. Grey, 7 December 1955, ibid.

19 A.P. Craig to L.A. Landreville, 13 February 1956, ibid. Craig sent a blind copy of this correspondence to Farris, along with the observation that 'Trans-Canada hopes very much that this whole Sudbury and International Nickel Company situation will "gel" soon enough to enable at least a Precedent Agreement with the certified franchise holder by early March at the very latest.' A.P. Craig to R.K. Farris, 14 February 1956, ibid.

20 L.A. Landreville to G.J. Monaghan, 20 February 1956, ibid.

21 Meeting of the Board of Control, 21 February 1956, ibid.

22 *In the Matter of NONG, etc.*, evidence of Ralph K. Farris, 17 October 1962, 42ff

23 William Kilbourn, *PipeLine: TransCanada and the Great Debate, A History of Business and Politics* (Toronto: Clarke, Irwin 1970), vii–viii

24 Canada, House of Commons, *Debates*, 15 March 1956, 2169; 14 May 1956, 3864

25 Dale C. Thomson, *Louis St. Laurent: Canadian* (Toronto: Macmillan 1967), 421

26 Needless to say, it was not just Liberals who supported an all-Canadian route. Some Conservatives did so as well. See, for example, Ontario, Legislative Assembly, *Debates*, 21 February 1956, 377ff, where Attorney General Dana Porter moved second reading on the Northern Ontario Pipe Line Act, which provided for Ontario's $35 million contribution to the scheme.

27 William Kilbourn, 'The 1950s,' in J.M.S. Careless and R. Craig Brown, eds., *The Canadians: 1867–1967* (Toronto: Macmillan 1967), 319

28 House of Commons, *Debates*, 22 May 1956, 4173–4

29 Ibid., 17 May 1956, 4025. In his speech, Howe is quoting from an earlier speech given to the Calgary Petroleum Institute.

30 *Financial Post*, 2 June 1956
31 Robert Bothwell and William Kilbourn, *C.D. Howe: A Biography* (Toronto: McClelland and Stewart 1979), 303
32 L.A. Landreville to C.D. Howe, 3 May 1956, Landreville Papers
33 C.D. Howe to L.A. Landreville, 4 May 1956, ibid.
34 L.A. Landreville to R.K. Farris, 3 May 1956, ibid.
35 R.K. Farris to L.A. Landreville, 8 May 1956, ibid. See chapter 7, 132.
36 Minutes of Meeting of Council, 22 May 1956, ibid.
37 J.J. Kelly to L.A. Landreville, 19 June 1956, ibid. Indeed, even though Kelly's retirement was approaching – he had accepted a new position in Kitchener – he volunteered to continue working on this matter for no fee in order to secure 'the most advantageous gas distribution system whether by way of franchise agreement or otherwise for the inhabitants of the City of Sudbury.'
38 Minutes of City Council, 19 June 1956, ibid.
39 Minutes of Board of Control, 20 June 1956, ibid.
40 Notes on Hearing before Ontario Fuel Board, 21 June 1956, ibid.
41 Ibid.
42 *In the Matter of NONG, etc.*, evidence of L.A. Landreville, 3 and 4 October 1962, 155
43 Kelly apparently believed that the Fuel Board would set a flat rate on return on investment, and if a separate company held Sudbury's distribution rights, the city could end up with a lower rate because of INCO's high consumption. This was not, in fact, how the system was expected to work. The OFB would set fuel rates, and those rates were expected to be uniform throughout the north. Moreover, there was every reason to believe that it might be difficult to market the subsidiary shares.
44 Arthur Crawley and Company were retained to report on the feasibility of establishing a NONG subsidiary to serve the Sudbury area, and reported that there would be no benefit to Sudbury in doing so.
45 According to city engineer T.L. Hennessy, who, along with Kelly, was in charge of negotiating the deal with NONG, 'we had probably through our efforts managed to get a better contract than any other municipality in Northern Ontario.' Hennessy did, however, qualify his opinion: 'I don't think we were completely satisfied we had done as well as we might have.' See Sypnowich, 'The Case of Mr. Justice Landreville,' 6.
46 Minutes of Sudbury City Council, 17 July 1956, Landreville Papers
47 In fact, that did not take place until 1958.
48 Ontario Securities Commission, *Final Report*, 22 July 1963 (Counsel: H.S. Bray), 135
49 *In the Matter of NONG, etc.*, evidence of Ralph K. Farris, 17 October 1962, 89–90

Farris's evidence on this point was fully corroborated by both C. Spencer Clark and, of course, Leo Landreville.

50 R.K. Farris and C.S. Clark to L.A. Landreville, 20 July 1956, Landreville Papers

51 L.A. Landreville to R.K. Farris, 30 July 1956, ibid. Landreville had by this time established a warm friendship with Farris. Visiting New York at the invitation of one of the directors of NONG, Landreville wrote to Farris about the trip, concluding: 'All the time thinking of our friendship and your kindness.' L.A. Landreville to R.K. Farris, August 1956, ibid.

52 The bubble eventually burst. Fabbro, who had taken the largest number of units for himself, held on to his units for too long and watched them slip below his acquisition price. He arranged through Farris for John McGraw of Convesto to buy them back at $30 each when they were trading for much less. McGraw absorbed the loss. See Ontario Securities Commission, *Final Report*, 176.

53 Northern Ontario Natural Gas Company, *Annual Report*, 28 April 1958, 14

54 Ibid., 9

55 Toronto *Globe and Mail*, 5 July 1958

56 *Sudbury Star*, 30 August 1956, L.A. Landreville Scrapbook, private collection, Ottawa

57 *Proceedings of Inquiry ... before the Honourable Ivan Cleveland Rand*, evidence of C. Spencer Clark, Vancouver, 14 March 1966, 132–3

58 L.A. Landreville to R.K. Farris, 19 September 1956, Landreville Papers

59 R.K. Farris to L.A. Landreville, 1 October 1956, ibid.

60 Special Joint Committee of the Senate and the House of Commons respecting Mr. Justice Landreville, *Minutes of Proceedings and Evidence*, no. 5, 9 March 1967 (Co-chairs: Daniel Lang and Ovide Laflamme), 165

61 'Inter Alia,' *Fortnightly Law Journal*, 6 (1936): 1

62 Royal Commission, *Report* (Commissioner: the Hon. Ivan C. Rand), 35

63 J. McGraw to L.A. Landreville, 12 February 1957, Landreville Papers

64 L.A. Landreville to Continental Investments Corporation, 16 February 1957, ibid.

65 Special Joint Committee, *Minutes of Proceedings and Evidence*, no. 5, 9 March 1967, 160

66 For McLean's account of this event, see *R. v. Farris*, Transcript, 10 April 1964, 458ff, Landreville Papers

67 Earl Cherniak interview, Toronto, 20 March 1995

68 L.A. Landreville to P.E. Trudeau, 9 May 1967, Landreville Papers

3 SCANDAL

1 Ottawa *Citizen*, 25 January 1966

2 Ontario Archives, Attorney General's Papers, RG 49, Series 19, box 2-99, Ontario Government Press Releases, press release, 4 July 1958

3 Ontario Securities Commission, *Final Report*, 22 July 1963 (Counsel: H.S. Bray), 240, 263

4 Donald C. MacDonald, *The Happy Warrior: Political Memoirs* (Markham, Ontario: Fitzhenry and Whiteside 1988), 79

5 Ontario, Legislative Assembly, *Debates*, 18 March 1959, 1329

6 Memorandum, 29 August 1972, 4, box 8, file 18, Leslie Frost Papers, 77-024, Trent University Archives, Peterborough, Ontario

7 According to Kelly, Griesinger began pressing him for some shares after the northern route was chosen in 1955. Griesinger formally subscribed for his shares by a letter dated 19 October 1956. See *In the Matter of the Securities Act and In the Matter of NONG Ltd.*, evidence of Philip Kelly, 18 June 1958, 96, 116

8 The following section is derived, in part, from MacDonald, *The Happy Warrior*, 75ff.

9 Toronto *Globe and Mail*, 5 July 1958. For the resignation letter, see P. Kelly to L. Frost, 8 July 1957, box 8, file 9, Frost Papers. See also *Globe and Mail*, 6 February 1959.

10 Legislative Assembly, *Debates*, 10 March 1958, 670, 673, 676

11 Ibid., 11 March 1958, 694

12 *Toronto Star* (hereafter *Star*), 5 May 1958

13 Legislative Assembly, *Debates*, 11 March 1958, 698, 702

14 *Star*, 5 May 1958

15 Toronto *Telegram*, 12 March 1958. See also Legislative Assembly, *Debates*, 12 March 1958, 745.

16 Quoted in MacDonald, *The Happy Warrior*, 78. See also Roger Graham, *Old Man Ontario: Leslie M. Frost* (Toronto: University of Toronto Press 1990), 344.

17 Legislative Assembly, *Debates*, 12 March 1958, 746

18 *Star*, 3 May 1958; *Telegram*, 3 May 1958

19 *Globe and Mail*, 13 February 1959

20 *In the Matter of the Securities Act and In the Matter of NONG Ltd.*, evidence of Philip Kelly, 18 June 1958, 31ff, 75ff

21 Attorney General's Papers, RG 4-02, file 249.12, Interim Report, 2 July 1958, 13. See also *Star*, 5 May 1958; *Globe and Mail*, 7 May 1958.

22 Legislative Assembly, *Debates*, 2 February 1959, 89–90. The OSC investigators found otherwise. According to them, Wintermeyer bought his shares on 21 January 1957 for $2745. He sold them on 12 May 1958 for $6757. See Attorney General's Papers, RG 4-02, file 249.12, Interim Report, 2 July 1958, 13.

23 *Globe and Mail*, 5 July 1958

24 Ibid., 9 May 1958

25 *Telegram,* 14 February 1959

26 Ibid., 8 May 1958

27 The *Toronto Star* accused the government of hiding 'behind a limited, semi-secret investigation by a limited committee of its own people' (16 May 1958).

28 A. Kelso Roberts, *Thirty Years of Ontario Political Action* (Private edition 1969), 94

29 Northern Ontario Natural Gas Company, *Annual Report,* 28 April 1958. See also Legislative Assembly, *Debates,* 12 February 1959, 319; Ontario Securities Commission, *Final Report,* 22 July 1963 (Counsel: H.S. Bray), 58.

30 Attorney General's Papers, RG 4-02, file 249.12, OSC, Interim Report, 2 July 1958

31 *Telegram,* 4 July 1958. See also Attorney General's Papers, RG 49, Series 19, box 2-99, file Ontario Government Press Releases, press release, 4 July 1958.

32 *Globe and Mail,* 5 July 1958. See W. Griesinger to L. Frost, 14 May 1958, box 8, file 12, Frost Papers.

33 Attorney General's Papers, RG 4-02, file 249.12, OSC, Interim Report, 2 July 1958, 12. See also Ontario Securities Commission, *Final Report,* 58–9.

34 Press Release, 4 July 1958, box 8, file 12, Frost Papers

35 *Star,* 5 July 1958

36 *Telegram,* 5 July 1958

37 *Final Report of Messrs. Ford, Bray and Chisholm Re NONG Investigation,* 29 August 1958, 15, Ontario Archives, Ontario Securities Commission Papers, RG 4, Series 4-02, box 249, file 249.12.

38 There may also have been some other factors at work. See *Star,* 8 July 1958, and Roberts, *Thirty Years of Ontario Political Action,* 97–8.

39 The full text of the report is set out in the *Globe and Mail,* 13 February 1959.

40 On Robinette, see Jack Batten, *Robinette: The Dean of Canadian Lawyers* (Toronto: Macmillan 1984).

41 *R. v. NONG,* Argument, 23 September 1958 at 12, Ontario Archives, Ontario Securities Commission Papers, RG 4-02, file 249.10

42 Ibid., 48

43 *Star,* 24 September 1958; *Globe and Mail,* 24 September 1958

44 *Her Majesty the Queen v. NONG Ltd., R.K. Farris, C.S. Clark* (24 November 1958) (Magistrates' Court, Toronto) [unreported decision] at 8, Magistrate Elmore, Ontario Archives, Ontario Securities Commission Papers, RG 4, Series 4-02, box 249, file 249.12

45 Legislative Assembly, *Debates,* 5 February 1959, 183

46 L.A. Landreville to R.K. Farris, 25 November 1958, L.A. Landreville Papers,

private collection, Ottawa; R.K. Farris to L.A. Landreville, 20 January 1959, ibid.

47 Cited in MacDonald, *The Happy Warrior*, 80

48 *Star*, 6 February 1959; Legislative Assembly, *Debates*, 6 February 1959, 197

49 *In the Matter of the Securities Act and In the matter of NONG Ltd.*, evidence of P.T. Kelly, 18 June 1958, 170, Ontario Archives, Ontario Securities Commission Papers, RG 4-02, file 249.1

50 Legislative Assembly, *Debates*, 6 February 1959, 198

51 *Star*, 9 February 1959

52 For Frost's view, see Graham, *Old Man Ontario*, 350. See also Memorandum, nd, box 8, file 18, Frost Papers.

53 Alexander Ross, 'The Life and Times of a Wheeler-Dealer,' *Maclean's*, September 1963, 67

54 *Star*, 6 February 1959

55 *Globe and Mail*, 7 February 1959

56 Ibid., 5 February 1959

57 Legislative Assembly, *Debates*, 6 February 1959, 198

58 *In the Matter of the Securities Act and In the Matter of NONG Ltd.*, evidence of Philip Kelly, 18 June 1958, 39

59 The full text of the retainer letter is reproduced in *Star*, 6 February 1959. See also box 8, file 12, Frost Papers.

60 For Donald MacDonald's explanation, see Legislative Assembly, *Debates*, 18 March 1959, 1329ff.

61 According to Griesinger, 'everyone' knew that he and other ministers owned NONG stock. 'Mr. Griesinger pointed out that Alec Mackenzie did a lot of work for NONG and made it pretty clear that Alec Mackenzie was instrumental in helping that company win the concession it needed from the government in order to proceed.' W. Griesinger, interview, Ontario Archives, OHSS, RG 47-27-1-47

62 Griesinger later stated that 'Premier Frost must have known who else had stock, since there was a fairly wide circle who had discussed these matters at the Royal York breakfast meetings. Griesinger was sure that Frost knew Mackenzie had stock in NONG.' Ibid. Moreover, Kelly testified before the OSC that his involvement in the NONG play was common knowledge: 'It was no secret; it was quite open around the hotel, the Royal York; everybody knew [by mid-1955 at least] I was backing this play for McLean.' Cited in Legislative Assembly, *Debates*, 18 March 1959, 1339

63 *Star*, 6 February 1959; Legislative Assembly, *Debates*, 18 March 1959, 1356

64 Ford later told the attorney general that they never went to see McGraw

because they believed they had all the information they required and that McGraw's evidence was therefore 'not necessary.' See Attorney General's Papers, RG 49, Series 19, box 2-99, Sessional Paper No. 63, file Further Documents Relating to NONG, Gordon Ford to Kelso Roberts, 23 February 1959.
65 Much of the following section has been reconstructed making use of Ontario Security Commission, *Final Report*, 22 July 1963 (Counsel: H.S. Bray).
66 *In the Matter of NONG, etc.*, evidence of Ralph K. Farris, 23 October 1962, 342
67 Ontario Securities Commission, *Final Report*, 75–6
68 Ibid., 94–5, 96
69 Ibid., 68
70 Legislative Assembly, *Debates*, 12 February 1959, 325, 326, 337
71 A.K. Roberts to L. Frost, 17 June 1957, box 8, file 6, Frost Papers
72 Legislative Assembly, *Debates*, 12 February 1959, 333
73 Ibid., 6 February 1959, 200
74 Ibid., 18 March 1959, 1318
75 Donald C. MacDonald interview, Toronto, 5 February 1995
76 Legislative Assembly, *Debates*, 18 March 1959, 1341, 1346
77 Ibid., 1347
78 Ibid., 1348
79 Ibid., 1352–9
80 Jonathan Manthorpe, *The Power and the Tories: Ontario Politics – 1943 to the Present* (Toronto: Macmillan 1974), 53
81 Legislative Assembly, *Debates*, 19 March 1959, 1368, 1369

4 THE POLICE COME CALLING

1 Peter Sypnowich, 'The Case of Mr. Justice Landreville,' *Canadian Weekly*, 13 December 1965, 6
2 Report of C.W.J. Goldsmith, nd, 61 HQ-1130-Q-3-1, RCMP Papers, Ottawa, Leo Landreville Privacy Act Request 89HR-0953 (copy in author's files).
3 File 59E112-193, RCMP Papers, Privacy Act Request 89HR-0953
4 Report of C.W.J. Goldsmith, nd, 61 HQ-1130-E-1
5 That was undoubtedly correct. However, the RCMP was also acting, it was later learned, on the basis of information supplied by the Department of National Revenue, which had apparently raised questions about Landreville's income as a result of processing his income tax forms. See Toronto *Globe and Mail*, 15 November 1977.
6 Memorandum of interview, RCMP, 11 September 1962, L.A. Landreville Papers, private collection, Ottawa; Résumé of interviews, 11 and 12 September 1962, ibid.

7 A. Kelso Roberts, *Thirty Years of Ontario Political Action* (Private edition 1969), 103

8 Report of A.R. Bates, 14 September 1962, RCMP Papers, Privacy Act Request 89HR-0953

9 *Proceedings of Inquiry into the Dealings of the Honourable Mr Justice Leo A. Landreville with NONG Ltd. before the Honourable Ivan Cleveland Rand*, Toronto, 5 April 1966, 873

10 Toronto *Telegram*, 18 September 1962

11 Ontario, Legislative Assembly, *Debates*, 24 April 1963, 2753. The premier and the attorney general were warned in advance that Roberts intended to take the government to task, but were unsuccessful in persuading him to await release of the final OSC report. See Ontario Archives, Attorney General's Papers, RG 4-02, Access Unit interim box 017, file 210.5, NONG 1963, Roberts to Cass, 29 March 1963, Cass to Roberts, 4 April 1963.

12 Legislative Assembly, *Debates*, 24 April 1963, 2753, 2754

13 A.K. McDougall, *John P. Robarts: His Life and Government* (Toronto: University of Toronto Press 1986), 115

14 Legislative Assembly, *Debates*, 25 April 1963, 2767–8, 2842, 2838

15 *Toronto Star* (hereafter *Star*), 27 April 1963

16 *Star*, 26 April 1963. In fact, Landreville had been making this claim for some time. See *Star*, 2 October 1962.

17 *Telegram*, 27 April 1963

18 L.A. Landreville to J.P. Robarts, 24 October 1962, Landreville Papers

19 L.A. Landreville to F. Cass, 8 November 1962; F. Cass to L.A. Landreville, 26 November 1962, ibid.

20 Ontario Securities Commission, *Final Report*, 22 July 1963 (Counsel: H.S. Bray), 44–5

21 Ibid., 80ff

22 *In the Matter of NONG, etc.*, evidence of Ralph K. Farris, 17 October 1962, 127–8

23 P.B.C. Pepper interview, Toronto, 1 May 1995

24 *In the Matter of NONG, etc.*, examination of L.A. Landreville, 3 and 4 October 1962, 62–3

25 Ibid., 149

26 Ontario Securities Commission, *Final Report*, 151

27 *In the Matter of NONG, etc.*, evidence of L.A. Landreville, 3 and 4 October 1962, 160

28 Ontario Securities Commission, *Final Report*, 149

29 *In the Matter of NONG, etc.*, evidence of L.A. Landreville, 3 and 4 October 1962, 164, 167

30 Ibid., 177–8
31 *In the Matter of NONG, etc.*, evidence of R.K. Farris, 17 October 1962, 7
32 Ontario Securities Commission, *Final Report*, 142–3
33 *In the Matter of NONG, etc.*, evidence of R.K. Farris, 17 October 1962, 93–5
34 Ibid., 200
35 Ibid., 64
36 Ontario Securities Commission, *Final Report*, 155–6
37 *In the Matter of NONG, etc.*, evidence of R.K. Farris, 17 October 1962, 64–5, 96–7
38 Ontario Securities Commission, *Final Report*, 163
39 *In the Matter of NONG, etc.*, evidence of R.K. Farris, 17 October 1962, 107–8, 150
40 Ontario Securities Commission, *Final Report*, 92ff
41 *In the Matter of NONG, etc.*, evidence of R.K. Farris, 17 October 1962, 191–2
42 Ontario Securities Commission, *Final Report*, 93
43 *In the Matter of NONG, etc.*, evidence of R.K. Farris, 17 October 1962, 188, 190
44 Ibid., 120, 185, 171–2, 177ff
45 Ibid., 23 October 1962, 219
46 Ibid., 224–8
47 Ibid., 264ff
48 Ibid., 228–30, 235, 253–4
49 Ibid., 330, 332
50 Ibid., 342
51 Ibid., 360–1
52 Ontario Securities Commission, *Final Report*, 186–9
53 The Ontario Securities Commission also learned that Miller sent NONG a bill
   for legal services after Orillia granted the franchise to NONG, but it was not
   apparent, given that Moore acted for Orillia and not for NONG, just what professional services were involved. Ibid., 200
54 Ibid., 214ff , 222–3
55 Ibid., 271
56 P.B.C. Pepper to F. Cass, 30 April 1963, Landreville Papers
57 F. Cass to P.B.C. Pepper, 7 May 1963, ibid.
58 P.B.C. Pepper to F. Cass, 18 February 1963, ibid.
59 Attorney General's Papers, RG 4-02, Access Unit interim box 017, file 210.5,
   NONG, 1963, Re Proposed Prosecution Arising out of 1962–63 Inquiry by the
   OSC relating to NONG Ltd.

5 TRIALS AND TRIBULATIONS

1 Alexander Ross, 'The Life and Times of a Wheeler-Dealer,' *Maclean's*, September 1963, 17

2 Ibid., 64
3 Toronto *Globe and Mail*, 10 April 1964
4 *R. v. Farris*, Transcript, 16 April 1964, 977
5 Ibid., 13 April 1964, 525
6 Ibid., 587ff
7 *Toronto Star* (hereafter *Star*), 15 April 1964
8 *R. v. Farris*, Transcript, 14 April 1964, 687–8, 695
9 Ontario Securities Commission, *Final Report*, 22 July 1963 (Counsel: H.S. Bray), 34
10 *Farris* v. *R.*, [1965] 2 OR 396, 398 (CA)
11 *R. v. Farris*, Charge to Jury, 23 April 1964, 1527. See also Toronto *Telegram*, 23 April 1964.
12 *R. v. Farris*, Charge to Jury, 23 April 1964, 1574
13 *Telegram*, 23 April 1964
14 *Globe and Mail*, 25 April 1964
15 Ibid.
16 *Farris* v. *R.*, [1965] 2 OR 396, 401 (CA)
17 Ibid., 410
18 Ibid.
19 The truth of his illness was later questioned. See *Telegram*, 7 March 1968, and Ontario Archives, Attorney General's Papers, RG 4-32, Access Unit interim box 0-27, file 248, J.A. Inch to A.R. Dick, 12 March 1958. Inch reported that 'in July 1964, this Department had reliable information that he had cancer. A subsequent medical report in March 1965 indicated that perhaps Farris did not have cancer.'
20 L.A. Landreville to G. Favreau, 12 June 1964, L.A. Landreville Papers, private collection, Ottawa; G. Favreau to L.A. Landreville, 29 June 1964, ibid.
21 P.B.C. Pepper to L.A. Landreville, 30 July 1964, ibid. For his part, Cass was, initially at least, reluctant to lay charges. At a meeting with the RCMP, Attorney General Cass 'stated that unless they were absolutely sure of a conviction against Mr. Justice Landreville, they would hesitate to proceed in view of the damage it would do in the eyes of the public, for the position held by Mr. Justice Landreville.' Report, 17 January 1963, RCMP Papers, Ottawa, L.A. Landreville, Privacy Act Request 89HR-0953 (copy in author's files)
22 Arthur A. Wishart, interview by Christine J.N. Kates, Osgoode Society, June 1984–April 1985, 204
23 Municipal Act, RSO 1950, c. 243, s. 56(5)
24 *Re L'Abbe and Blind River* (1904), 7 OLR 230 (Div Ct)
25 An Act to Amend the Municipal Act, SO 1960–61, c. 59, s. 6
26 Ontario Archives, Attorney General's Papers, RG 4-02, Access Unit interim

box 017, file 210.5, NONG, 1963, Re Proposed Prosecution Arising Out of 1962–63 Inquiry by the OSC relating to NONG Ltd.

27 P.B.C. Pepper to L.A. Landreville, 30 July 1964, Landreville Papers

28 Section 104 of the Criminal Code provided: 'Every one who (b) being a municipal official, demands, accepts or offers or agrees to accept from any person, a loan, reward, advantage or benefit of any kind as consideration for the official (c) to abstain from voting at a meeting of the municipal council or a committee thereof (d) to vote in favour of or against a measure, motion or resolution, or (e) to aid in procuring or preventing the adoption of a measure, motion or resolution, or (f) to perform or fail to perform an official act, is guilty of an indictable offence and is liable for imprisonment for two years.'

Section 408(2) provided: 'Every one who conspires with any one (a) to effect an unlawful purpose, or (b) to effect a lawful purpose by unlawful means, is guilty of an indictable offence and is liable to imprisonment for two years.'

29 Farris was also charged, but because of the declining state of his health, these charges were not pursued.

30 L.A. Landreville to Chief Justice D. Porter, 27 November 1963, Landreville Papers

31 L.A. Landreville to G. Favreau, 5 August 1964, ibid.

32 P.B.C. Pepper interview, Toronto, 1 May 1995

33 Peter Sypnowich, 'The Case of Mr. Justice Landreville,' *Canadian Weekly*, 13 December 1965, 4

34 *Telegram*, 1 October 1964

35 *Re Mr. Justice Landreville* (8 October 1964) (Magistrates' Court) [unreported], 6, Magistrate Marck, Landreville Papers

36 Ibid., 8

37 *Star*, 26 October 1964

38 *Globe and Mail*, 26 October 1964

39 *Star*, 26 October 1964

40 *Globe and Mail*, 27 October 1964

41 *Star*, 24 October 1964

42 *Globe and Mail*, 8 June 1965

43 Orillia *Packet and Times*, 17 June 1965; *Globe and Mail*, 17 June 1965

44 *Telegram*, 7 October 1964

45 Sypnowich, 'The Case of Mr. Justice Landreville,' 6

46 *Telegram*, 22 October 1964

47 *Landreville v. R.* (No. 2), [1977] 2 FC 725, 75 DLR (3d) 380 (TD), Collier J. See also *Globe and Mail*, 22 October 1964.

48 A.A. Wishart to L.A. Landreville, 8 October 1964, Landreville Papers

49 *Telegram*, 21 October 1964

50 *Globe and Mail*, 9 October 1964

51 See Canada, House of Commons, *Debates*, 19 October 1964, 9177.

52 *Telegram*, 20 October 1964; L.A. Landreville to G. Favreau, 28 April 1965, Landreville Papers

53 *Star*, 20 October 1964

54 Deputy minister of justice to Chief Justice G.A. Gale, 28 October 1964, Landreville Papers

55 J.M. Cooper to L.A. Landreville, 6 November 1964, ibid.

56 *Telegram*, 24 October 1964; *Star*, 26 October 1964; *Globe and Mail*, 22 October 1964; Belleville *Intelligencer*, 14 October 1964

57 P.B.C. Pepper interview, Toronto, 1 May 1995

58 See, for example, Ottawa *Citizen*, 24 October 1964.

59 J.J. Robinette interview, Toronto, 5 April 1991

60 Canada, House of Commons, *Debates*, 19 October 1964, 9177; 22 October 1964, 9315

61 *Star*, 25 October 1964

62 *Globe and Mail*, 10 October 1964

6 A KANGAROO COURT

1 J.J. Robinette to L.A. Landreville, 3 December 1964, L.A. Landreville Papers, private collection, Ottawa

2 Peter Sypnowich, 'The Case of Mr. Justice Landreville,' *Canadian Weekly*, 13 December 1965, 4

3 J.D. Arnup to G. Favreau, 17 February 1965, Law Society of Upper Canada Papers, Toronto

4 W.S. Martin to J. Matheson, 10 April 1967, N4 Series, volume 136, file 345 (Landreville), Lester Pearson Papers, MG 26, National Archives of Canada, Ottawa. Martin, one of the benchers who opposed the Law Society's vendetta against Landreville, later wrote that Landreville, in the aftermath of his acquittal, 'was accepted by the Bar and the public and as far as I was aware there has never been any criticism of Mr. Justice Landreville in the discharge of his official duties.'

5 J.D. Arnup to G. Favreau, 17 February 1965, Law Society Papers

6 John D. Arnup interview, Toronto, 12 February 1995

7 Ibid. Both of these interventions concerned complaints of discourtesy of the bench to the bar.

8 John D. Arnup, interview with Christine J.N. Kates, Osgoode Society, November 1982–April 1983, 301–7

9 J.D. Arnup to G. Favreau, 17 February 1965, Law Society Papers

10 Law Society of Upper Canada, *Report of the Special Committee re Landreville J.*, 17 March 1965, adopted by Convocation 23 April 1965, 1

11 Ibid., 5

12 Ibid., 6

13 P. Wright to treasurer J.D. Arnup, 24 April 1965, Law Society Papers. Wright asked Arnup to consider his letter a letter of resignation, to take effect if and when the Law Society issued its report.

14 According to John Arnup, there was no need to interview Landreville, or to provide him with an opportunity to make submissions, because the Law Society was not sitting as a court. Rather, it was acting in its capacity as the representative of lawyers in Ontario, and it was suggesting that the minister of justice convene an inquiry. It was true enough that the Law Society was of the view that Landreville was not fit to continue as a judge, but that finding was made, Arnup states, only in the context of raising its concerns with the minister of justice, who was, after all, responsible for the superior court judiciary. John D. Arnup interview, Toronto, 12 February 1995

15 *Mehr* v. *Law Society of Upper Canada*, [1955] SCR 344

16 A.J. Marck to W.E. Smith, 12 June 1965, Landreville Papers. Smith would probably not have known, but the letter appears to have been drafted by Landreville and sent to the Law Society and the attorney general of Ontario at Landreville's request.

17 W.E. Smith to A.J. Marck, 28 June 1965, Landreville file, Law Society Archives, Toronto

18 L.A. Landreville to G. Favreau, 28 April 1965, Landreville Papers

19 L.A. Landreville to G. Favreau, 7 May 1965, ibid.

20 L.A. Landreville to G. Favreau, 13 May 1965, ibid.

21 J.J. Robinette to G. Favreau, 22 February 1965, ibid. On 29 April 1965 Robinette sent a copy of this letter to Landreville.

22 Canada, House of Commons, *Debates*, 19 May 1965, 1190

23 Statement of John D. Arnup, QC, treasurer, on behalf of the Law Society of Upper Canada, 13 December 1965, Law Society Papers

24 Ibid.

25 W.S. Martin to J.D. Arnup, 3 December 1965, Law Society Papers. Moreover, as Martin later pointed out to John Matheson, a number of the benchers who abstained, notably Robinette, Sedgwick, and G. Arthur Martin, did so because of their direct involvement with either Landreville or the Farris prosecution. See W.S. Martin to J. Matheson, 10 April 1967, N4 Series, volume 136, file 345 (Landreville), Pearson Papers.

26 W.S. Martin to J.D. Arnup, 25 November 1965, Law Society Papers

27 L. Cardin to L.B. Pearson, 2 June 1965, N3 Series, volume 158, file 345 (Landreville), Pearson Papers

28 L. Cardin to L.A. Landreville, 29 July 1965, N3 Series, volume 158, file 345 (Landreville), Pearson Papers

29 L.A. Landreville to L. Cardin, 4 August 1965, Landreville Papers

30 L. Cardin to L.A. Landreville, 18 August 1965, ibid.

31 Peter Russell, *The Judiciary in Canada: The Third Branch of Government* (Toronto: McGraw-Hill Ryerson 1987), 179

32 *Toronto Star*, 23 November 1965; Toronto *Globe and Mail*, 17 December 1965

33 Canada, House of Commons, *Debates*, 3 February 1966, 671

34 Toronto *Telegram*, 23 November 1966

35 Alpheus Todd, *On Parliamentary Government in England: Its Origin, Development, and Practical Operation*, 2nd ed., vol. 2 (London: Longmans, Green 1887), 857–8

36 *The Canadian Annual Review of Public Affairs* (Toronto: Canadian Review Company 1933), 109–10

37 Dale Gibson and Lee Gibson, *Substantial Justice: Law and Lawyers in Manitoba, 1670–1970* (Winnipeg: Peguis 1972), 240

38 For an account of the Stubbs controversy, see ibid., 258–65.

39 Special Joint Committee of the Senate and the House of Commons respecting Mr. Justice Landreville, *Minutes of Proceedings and Evidence*, no. 1, 1 February 1967 (Co-chairs: Daniel Lang and Ovide Laflamme), 17ff. See also Eugene Forsey, 'Removal of Superior Court Judges,' *Commentator* 10 (1966): 17.

40 See J.D. Arnup to all benchers, 23 November 1965, Law Society Papers

41 J.J. Robinette to L. Cardin, 29 November 1965, Landreville Papers

42 L. Cardin to J.J. Robinette, 28 December 1965, ibid.

43 J.J. Robinette to L.A. Landreville, 29 December 1965, ibid.

44 J.J. Robinette interview, Toronto, 5 April 1991. In one case, *Thomson* v. *MNR*, [1945] SCR 209, Rand had indicated his disapproval for the lifestyles of the rich and famous. The issue in the case was Thomson's place of domicile, Bermuda, the United States, or Canada. Ultimately, the court found that he was domiciled in Canada and liable to pay Canadian income taxation. Rand paid special attention to Thomson's lifestyle: he had several houses, all of which were kept in readiness for him. He spent the winter months moving from one house to another. 'With him in these mass movements are his wife and only child, motor cars and servants, and at all three places he indulges himself as an addict of golf, to which he devotes most of his time and a substantial part of his money' (222). Rand later added that Thomson's life was 'a good example of what Viscount Sumner ... had in mind when he spoke of the "fluid and restless character of social habits" to which modern life has introduced us' (225). Rand would develop this theme in his Landreville report.

45 J.J. Robinette to L.A. Landreville, 11 January 1966, Landreville Papers; J.J. Robinette to L. Cardin, 17 January 1966, ibid.

46 Deputy Minister of Justice E.A. Driedger to minister, 2 February 1967, ibid.; Driedger to minister, 3 February 1967, ibid.

47 Cabinet Minutes, 17 January 1966, Privy Council Office, Access to Information Act Request No. 135-2/9293029

48 John D. Arnup interview, Toronto, 12 February 1995

49 I.C. Rand to L. Cardin, 24 July 1965, Landreville Papers

50 PC 1966-128, 19 January 1966

7 CANADIAN GOTHIC MEETS THE MAMBO KING

1 Thomas J. Lockwood, 'A History of Royal Commissions,' *Osgoode Hall Law Journal* 5 (1967): 173

2 *Time Magazine*, 28 January 1966

3 W.G. Morrow to Deputy Minister of Justice E.A. Driedger, 28 February 1966, and attached documents, L.A. Landreville Papers, private collection, Ottawa

4 *Proceedings of Inquiry into the Dealings of the Honourable Mr. Justice Leo A. Landreville with NONG Ltd. before the Honourable Ivan Cleveland Rand*, evidence of Ralph Farris, 16 March 1966, 375–6, 354, 364

5 Ibid., 378

6 *Proceedings of Inquiry ... before the Honourable Ivan Cleveland Rand*, Vancouver, 15 March 1966, 221

7 W.J. Morrow to J.J. Robinette, 29 March 1966, E 77 Series, volume 4, Landreville Correspondence file, I.C. Rand Papers, MG 30, National Archives of Canada, Ottawa

8 *Proceedings of Inquiry ... before the Honourable Ivan Cleveland Rand*, evidence of A.R. Crozier, Toronto, 6 April 1966, 820–1

9 *Sudbury Star*, 23 March 1966

10 *Proceedings of Inquiry ... before the Honourable Ivan Cleveland Rand*, Sudbury, 21 March 1966, 499

11 Ibid., 22 March 1966, 524ff, 528

12 Ibid., 621–4, 625–6, 658, 753

13 Report, nd, RCMP Papers, Ottawa, Landreville Privacy Act Request 89HR-0953 (copy in author's files)

14 J.D. Arnup to A.S. Pattillo, 14 February 1966, Law Society Papers, Toronto

15 A.S. Pattillo to J.D. Arnup, 4 March 1966, ibid.

16 J.D. Arnup to W.G. Morrow, 21 March 1966, ibid.

17 J.D. Arnup to I.C. Rand, 10 March 1966, ibid.

18 A.A. Wishart to I.C. Rand, 16 March 1966, E 77 Series, box, 3, Landreville Correspondence file, Rand Papers

19 Toronto *Globe and Mail*, 26 April 1966

20 *Proceedings of Inquiry ... before the Honourable Ivan Cleveland Rand*, Ottawa, 25 April 1966, 1082–3

21 Ibid., 26 April 1966, 1138

22 Ibid., 27 April 1966, 1270

23 Ibid., 1274–6

24 Ibid., 1279

25 Ibid., 1285

26 Ibid., 1286

27 Ibid., 1290

28 Ibid., 1291

29 Ibid., 1301–2

30 Ibid., 1322

31 Jack Batten, *Robinette: The Dean of Canadian Lawyers* (Toronto: Macmillan 1984), 188

32 *Proceedings of Inquiry ... before the Honourable Ivan Cleveland Rand*, Ottawa, 27 April 1966, 1325–6

33 Ibid., 1329

34 L.A. Landreville to J.J. Robinette, 29 April 1966, Landreville Papers. This, of course, was both literally and figuratively correct.

35 Royal Commission, *Report: Inquiry Re: the Honourable Mr. Justice Leo A. Landreville* (Ottawa: Queen's Printer 1966) (Commissioner: The Hon. Ivan C. Rand), 4

36 Ibid., 17, 68, 68–71

37 Ibid., 71–2

38 Ibid., 4

39 Ibid., 73, 65

40 Ibid., 75

41 Ibid., 79–81

42 Ibid., 92–5

43 Ibid., 98

44 Ibid., 107–8

45 Ibid., 108, 106

46 Cabinet Minutes, 23 August 1966, Privy Council Office, Access to Information Act Requests 9293029 and 9495083

47 *Globe and Mail*, 25 August 1966

48 Toronto *Telegram*, 25 August 1966

49 *Globe and Mail*, 26 August 1966

50 *Landreville* v. *R.*, T-2205-72, Agreed Statement of Facts, Landreville Papers. See also L.A. Landreville to L. Cardin, 21 September 1966, ibid.

51 Cabinet Minutes, 29 August 1966, Privy Council Office, Access to Information Act Requests 9293029 and 9495083

52 Ibid., 25 August 1966, Privy Council Office, Access to Information Act Request 9293029

53 Canada, House of Commons, *Debates*, 29 August 1966, 7742

54 See L.A. Landreville to L. Cardin, 21 September 1966, Landreville Papers.

55 *Sudbury Star*, 30 August 1966

56 M.L. Tyrwhitt-Drake, 'Mr. Rand and the Public Interest,' *Law Society Gazette*, September 1967, 15

57 'Editorial,' ibid., 4

58 Ottawa *Journal*, 30 August 1966

59 Royal Commission, *Report*, 70

60 *Proceedings of Inquiry ... before the Honourable Ivan Cleveland Rand*, evidence of L.A. Landreville, Ottawa, 25 April 1966, 1047–8

61 Royal Commission, *Report*, 70

62 House of Commons, *Debates*, 12 May 1966, 5063

63 J.J. Robinette interview, Toronto, 5 April 1991

64 *Toronto Star*, 30 August 1966

65 Ibid., 26 August 1966. Landreville later clarified his remarks. He had never said that he had arranged for Kirby to get the sack: 'I had had Kirby barred from my office at City Hall when I was mayor because of inaccurate and prejudicial reporting affecting city hall news; not just me.' *Sudbury Star*, 26 August 1966

66 *Sudbury Star*, 30 August 1966

67 D.G. Humphrey to L. Cardin, 21 September 1966, Landreville Papers

68 Special Joint Committee of the Senate and the House of Commons respecting Mr. Justice Landreville, *Minutes of Proceedings and Evidence*, no. 2, 20 February 1967 (Co-chairs: Daniel Lang and Ovide Laflamme), 31

69 House of Commons, *Debates*, 21 November 1966, 10140

70 D.G. Humphrey to L. Cardin, 26 October 1966, Landreville Papers

71 D.G. Humphrey to L. Cardin, 5 January 1967, ibid.

8 'PLEADING FOR MY HONOUR'

1 Prior to Confederation, however, attempts had been made on several occasions to impeach a judge. Indeed, in colonial times, judges were appointed 'at pleasure,' and were sometimes dismissed for offending the government.

2 Special Joint Committee of the Senate and the House of Commons respecting

Mr. Justice Landreville, *Minutes of Proceedings and Evidence,* no. 2, 20 February 1967 (Co-chairs: Daniel Lang and Ovide Laflamme), 31

3 Ibid., 31, 33, 36

4 Toronto *Telegram,* 21 February 1967

5 *Toronto Star,* 22 February 1967

6 Special Joint Committee, *Minutes of Proceedings,* no. 2, 23 February 1967, 56; Yves Fortier interview, Toronto, 10 March 1995

7 Special Joint Committee, *Minutes of Proceedings,* no. 3, 28 February 1967, 92

8 Ibid., no. 2, 23 February 1967, 57

9 Toronto *Globe and Mail,* 1 March 1967

10 Special Joint Committee, *Minutes of Proceedings,* no. 6, 14 March 1967, 239, 234, 235

11 Ibid., no. 5, 9 March 1967, 184

12 *Globe and Mail,* 4 November 1966

13 Special Joint Committee, *Minutes of Proceedings,* no. 4, 2 March 1967, 131

14 Ibid., no. 6, 10 March 1967, 205

15 Ibid., 231

16 Ibid., 231, 258

17 Yves Fortier interview, Toronto, 10 March 1995

18 Gordon Fairweather to William Kaplan, 28 April 1995

19 Special Joint Committee of the Senate and House of Commons respecting Mr. Justice Landreville, *Second Report* (Co-chairs: Daniel Lang and Ovide Laflamme), Ottawa, 17 March 1967

20 *Telegram,* 20 March 1967

21 L.A. Landreville to L.B. Pearson, 22 March 1967, L.A. Landreville Papers, private collection, Ottawa

22 *Globe and Mail,* 31 March 1967

23 L. Cardin to L.B. Pearson, 30 March 1967, N4 Series, volume 136, file 345 (Landreville), Lester Pearson Papers, MG 26, National Archives of Canada, Ottawa

24 L.A. Landreville to L.B. Pearson, 22 March 1967, Landreville Papers

25 Memorandum for the prime minister, 5 April 1967, N4 Series, volume 26, file 345 (Landreville), Pearson Papers

26 L. Cardin to L.B. Pearson, 30 March 1967, N4 Series, volume 136, ibid.

27 Victoria *Daily Colonist,* 5 June 1967. In cabinet meetings, Trudeau privately and repeatedly insisted that Landreville be accorded 'all of the guarantees of natural justice.' See, for example, Cabinet Minutes, 23 August 1966, Privy Council Office, Access to Information Act Request 9293029.

28 Canada, House of Commons, *Debates,* 21 March 1967, 14255; 4 April 1967, 14483; and 11 April 1967, 14761. On 11 April 1967 Social Credit leader Réal Caouette suggested that Landreville be given the opportunity to appear in

light of the 'rumour' that he was 'discriminated against because he is a French Canadian' (14761–2).

29 Gordon Robertson, clerk of the Privy Council, prepared a detailed memorandum for the prime minister outlining a strategy for securing Landreville's resignation, with a pension, and with minimal political fallout. Another senior adviser, Jean Beetz, a Quebec lawyer destined to serve on the Supreme Court, liked the plan. It was ingenious and subtle, Beetz wrote, but what worried him was that the public would be confirmed in its widely held beliefs that 'highly placed persons always manage to get away with it.' Robertson agreed that this was a 'good point.' See Memorandum for the prime minister, 20 April 1967, N4 Series, volume 136, file 345 (Landreville), Pearson Papers; G. Robertson to J. Beetz, 21 April 1967, ibid.

30 House of Commons, *Debates*, 31 May 1967, 789

31 Cabinet Minutes, 6 April 1967, Privy Council Office, Access to Information Act Request 9293029

32 See, for instance, N4 Series, volume 136, file 345 (Landreville), Pearson Papers, for copies of correspondence received.

33 Cabinet Minutes, 4 May 1967, Privy Council Office, Access to Information Act Request 9293029

34 J. Matheson to L.B. Pearson, 30 March 1967, N4 Series, volume 136, file 345 (Landreville), Pearson Papers

35 L.A. Landreville to P.E. Trudeau, 4 March 1968, Landreville Papers. This account is confirmed by the Cabinet Minutes that have been released. See Cabinet Minutes, 8 June 1967, Privy Council Office, Access to Information Act Request 9495083.

36 John Matheson, telephone conversation with author, 17 January 1995

37 Cabinet Minutes, 4 May 1967, Access to Information Act Request 9293029

38 This account is based on various memoranda in the Landreville Papers, on interviews with Landreville, and on the evidence in Collier J's pension judgment, *Landreville v. R. (No. 3)* (1980), [1981] 1 FC 15, 111 DLR (3d) 36 (TD).

39 L.A. Landreville to P.E. Trudeau, 4 March 1968, Landreville Papers

40 L.A. Landreville to P.E. Trudeau, 7 June 1967, ibid.

41 Cabinet Minutes, 8 June 1967, Access to Information Act Request 9293029

42 Ibid. Soon enough, Justice Minister Trudeau and other members of the government began receiving letters to the effect that no pension should be granted. Giving Landreville a pension, a typical letter stated, would be unjustified 'morally, politically or on any grounds of common sense.' See R.C. Honey to P.E. Trudeau, 16 June 1967, Landreville Papers.

43 House of Commons, *Debates*, 8 June 1967, 1283–4

44 Edgar Benson interview, Ottawa, October 11, 1994

45 House of Commons, *Debates*, 9 June 1967, 1342; 13 June 1967, 1506
46 Ibid., 20 June 1967, 1715–16
47 The full provision reads: 'The Governor in Council may grant to (c) a judge who has become afflicted with some permanent infirmity disabling him from the due execution of his office, if he resigns his office or by reason of such infirmity is removed from office ...' *Judges Act*, RSC 1952, c. 159, as amended by SC 1960, c. 46, s. 3
48 A.M. Doyle to 'Whom it may concern,' 21 June 1967, Landreville Papers
49 L.A. Landreville to P.E. Trudeau, 23 June 1967, ibid.
50 Cabinet Minutes, 29 June 1967, Access to Information Act Request 9293029
51 Ibid., Access to Information Act Request 9495083
52 House of Commons, *Debates*, 5 July 1967, 2274
53 L.A. Landreville to P.E. Trudeau, 12 September 1967, Landreville Papers
54 See Memorandum to file, 22 November 1967, ibid., regarding the interview with Trudeau.
55 John Saywell, ed., *Canadian Annual Review for 1968* (Toronto: University of Toronto Press 1969), 15–19
56 L.A. Landreville to L.B. Pearson, 17 February 1968, Landreville Papers
57 L.A. Landreville to P.E. Trudeau, 4 March 1968, ibid.
58 J.J. Connolly to P.E. Trudeau, 20 December 1967, N4 Series, volume 136, file 345 (Landreville), Pearson Papers; J.J. Connolly to L.B. Pearson, 29 January 1968, ibid.
59 P.E. Trudeau to L.A. Landreville, 5 March 1968, Landreville Papers
60 Cabinet Minutes, 7 March 1968, Privy Council Office, Access to Information Act Request 9293029. As Mitchell Sharp noted in his reply to Landreville, dated 6 March 1968, 'You will appreciate that the primary responsibility in bringing this matter up rests with the Minister of Justice so that I can only assure you that I shall bear your representations in mind when that time comes' (M. Sharp to L.A. Landreville, 6 March 1968, Landreville Papers). There are other letters from P. Hellyer (25 March 1968), J. Marchand (7 March 1968), and J. Turner (6 March 1968) in the Landreville Papers, all, in varying degrees, indicating that they would give the matter consideration or that they would discuss the matter with the minister.
61 L.A. Landreville to P.E. Trudeau, 13 March 1968, Landreville Papers
62 P.E. Trudeau to L.A. Landreville, 22 March 1968, ibid.
63 House of Commons, *Debates*, 18 March 1968, 7723
64 John English suggests the importance of Pearson's role in Trudeau's campaign in *The Worldly Years: 1949–1972*, volume 2 of *The Life of Lester Pearson* (Toronto: Knopf 1992), 383. Saywell, *Canadian Annual Review for 1968*, 29
65 Saywell, *Canadian Annual Review for 1968*, 50–1

66 J. Turner to L.A. Landreville, 23 July 1968, Landreville Papers

67 L.B. Pearson to L.A. Landreville, 23 October 1968, ibid.

68 Macdonald, however, has no recollection of this event. Donald Macdonald to William Kaplan, March 1995

69 Letter, 8 January 1969, Landreville Papers

70 L.A. Landreville to G.F. Henderson, 22 September 1971, ibid.; G.F. Henderson to L.A. Landreville, 28 September 1971, ibid.

9 VINDICATION?

1 Memorandum from J.R. Cartwright (dated 24 July 1972), 17 July 1972, L.A. Landreville Papers, private collection, Ottawa

2 *Landreville v. R.*, [1973] FC 1223 at 1228, 41 DLR (3d) 574 at 579 (TD), Pratte J. [hereafter *Landreville v. R.* cited to FC]

3 Ibid., 1229

4 Gordon Henderson interview, Ottawa, 4 March 1989

5 *Landreville v. R. (No. 2)*, [1977] 2 FC 726 at 747, 75 DLR (3d) 280 at 396 (TD) [hereafter *Landreville v. R. (No. 2)* cited to FC]

6 Ibid., 748

7 Ibid., 754

8 Royal Commission, *Report of the Commission of Inquiry into Matters Relating to Gerda Munsinger* (Ottawa: Queen's Printer 1966) (Commissioner: The Hon. Wishart F. Spence)

9 *Landreville v. R. (No. 2)*, 756

10 Royal Commission, *Report: Inquiry Re: the Honourable Mr. Justice Leo A. Landreville* (Ottawa: Queen's Printer 1966) (Commissioner: The Hon. Ivan C. Rand), 94–5

11 *Landreville v. R. (No. 2)*, 757

12 Ibid.

13 Ibid., 759

14 Ibid., 760–1

15 L.A. Landreville to G.B. Henderson, 20 June 1977, Landreville Papers

16 R. Basford to G.B. Henderson, 5 April 1978, ibid.

17 'Subject to the provisions of any other Act and to subsection (2), when a Minister of the Crown certifies to any court by affidavit that a document belongs to a class or contains information which on grounds of public interest specified in the affidavit should be withheld from production and discovery, the court may examine the document and order its production and discovery to the parties, subject to such restrictions or conditions as it deems appropriate, if it concludes in the circumstances of the case that the public interest in the proper

administration of justice outweighs in importance the public interest specified in the affidavit.

'(2) When a Minister of the Crown certifies to any court by affidavit that the production or discovery of a document or its contents would be injurious to international relations, national defence of security, or to federal-provincial relations, or that it would disclose a confidence of the Queen's Privy Council for Canada, discovery and production shall be refused without any examination of the document by the court.' *Federal Court Act*, RSC 1970 (2nd Supp.), c. 10, s. 41

18 In fact, Drury swore two affidavits. The first was dated 26 November 1975. In that affidavit, Drury swore that he had examined and read the Cabinet Minutes dated 17 October 1967, 26 October 1967, and 7 March 1968,and that he certified that their production would disclose a confidence of the Queen's Privy Council for Canada. In Henderson's view, this affidavit was inadequate, and he brought a motion directing the Crown to produce a list of all relevant documents. After all, it was inconceivable that there were only three references to Landreville and his pension application. Moreover, Drury's affidavit did not indicate whether Landreville's pension application was considered on the indicated dates. The motion came before Mr Justice Gibson who, on 19 December 1975, effectively ordered the Crown, if claiming under section 41(2) of the *Federal Court Act*, to file a new affidavit comprehensively responding to Henderson's request. On 27 May 1976 a second, more comprehensive affidavit was filed. This one indicated that the cabinet, on seven occasions, generally discussed the matter of granting Landreville a pension. It further indicated that there were four cabinet minutes 'relating specifically to the request of former Mr. Justice Landreville for a pension in his letter to the then Minister of Justice and the Governor in Council of June 23, 1967.' And there were three different cabinet memoranda relating generally to the question of granting a pension to Landreville. What was most important about this affidavit was what it did not say. It nowhere indicated that the cabinet ever considered and decided Landreville's pension request. This, of course, would turn out to be the deciding factor in Landreville's pension suit.

Drury was an appropriate minister to submit the affidavit. Privy Council policy is not to disclose cabinet documents generated during the tenure of a particular prime minister to ministers who did not serve during that tenure. All the documents sought in this case were generated during the tenure of Prime Minister Pearson. Drury was one of a limited number of cabinet ministers who had served under Pearson and who were still in the cabinet, and so could examine the documents in question.

19 Affidavit of Charles Mills Drury, 27 May 1976, Landreville Papers

20 Cabinet Minutes, 7 March 1968, Privy Council Office, Access to Information Act Request 9495083. As will be seen from the discussion that follows, this was not the usual practice for the consideration of pension requests.
21 Memorandum to file, 3 May 1978, Landreville Papers
22 Memorandum to file, 2 October 1978, ibid.
23 G.B. Henderson to G. Ainslie, 3 October 1978, ibid.
24 G.B. Henderson to G. Ainslie, 12 December 1978, ibid.
25 Memorandum to file, 18 January 1979, ibid. See also G.B. Henderson to G. Ainslie, 5 February 1979, ibid.
26 Memorandum to file, 31 March 1979, ibid.
27 Memorandum to file, 11 July 1979, ibid.
28 G.B. Henderson to R. Tassé, 8 August 1979, ibid.
29 *Landreville* v. *R.*, Federal Court, T-2204-72, Transcript, 1 November 1979
30 *Landreville* v. *R. (No. 3)* (1980), [1981] 1 FC 15 at 27, 111 DLR (3d) 36 at 47–8 (TD), Collier J [hereafter *Landreville* v. *R. (No. 3)* cited to FC]
31 Ibid., 43, 44
32 Ibid.
33 Ibid., 51–2
34 Ibid., 52
35 Ibid., 56
36 Ibid., 57–8
37 Ibid., 59
38 Toronto *Globe and Mail*, 6 May 1980
39 G.B. Henderson to J.A. Scollin, 20 June 1980, Landreville Papers
40 L.S. Holland to G.B. Henderson, 4 July 1980, ibid.
41 PC 1981–3/468, 19 February 1981

CONCLUSION

1 R.K. Farris to L.A. Landreville, 8 May 1956, L.A. Landreville Papers, private collection, Ottawa
2 Tom Alderman, 'A disgraced judge fights to clear his name,' *Canadian Magazine*, 16 November 1968, 3–6
3 L. Frost to P. Quinn, 21 July 1972, box 8, file 18, Leslie Frost Papers, 77-024, Trent University Archives, Peterborough, Ontario
4 J. Matheson to L.B. Pearson, 30 March 1967, N4 Series, volume 136, file 345 (Landreville), Lester Pearson Papers, MG 26, National Archives of Canada, Ottawa
5 M.A. MacPherson to L.A. Landreville, nd, Landreville Papers
6 Cited in Ontario, Legislative Assembly, *Debates*, 9 March 1961, 1981

7 Ibid., 1985

8 W.P. Rosenfeld, 'Conflict of Interest and the Ontario Municipal Act,' *University of Toronto Faculty of Law Review* 20 (1962): 92

9 *An Act Respecting Conflict of Interest of Members of Municipal Councils and Local Boards*, SO 1972, c. 142

10 J. Matheson to L.B. Pearson, 30 March 1967, N4 Series, volume 136, file 345 (Landreville), Pearson Papers

11 *Toronto Star*, 26 October 1964

12 See *Landreville v. R. (No. 2)*, [1977] 2 FC 726 at 740, 75 DLR 380 at 391, and Peter Russell, *The Judiciary in Canada: The Third Branch of Government* (Toronto: McGraw-Hill Ryerson 1977), 177.

13 J. Matheson to L.B. Pearson, 23 October 1967, N4 Series, volume 136, file 345 (Landreville), Pearson Papers

14 I am grateful to Martin Friedland for sharing with me a copy of his draft study, 'A Place Apart: Judicial Independence and Accountability in Canada,' from which much of the following section is drawn.

15 Canada, House of Commons, *Debates*, 14 June 1971, 6666

16 See, generally, *Gratton v. Canadian Judicial Council* (1994) 115 DLR (4th) 81 (FCTD)

17 Russell, *The Judiciary in Canada*, 184

18 E. Haines to J. Matheson, 16 April 1967, N4 Series, volume 136, file 345 (Landreville), Pearson Papers

19 Northern Ontario Natural Gas Company, *Annual Report, 1964* (Toronto 1965)

Index

PUBLICATIONS OF THE OSGOODE SOCIETY FOR CANADIAN LEGAL HISTORY

1995 David Williams, *Just Lawyers: Seven Portraits*

Hamar Foster and John McLaren, eds., *Essays in the History of Canadian Law, vol. VI, British Columbia and the Yukon*

W.H. Morrow, ed., *Northern Justice: The Memoirs of Mr Justice William G. Morrow*

Beverley Boissery, *A Deep Sense of Wrong: The Treason, Trials, and Transportation of Lower Canadian Rebels to New South Wales after the 1838 Rebellion*

1996 William Kaplan, *Bad Judgment: The Case of Mr Justice Leo A. Landreville*